ANTI-SUBMARINE WARFARE

BRASSEY'S SEA POWER: Naval Vessels,
Weapons Systems and Technology Series:
Volume 11

Brassey's Sea Power:
Naval Vessels, Weapon Systems and Technology Series

General Editor: PROFESSOR G. TILL, Royal Naval College, Greenwich and Department of War Studies, King's College London

This series, consisting of twelve volumes, aims to explore the impact of modern technology on the shape, size and role of contemporary navies. Using case studies from around the world it explains the principles of naval operations and functions of naval vessels, aircraft and weapon systems. Each volume is written by an acknowledged expert in a clear, easy to understand style, and is well illustrated with photographs and diagrams. The series will be invaluable for naval officers under training and also will be of great interest to young professionals and naval enthusiasts.

Volume 1 – Modern Sea Power: An Introduction
DR. G. TILL

Volume 2 – Ships, Submarines and the Sea
DR P. J. GATES & N. M. LYNN

Volume 3 – Surface Warships
DR P. J. GATES

Volume 4 – Amphibious Operations
COLONEL M. H. H. EVANS

Volume 5 – Naval Electronic Warfare
DR D. G. KIELY

Volume 6 – Naval Surface Weapons
DR D. G. KIELY

Volume 7 – Submarines
REAR ADMIRAL J. B. HERVEY CB OBE

Volume 8 – Naval Command and Control
CAPTAIN W. T. T. PAKENHAM

Volume 9 – Merchant Shipping
ED. PROF. G. TILL

Volume 10 – Coastal Forces
ED. PROF. G. TILL

Volume 11 – Anti-Submarine Warfare
W. J. R. GARDNER

ANTI-SUBMARINE WARFARE

by

W J R GARDNER

BRASSEY'S
LONDON * WASHINGTON

First English Edition 1996

UK editorial offices: Brassey's, 33 John Street, London WC1N 2AT

UK orders: Marston Book Services, PO Box 269, Abingdon, OX14 4SD

North American orders: Brassey's Inc., PO Box 960,
Herndon, VA 22070, USA

W J R Gardner has asserted his moral right to be identified as the author of this work.

Library of Congress Cataloging in Publication Data
available

British Library Cataloguing in Publication Data
A catalogue record for this book is available from the British Library

ISBN 1 85753 120 5 Flexicover

Typeset by Florencetype Ltd., Stoodleigh, Devon
Printed in Great Britain by Alden Press, Oxford

Cover Photograph:
An EH101 Merlin helicopter operating with HMS *Iron Duke* (Westland Helicopters)

Contents

Acknowledgements

A book may only have one author but it is rarely the unaided work of one person. What follows in this volume owes a great deal to many other people. Firstly, I would like to thank collectively all those defence manufacturers who so very kindly supplied me with illustrations for the book; their specific contributions are mentioned where their photographs appear in the text.

Next, it is absolutely necessary to mention Commander Ian Gallett, Royal Navy, a colleague and friend of many years' standing. As Ian and I took part in one of the pioneer towed array patrols, wondering nervously whether our ageing frigate was going to reach the end of it in one piece, I do not supposed it occurred to either of us that we might later collaborate on a book. Ian took on the unenviable task of making sense of my first draft of Chapter 5. He deserves credit for correcting my errors as well as imposing clarity where none previously existed: I still claim the responsibility for any residual difficulties a reader may have with this chapter.

A long-time collaborator on many projects has been Miss Mavis Simpson of the Ministry of Defence Library in Whitehall and, yet again, I must thank her and many of her colleagues for their help, often in the face of considerable difficulties. Mrs Elisabeth Ingham provided very useful advice on indexing, a field in which she is a consummate professional.

The General Editor of the series, Professor Geoffrey Till, asked me to write this book in such splendid surroundings that modesty forbids their repetition here; suffice it to say that it has provided a useful after-dinner story ever since. More importantly, I am grateful to Geoffrey for his advice. Squadron Leader John Green (now retired from the Royal Air Force) in a past existence managed to put certain useful ASW experiences my way. More recently, he has served as an extremely trenchant critic of my writing, a very necessary task I am afraid. At Brassey's, Jenny Shaw and Robert Zealley have provided me with a (relatively) pain-free introduction to publishing.

Lastly, I must mention Lieutenant Commander Don Hillman, retired from the Royal Navy and now from the defence industry. If I learned much of use as an ASW officer, it was from him. This extended well beyond the mere marshalling of facts. He was wise enough to see that his students' knowledge of ASW should be founded in their understanding of submarines, their crews and what they were trying to achieve. Thus I owe my only time at sea in a nuclear submarine to his foresight.

He was also a highly significant, if now unrecognised, force in the vast strides made by the Royal Navy in passive ASW during the 1980s. More importantly, although I do not think I ever heard him once use the term, he transmitted an understanding of the philosophy of ASW to at least one of his students.

Glossary

ADCAP	Added capability – torpedo upgrade
AIO	Action information organisation (see also CIC)
AIP	Air independent propulsion
Asdic	Early term for Sonar (qv)
ASROC	Anti-submarine rocket (delivering a homing torpedo)
ASUW	Anti-surface warfare
ASW	Anti-submarine warfare
Autolycus	Airborne exhaust trail indicator (obsolete)
BB	Bottom bounce
BDA	Battle damage assessment
C3	Command, control and communications
CAMBS	Command activated multi-beam sonobuoy
CIC	Combat information centre (see also AIO)
CPP	Controllable pitch propeller
CVBG	Aircraft carrier battle group
CZ	Convergence zone
DASH	Drone anti-submarine helicopter
dB	Decibel
DP	Direct path
ERAPS	Expendable reliable acoustic path sonobuoy
ESM	Electronic support measures
FAC	Fast attack craft
FLIR	Forward looking infra red (sensor)
FSU	Former Soviet Union
GPS	Global positioning system
GRIUK	Greeenland-Iceland-United Kingdom (gap)
HEAT	High explosive anti-tank

HF DF	High frequency (radio) direction finding
Hz	Hertz
IUSS	Integrated Underwater Surveillance System
kHz	Kilohertz
km	Kilometre
kts	Knots
LAMPS	Light airborne multi-purpose system (helicopter)
MAD	Magnetic anomaly detection (or detector)
MATCH	Medium anti-submarine torpedo-carrying helicopter
MIZ	Marginal ice zone
MPA	Maritime patrol aircraft
MRS	Medium range sonar
NATO	North Atlantic Treaty Organisation
NDB	Nuclear depth bomb
nm	Nautical mile
OA	Operations analysis
OR	Operational research
PGM	Precision guided missile (or munition)
PWR	Pressurised water reactor
RAP	Reliable acoustic path
RF	Radio frequency
SACLANT	Supreme Allied Commander, Atlantic
SATCOM	Satellite Communications
Scud	Type of SRBM (qv)
SDI	Strategic Defense Initiative
Shaddock	NATO codename for Soviet submarine-launched anti-ship missile
SIGINT	Signals intelligence
SLCM	Submarine-launched cruise missile
SLBM	Submarine-launched ballistic missile (system)
SOSUS	Sound surveillance system
SRBM	Short-range ballistic missile
SSB	Diesel-electric ballistic missile-firing submarine
SSBN	Nuclear-powered ballistic missile-firing submarine
SSG	Diesel-electric antiship missile-firing submarine
SSGN	Nuclear-powered antiship missile-firing submarine
SS-N-	NATO designator for Soviet surface-to-surface missile
SSN	Nuclear powered attack submarine
SSTD	Surface ship torpedo defence

SURTASS	Surveillance towed array sonar system
TACTASS	Tactical towed array sonar system
T-AGOS	Towed array ocean surveillance ship (system)
TERCOM	Terrain comparison – guidance technique for cruise missile
UHF	Ultra-high (radio) frequency
ULF	Ultra-low frequency (of radio – below VLF (qv))
VDS	Variable depth sonar
VLF	Very-low frequency (of radio – above ULF (qv))

List of Figures

List of Plates

1

Introduction

Anti-submarine warfare (ASW) is the art and science of depriving the enemy of the effectiveness of his submarines. It is easy to define, but requires rather more to explain it adequately: that is the purpose of this book. It should first be understood that ASW does not have a truly independent existence, and that it should be placed in the context of two other environments.

There can be no ASW without submarines. Before the invention of the practicable submarine in the early 20th century, there was no need for ASW: if the nations of the world ban or otherwise dispose of all submarines, there will again be no need for ASW. But the submarine like the nuclear bomb probably cannot be uninvented – a submarine-free world appears highly unlikely. Thus, to jump ahead to the end of the book, the future of ASW, if only as a requirement, seems assured.

The two other environments that have to be considered are the maritime one as a whole (including naval combat) and the whole spectrum of warfare. The former is the more obvious and easier to explain. All naval activities have to take into account the physical characteristics of the sea and the atmosphere, but few can be quite so reliant on this factor as ASW. The ocean is largely an opaque medium, working to the advantage of the submarine. There are ways of overcoming this important limitation, but any form of ASW which does not acknowledge this factor and take full account of it is doomed to failure.

Further, any form of ASW is unlikely to be conducted in a strategic vacuum. The units which have to practice ASW will almost certainly have other problems to deal with: firstly, there will be the competing priorities of other tasks to do; secondly, these forces may well have to deal with other problems at the same time, such as enemy surface forces, missiles or aircraft; and lastly, and often most importantly, their enemy may be one much older than the submarine – time.

Naval warfare is not the only form of conflict likely to be practised at any time: land and air campaigns can also have an important impact on ASW. Perhaps this may best be illustrated by means of two historical examples. Arguably the worst ASW setback suffered by the British in the Second World War occurred not at the hands of Admiral Dönitz, the commander of the German Navy's submarines, but because of the activities of General Heinz Guderian and the panzer generals whose very successful strategy and tactics in the Battle of France in 1940 led to greatly improved access for German submarines to the Atlantic. Air superiority later in the same war allowed Allied air power to disrupt very successfully the German construction and deployment of advanced technology submarines.

This book will examine ASW in several different ways. In Chapter 2, a brief historical survey will be made of ASW in the near-century of its practice. This is important as the best way of revealing and illuminating key principles of ASW. Such illustrations may also be used in further chapters: one historical example may be more telling than a thousand more theoretical words. Next, Chapter 3 considers the submarine. No apologies are made for covering this topic at such length, notwithstanding there being an excellent volume on this subject in the Brassey's Sea Power series by Rear Admiral John Hervey. Although there are references to that work in this book, it is essential that a knowledge of the submarine, both as a technical device and as an operating warship, should inform any study of ASW.

Having established ASW in terms of history and opposition, it will then be possible to look at ASW in greater depth, considering the whole range of the subject. Some aspects of the topic will be sketched in Chapter 4, which will not necessarily receive any further detailed treatment in the book: this is not because they are unimportant, but because a full treatment belongs in other places, both in other volumes of this series and elsewhere. Next for discussion, in Chapter 5, is the environment of the sea itself. Like the submarine, this is a most important area to consider. As previously mentioned, the sea tends to shrug off attempts to render it transparent. Given such a difficult medium, ASW should not attempt to fight both submarine and sea.

From there, we move into the area of ASW hardware proper and examine the ways in which submarines can be detected. Although this is largely the domain of sonar, both active and passive, other sensors can also be used. These are all described in Chapter 6, together with examples. It is little use, however, merely to find and track a submarine: it will nearly always be necessary to attack it, and Chapter 7 addresses the topic of prosecuting a submarine contact and the weapons necessary for this task.

Detection and attack are the core activities of ASW, but they could not occur without a number of other important supporting activities, some of which are not always very obvious, and which are discussed in Chapter 8. These include the ability to measure key variables in the oceanic environment; acoustic measurement and quietening; training; and operations analysis. Such areas may not have the obvious interest of 'pinging' and 'banging', but they are significant in maintaining a useful ASW capability. These factors underpin professional ASW, but it is also important to realise that all these activities have to be brought together so that the whole may form an ASW system and not just a collection of parts, useful as any of these may be by themselves. The way in which this 'bringing together' takes place is decsribed in Chapter 9.

Lastly, before concluding, a limited glimpse of the future for ASW is given in Chapter 10. This is not merely a matter of considering what sensors and weapons may be in the pipeline and then making some mild extrapolations. Here, the overriding importance of the submarine to ASW is the theme which restates itself. Who is going to own submarines; what use will they be put to; what type of boats will be at sea in the future; and what the total size of the world submarine fleet is likely to be are the important questions which have to be assessed before even attempting a rudimentary look into the future of ASW.

In all of what follows little more can be done than to indicate the outlines of a very large subject: each chapter could easily form the basis of a book by itself. However, it is hoped that there will be sufficient material here to both interest and inform the reader wishing to learn more about this fascinating topic.

2

Twentieth Century ASW – the Story So Far

EARLY DAYS – UP TO 1918

In this chapter we look at ASW in the 20th century, noting its triumphs and disasters. Above all, a theme emerges of ASW reacting to the submarine as it developed with all its inherent capabilities and drawbacks. ASW has been around for the same length of time as the submarine, which means in effect from the beginning of the 20th century. The earliest submarines were crude, slow and probably as dangerous to their crews as they were to any potential enemy. Perhaps their greatest drawback initially was the lack of a suitable weapon, consistent with their operations and the then perceived constraints of international law.

Nevertheless, their potential was evident to many and the ability of a warship of any kind to make itself invisible – if only for some of the time – could hardly be ignored. Established navies with large fleets of conventional surface warships might be very worried. But those that had most to fear were nations which depended on seaborne trade both for subsistence and the generation of wealth. But there were three immediate and interconnected barriers to the submarine living up to its promise:

- ► Lack of tactical doctrine for attack on either warships or merchant vessels.
- ► Practical difficulties in taking over, attacking or sinking an enemy.
- ► Even if the above were overcome, constraints of international law.

In a sense these were an unrecognised form of ASW, particularly in view of the broad definition of ASW adopted in the previous chapter.

Taken together, they rendered the early submarine incapable of doing much damage. Submarines could scout, but without the benefit of radio, which only reached a maturity of reliable long-range communication some time later, they did not have the capability of transmitting their findings over useful distances. Destroyers were faster, had a higher and more useful height of eye – greatly increasing the range of the visible horizon – and possessed better communications.

Early submarines could also attack warships, but this almost certainly implied the use of the torpedo. Early torpedoes were not reliable, tending to run erratically. Further, the relatively slow submarine had to reach a tightly defined firing position, often against a much faster target. Submarines were often armed with guns too, but despite the submarine being a smaller target, gun duels with almost any form of warship were considered suicidal. Surface warships were usually more heavily armed, as well as being superior gun platforms under most circumstances. The ultimate weapon to deal with a submarine was ramming and an obvious disadvantage of the minuscule early submarines, despite being constructed strongly to resist water pressure, was their susceptibility to this tactic, especially from armoured ships. Lastly, in circumstances when none of these disadvantages applied, for example when engaging a merchant ship, there were strong legal constraints, even if untested prior to the First World War. In broad terms, such encounters were governed by 'Prize Rules', which allowed warships (including submarines) to capture merchant vessels of belligerent nations. But there were many conditions laid down including warning, care of merchant ship crews and the use of prize crews (that is, using part of the attacker's crew to secure the vessel assailed and bring it to port after a successful capture). In practice, a small submarine could not give the degree of care to merchant crews, nor was the provision of prize crews practical. Thus the only practical option was to sink the ship. Legally this could be done, but the problem of dealing with merchant crews remained. How this developed under the stimulus of war will be seen.

By 1914, the submarine had adopted the torpedo as the weapon of choice. This allowed some successes against warships, especially slow ones. Thus the old cruisers, *Aboukir*, *Cressy* and *Hogue* were sunk in quick succession in September 1914. The threat was similar to that which had been perceived from torpedo boats for several decades, with the added twist of the firer being invisible, or virtually so.

How was this to be dealt with? Both material and tactical measures were tried. The problem of locating submarines underwater was not to be solved for some

PLATE 2.1 British World War I R-Class Submarine *(Photo: VSEL)*

time and tactical measures were little more effective. Much time was spent pursuing submarines by methods which owed more to cavalry tactics than rational thought. Fast area sweeps by destroyers were popular reactions to the submarine threat, but with the possible exception of operations in restricted areas such as the Baltic and Black Seas, these rarely resulted in the detection or destruction of submarines. The reason for failure is not difficult to find. A submarine, even on the surface, is a small visual target, whereas the hunters are relatively large, and this advantage would allow the submarine to dive before being detected.

Underwater detection was virtually impossible, except in a few areas where water clarity was exceptionally good. In the grey North Sea or blue Atlantic, such transparency was rare. Many methods were attempted to achieve detection. It would be easy in hindsight to mock many of them, but some do appear wildly optimistic: for example, attempts were made to train sealions from a well-known Glasgow circus to detect and indicate the presence of underwater moving objects.

More promising was the use of sound, one of the best ways in which energy can be transmitted underwater. There were two fundamental approaches, then as for the rest of the century, namely passive and active. The former relied on the ability to detect and classify the various sounds made by a submerged submarine, largely those connected with its propulsion system. This was to present problems which were beyond the reach of the technology of the day, not least because such systems had to be fitted to surface ships whose own noise was generally greater than that of the submarine. But active sound measures represented an even more difficult challenge of technology, and active equipment, known first as Asdic, later as Sonar, was not deployed in an effective way until after the First World War. Active sonar, on the other hand, involved the transmission of sound which on finding a submarine target would be reflected back to its point of origin; measuring its bearing and a calculation derived from time of transmission and reception (the speed of sound in water being known) produced the submarine's range, and thus position.

But submarines were to make their presence felt in the strongest possible way long before Asdic was fielded as an ASW measure. In a position of stalemate in the land war, and severely pressured by the Allied blockade of the continent, the Germans decided in February 1917 to retaliate by conducting a campaign of 'unrestricted' submarine warfare against shipping in the vicinity of the United Kingdom. Ultimately, this was to backfire politically by being a prime factor in bringing the United States into the war. But this did not happen before much shipping had been sunk, initiating the first – some would say the greatest ever – ASW challenge that has ever had to be faced.

German submarines had advanced only slightly in technical terms since 1914, but it was their deliberate flouting of previously perceived norms of international law which allowed them very much more tactical freedom in attacking shipping. Initially, a preferred method of sinking might be the surfaced gunnery attack, with or without warning to allow crews to abandon ship. But the increasing supply of radio to ships increased the probability that a warned ship might summon assistance and lead to the submarine itself being attacked by gunfire.

Thus, a tendency grew for no warning to be given and an attack could occur either by gunnery or, giving even less warning, by a submerged torpedo attack. With merchant ships sailing independently, there was little chance that the small number of warships devoted to ASW could be useful. After much experimenting and some British Admiralty reluctance, the expedient of the convoy, drawn from the centuries-old experience of anti-privateer warfare, was adopted. Merchant ships were concentrated and sailed as a formed body escorted by warships. This tactic succeeded where other measures had failed because:

- The resultant concentration of shipping made the submarine's task of finding targets much more difficult.
- Putting warships near merchantmen made them available for counter-attack at the time when the submarine was at its most dangerous.

These benefits largely offset the potency of the submarine and staunched the previous haemorrhaging.

The First World War also saw other developments which were continued later. Some, such as anti-torpedo nets, were not to be used again in the same form, only re-appearing in static defences rather than the ungainly skirts surrounding warships of all sizes. Others like the depth charge were refined later. Perhaps the most significant was the aircraft. These were poorly equipped to attack submarines but, having the advantage of an elevated height of eye, were able to sight submarines before they had any chance of harming a ship or convoy. As in the Second World War, the mere presence of an aircraft was often sufficient to deter a submarine attacker. This, too, is ASW.

ASW AGAIN – THE SECOND WORLD WAR

In their essentials the submarines available at the beginning of the Second World War were little different from those of 1918. They were a little larger, better in detail and probably more reliable. However, even the Germans, who were to make most use of submarines, had only a very few boats initially, and many of these were small, suitable only for coastal operations. In ASW, Britain and France entered the war with confidence, because of the work which had been carried out in the intervening years on Asdic. It was believed that this, together with the refinement of the depth charge, spelt an end to the previous submarine menace. This sense of assurance also meant that, in Britain at least, the air force had been steered away from ASW in maritime warfare towards scouting for capital ships and surface raiders.

A further measure, inducing some trust, was the early introduction of the convoy system, albeit to a limited extent. This was due to the small number of ships and aircraft suitable for escort, and the many other calls on them. But the Germans too were, to use a modern term, resource limited and this denied them not success but significance. For them the big breakthrough came not with the relatively slow buildup of submarines capable of oceanic warfare, but with the overrunning of most of France in the summer of 1940. This allowed them much easier access to the Atlantic by way of the Biscay ports, where huge bases were built, and also tied up many potential British convoy escorts in anti-invasion duties.

This led to what the Germans dubbed the 'First Happy Time' when they were able to sink significant merchant tonnage relatively easily. Most of this was unescorted, not by British choice, but because of the lack of resources. A good point emerges here about ASW in general: it is an expensive form of warfare, nearly always dearer than the submarine warfare requiring it, and often utilising scarce resources or causing difficult choices in building policy.

A year later, however, the vaunted German successes were first checked, then overturned. Despite some writers attributing this solely to the British ability to read German codes, the causes are more complex and include:

- ► Much greater British effort being put into the area west of the UK on the surface and in the air.
- ► A reactive German move to the mid-Atlantic increasing passage times, reducing productivity as measured in tons sunk per submarine deployed at sea per period, and making searching more difficult.
- ► The British extension of the convoy system, both in routes and numbers of ships included.
- ► Cryptographic success which allowed evasion and reinforcement of threatened convoys.

This British ASW success was achieved without the mass sinking of submarines, and shows that such sinking is but one of several means in ASW, albeit a very useful one, rather than the end itself.

Early 1942 saw a partial restaging of the first part of the German First World War campaign. This time, heavy sinking took place off the east coast of the USA. America was slow to establish convoys and, despite the long passages involved, the Germans enjoyed a 'Second Happy Time' sinking many hundreds of thousands of tons of shipping.

By mid-1942, this problem had largely been corrected and the anti-shipping campaign, and thus the burden of ASW, switched back to the central north Atlantic. By now qualitative as well as quantitative ASW improvements were evident. The Germans had developed so-called wolfpack tactics, the two main characteristics of which were the use of search lines to locate convoys and groups of submarines attacking convoys by night, on the surface.

The former made lavish use of long-range radio transmissions, allowing both opportunities for SIGINT with decryption ashore and tactical HF DF by ships of the convoy escort. Such ASW methods were only made possible by the technologies of machine decryption and electronics allowing direction-finding equipment to be miniaturised sufficiently to go to sea in even small warships, such as corvettes.

The German technique of attacking by night on the surface was intended to combat Asdic and in this context it worked, as Asdic was ineffective against such targets. Because of the limited and difficult visual target presented by the submarine, the tactic enjoyed much effectiveness in the early days of such tactics

PLATE 2.2 A World War II frigate – workhorse of the ASW war
(Photo: Conway Maritime Press)

from late 1940 onwards. By mid-1942, however, the increasing use of radar in Allied escorts was making life more difficult for submarines attacking on the surface. They could also be attacked by gunfire after identification by illuminants, another growing facet of ASW. A further severe pressure on submarines came from the growing number of capable long-range aircraft, which might make the submarine dive, even if nothing worse was done.

Should these techniques force the submarine underwater, it might now be subject not only to detection by improved Asdic but also to larger weapons which could now be projected some distance from the firing ship. Greater numbers of more capable ships and aircraft, with crews trained to a higher pitch and in co-operation with those in other units produced more effective ASW, leading to fewer merchant ships being sunk and yet more tactical pressures on submarines. The latter was often imperative as the Germans were now building submarines very quickly indeed.

At the same time, some efforts were made to attack the Biscay bases using bomber aircraft. This initiative was unfortunately delayed until after the bases had been completed. Thus their massive construction defied virtually all efforts to damage them. This failure does not, however, deny the principle of attacking bases and the submarines in them as a method of ASW.

Back in the mid-Atlantic the relentless pressure and scale of the Allied effort bore fruit in the early summer of 1943 when the Germans withdrew their submarines from these routes – arguably the most important ASW victory ever. Now submarines tended to be used singly and with great difficulty in coastal waters. For then and for the rest of the war, the Allies were able to shift a strategic gear, inflicting more damage on the Germans than they could on the Allies by the war often being taken to submarines, often before they had even reached their operational areas. There were residual concerns since the Germans continued development of their submarines, finally achieving the type of vessel that was to dominate post-war submarine warfare until the arrival of the nuclear submarine in the 1950s.

These advanced submarines, with much improved underwater endurance worried the Allies considerably, but a combination of Ultra – the Allies' ability to read encrypted German signal traffic – to monitor their progress to operational service and bombing of the production facilities prevented their playing any significant part in the war; this, too, is ASW. The Germans showed considerable innovation in such things as homing torpedoes, but these were quickly addressed by Allied countermeasures as well as deployment of a similar air-dropped weapon giving Allied aircraft the capability of attacking a submerged submarine for the first time.

It is important to note that many of the material developments in ASW did not so much harm submarines directly as deny them effectiveness and make carrying out their tasks more difficult. Radar, be it ship- or aircraft-mounted, often contributed to attacks on submarines, but its true importance lay in its denying the use of the surface to the submarine. This may sound paradoxical but it should be remembered that the pre-1945 submarine was a misnomer, since it was actually really a submersible torpedo boat.

Three last observations on the Second World War are useful. The vast Allied effort on ASW permitted them their choice of strategy on land. It was because they had the submarine problem sufficiently under control that they were able not only to mount the re-invasion of Europe, but also to choose the place of landing. Success in the battles of Normandy and on to Berlin were not assured by winning the Battle of the Atlantic, but the former could not have occurred without the ASW war being won.

On the other side of the world we find an example of what happens when a nation neglects ASW. Most will say that the war against Japan was won by the two atomic weapons dropped on Hiroshima and Nagasaki in 1945 and some, better informed, will also note the earlier strategic bombing of Japanese cities. Few, however, will credit the virtual destruction of the Japanese merchant fleet carried out by a relatively small number of American submarines, cutting Japan off from the necessary resources of her earlier conquests. Without disclaiming the skill and courage of these submarines, the result was largely attributable to the neglect of ASW by the Japanese.

Lastly, the diminishing prominence of international law applied to submarine warfare, both in itself and also by the *de facto* adoption by the Allied nations of the practice of sinking on sight as had been practised amidst legal controversy by the Germans in the First World War. Certain limits still remained, such as prohibitions against the gratuitous killing of survivors, but the Prize Rules could no longer be regarded as even a soft facet of ASW.

POST-1945 – THE COLD WAR

The Cold War presented a paradox in ASW. Greater attention was paid to it than ever before and advances continued, arguably at a greater rate than had occurred earlier, despite the fact that two enormous campaigns had already fired the rate of progress. But for all this movement, the period is distinguished by a lack of 'hot' war ASW action. The fundamental reason for this is that the nations most likely to be involved in submarine and anti-submarine warfare – and therefore large-scale warfare – were locked in an antagonistic relationship, the massive implications of which tended to preclude actual combat. There was plenty of war elsewhere, but this was generally local or regional and rarely involved opposing nations who were sufficiently advanced in military technology to deploy significant submarine or ASW resources.

Thus the story of the second half of the century is largely tied up with the Cold War protagonists themselves. Both sides had very considerable submarine and ASW forces but, as the largest number of submarines was owned by the USSR, much of what follows is skewed towards NATO ASW. Although this relationship is central to understanding the strategic role of ASW, part of the story is also concerned with technology. The two facets are interlinked, the politico-strategic conflict encouraging technology and the latter continuing if not causing the former.

It is often thought that a large Soviet submarine fleet is exclusively a post-war phenomenon, but this is not so. In 1939, the Soviet submarine fleet was the biggest in the world, although their quality was not good. Many were small, slow and of limited capability. This is indicated by the necessary transfer of several British submarines to the Soviet Union during the war. Nor, despite the courage of some of the crews, were numbers translated into significant results. This was partly due to the Germans bottling up the Baltic Fleet, and also because of sparse tactical doctrine and poor skills. The Soviet submarine fleet was clearly outstripped in scale and capability by the Germans by 1945, but the Soviets eventually gained access to German technology and skill. In the West, as relations with the former coalition partner deteriorated, it was feared that the Soviets would produce not only copies of late-model German submarines with all that implied in terms of underwater performance and general capability, but also develop them further. Beyond this, there was concern that such high-technology submarines could appear in the sort of numbers that both the USSR and Germany had recently demonstrated.

The naval leaders of NATO had every reason to regard this prospect with foreboding. Although the Germans had achieved little from mid-1943, the potential of the new-generation submarines had been regarded with respect and dread. The prospect of fighting this enemy again was unwelcome. But such an assessment seemed not only a worst, but also quite a probable, case. Accordingly research, ship and equipment programmes, plans and tactics not

PLATE 2.3 German Type XXI submarine – a new threat
(Photo: L & L van Ginderen)

only had to retain the best features of their Battle of the Atlantic predecessors, but would also have to deal with faster, deeper diving, and generally more capable submarines. Most importantly, they would have to allow for submarines which had little reliance on the surface compared with Germany's 1939 submarines. Stress would have to be laid on detecting submerged submarines earlier. Although warships of the general destroyer and frigate categories were still faster than any submarine likely to be encountered – an attribute of importance in the Battle of the Atlantic – much of this speed was effectively 'unusable' in ASW as sonar did not perform well at higher speeds.

Weapons would also have to improve: the errors inherent in attacking relatively lightly built submarines with depth charges and early thrown weapons at the slow speeds of the earlier submarines were acceptable; with the new submarines, agile at depth as well as fast, such inaccuracies were unacceptable. For this, more accurate weapons were needed with greater explosive power to compensate for the difficulties in delivering projected ordnance at a submarine. The two basic methods were more projectiles and the nuclear weapon. A more productive approach, however, was to apply mid-course guidance after the weapon entered the water, and this was to result in the full development of the homing torpedo.

The aircraft, too, was expected to play a vital part with its inherent mobility – enhanced by refinements of sonobuoy systems, first deployed during the war as well as depth charges, torpedoes and (for the rare cases when a submarine was surprised on the surface) rocket projectiles. In addition, improvements were made in radar to detect and deter, and also to ancillary equipment.

Important strides were made and it would be fair to say that by the early 1950s, the main ASW nations of NATO, the USA and UK, were reasonably well prepared to deal with numbers, if not masses, of Soviet submarines derived from the German Type XXIII. Much of this was to be nugatory. This occurred, firstly, because the Soviets did not field either many or modern submarines in any great hurry. The first post war submarine, designated by NATO as the *Whiskey* class, did not appear until 1950 and although the class was eventually to number over 230 boats, the initial delivery rate was quite low. As importantly, although the submarine was reasonably competent, German technology was not deployed to any significant extent. The *Whiskey* was followed in 1952 by the *Zulu* class, a bigger boat which incorporated German technology. Ninety units of this and its successor, the *Foxtrot*, were to be completed over the next 20 years.

But, ironically, the second and greatest challenge to the ASW of the early 1950s was to come from the USA, with the commissioning in 1955 of USS *Nautilus*, the world's first nuclear-powered submarine, which combined two features of significance – virtually unlimited underwater endurance and high submerged speed. The potential of this submarine indicated the futility of much of the hard work and investment in ASW development that had been carried out up to then. The Soviets took some time to follow suit but by the late 1950s were fielding comparable nuclear submarines.

At the same time, they had also been active in broadening submarine roles. For many years submarines had been limited to a main task of attack on ships, naval or merchant, with subsidiary tasks including reconnaissance, minelaying and supporting special forces. By the late 1950s, this had been widened, largely by the Soviets, to include attack on warships (especially aircraft carriers) by cruise missiles and, most importantly, the delivery of strategic nuclear missiles against an enemy's home territory.

The Soviets had worked hard on all these roles and by 1960 were fielding submarines capable of exercising them all. In most cases there were dual submarine classes, utilising both diesel-electric and nuclear power. Thus the *Golf* class SSB (diesel) was paired with the *Hotel* SSBN (nuclear), both deploying the SS-N-4 strategic ballistic missile. Although the missile only had a range of 350nm, this was sufficient to threaten the myriad of politico-economic targets on the US east coast, as well as useful military targets such as the Norfolk, Virginia, naval complex, whilst a firing submarine could occupy a huge area of ocean. At sea a NATO task force might be threatened by SS-N-3 cruise missile firing *Echo I/II* SSGN (nuclear) or *Juliett* SSG (diesel) submarines. In this instance the missile had a range of some 250nm and despite such submarines having to surface to launch and guide the missile, there was again a huge area in which they could operate effectively.

This double gain in speed and weapon range made ASW much more difficult. There were two immediate ways forward, but neither of these were entirely satisfactory. An option open to the Americans, but to almost nobody else, was to create hunter-killer groups comprising ASW escorts, ASW aircraft carriers and sometimes submarines separate from any convoy or heavy warship escorting group.

Even with this powerful collection of ASW capabilities, the group would still need some form of target indication to put it into a position where its strengths might be used: this implied intelligence in some form and it is not clear whether this was available in sufficient quantity and quality to permit full effectiveness. The other alternative was to consider dealing with the submarine before it reached its operational area. This could take a number of forms ranging from attack on submarine production facilities and bases – unlikely to be effective other than in a long war – to sinking submarines in transit.

Obviously, attempts were made to continue the impetus of improvements in relatively close-range ASW, such as medium range sonars, variable depth and convergence range sonars, better torpedoes together with faster, more accurate means of delivery such as the drone anti-submarine helicopter (DASH) and anti-submarine rocket (ASROC). But these were no real solution to the distant submarine. The speed of aircraft was one characteristic which might be harnessed, but in the early part of the period this was more than counterbalanced by a relatively poor underwater sensor fit. Progress in this direction was to be made by vast improvements in passive sonobuoy systems, described later.

Many of the innovations of the next 30 years were concerned with the expansion of ASW horizons to counter the much greater submarine threat. Developments were made across a broad spectrum of strategy, tactics and technology. New vehicles for ASW emerged such as the helicopter equipped with dipping sonar and sonobuoy systems and, more significantly, the submarine itself. Although there had been submarine-to-submarine encounters in the Second World War, these had generally been of a chance nature and most attacks had been against submarines on the surface or at periscope depth. Now advances in underwater sensors made the concept of totally submerged warfare feasible.

Some measures were relatively crude, such as the nuclear depth bomb (NDB), seen as necessary to deal with fast and very strongly constructed submarines, but since abandoned by the NATO nations; others, such as some sensor systems, were very sophisticated. Later policies, such as the USA's Maritime Strategy, in which both Soviet Northern Fleet bases and SSBNs at sea were threatened, were thoroughly aggressive, taking ASW conflict to a potential enemy. But the problem of ASW for the Soviets did not start with this policy. Admittedly, the main maritime challenge had probably been perceived as being the NATO, that is largely US, aircraft carrier battle groups (CVBG), but the underwater threat to surface operations in the Barents and Norwegian Seas was also a concern as were land-attack cruise missiles fired from nuclear-powered attack submarines (SSNs) in the latter part of the period. But perhaps the greatest ASW challenge to the Soviets was the vulnerability of their SSBNs to Western ASW.

In the early 1960s when Soviet SSBNs were first deployed, exposure along the American coasts was inevitable because of their missile range. Nor was there much the Soviets could do about this, operating thousands of miles from their bases and with the natural barriers of the Greenland-Iceland-United Kingdom (GRIUK) gaps on the transit routes. The late 1960s saw a missile range improvement in the *Yankee* class SSBN, but even this was insufficient to retain the submarines in home waters. Such came in the early 1970s with the *Delta* class, whose 4,500nm-range missiles allowed operations from waters close to Soviet bases. This was the most important step forward made by the Soviets, and it had nothing to do with underwater technology, but was rather the product of improvements in rocket propulsion and terminal guidance accuracy, illustrating that effective developments in underwater warfare may have unexpected origins. A further, arguably even more important, move by the Soviets was to conduct patrols under the Arctic ice. At a stroke, this rendered much of Western ASW inoperable. A combination of environmental factors and natural top-cover meant that only Western SSNs could attempt to detect, track and even destroy Soviet SSBNs. There was a drawback in that under-ice SSBNs might not be instantly ready for missile launch, but many commentators have suggested that the SSBN force was a reserve one.

Two further growth areas were broad area sensors, such as the Sound Surveillance System (SOSUS) and Command, Control and Communications (C3) systems and organisations to support ASW. More will be said about these in later chapters. Surface ships were to regain some of the ground lost in the 1950s and 1960s with the introduction of long-range passive towed sonar arrays and the greater availability of ASW aircraft at sea.

ASW has thus enjoyed an eventful near-century. The two German campaigns in the first half of the century demonstrated the potential of the submarine beyond any doubt and indicated in the strongest possible terms the degree of effort and resources necessary to counter it. Despite the generally accurate aphorism of war forcing development, the pace of progress has been maintained since 1945: it would probably not be going too far to say that post-war developments – especially the nuclear submarine – have led to the same broadening of strategic horizons as earlier seaborne airpower did compared with the gun. ASW would appear to have kept track with its enemy, the submarine, although that statement has not been put to the test significantly since 1945.

3

Know Your Enemy – the Submarine

INTRODUCTION

The previous chapter should have made it clear that ASW in its essence is reactive. Particular technologies and tactics may balance the potential of the submarine for harming the aims of the nation practising ASW, or even move ahead of it, but the submarine itself, its characteristics and roles, form the anvil on which the hammer of ASW has to work. For this reason it is necessary to consider the submarine in some detail before moving on to explain ASW further. Here submarines will be considered in terms of propulsion, roles and activities. Much more detail of this potent warship and its *modus operandi* can be found in the *Submarines* volume of this series by Rear Admiral John Hervey.

PROPULSION

The first way of classifying submarines is by their types as opposed to their roles. Here the main division is by propulsion method and this is to some extent further overlaid by age or technological generation. There are fundamentally two main propulsion divisions at present – diesel-electric and nuclear – and these have radically different natures, although the gap is not perhaps as wide in its effects as it was some decades ago. Technological developments such as Air Independent Propulsion (AIP) systems may even cross the divide, but these are only on the verge of operational deployment and it is too early to judge their full impact, which is considered in Chapter 10.

The diesel-electric submarine has a pedigree extending back virtually to the beginning of practical submarines. On the surface, it is propelled by one or more diesel reciprocating engines and a similar number of propellers. It has become common to avoid direct mechanical drive, instead using the intermediate devices of generators, batteries and electric motors.

This is done for a number of reasons. Firstly, indirect drive allows more flexibility in the design of machinery spaces and layouts. Secondly, this technique facilitates the acoustic isolation of the relatively noisy diesel engines from the rest of the propulsive equipment, known as the drive train. But most impor-

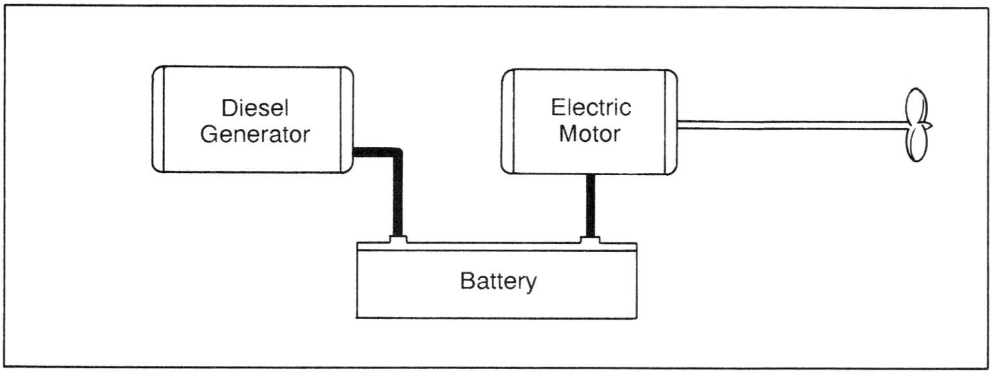

FIG. 3.1 Conventional submarine drive train

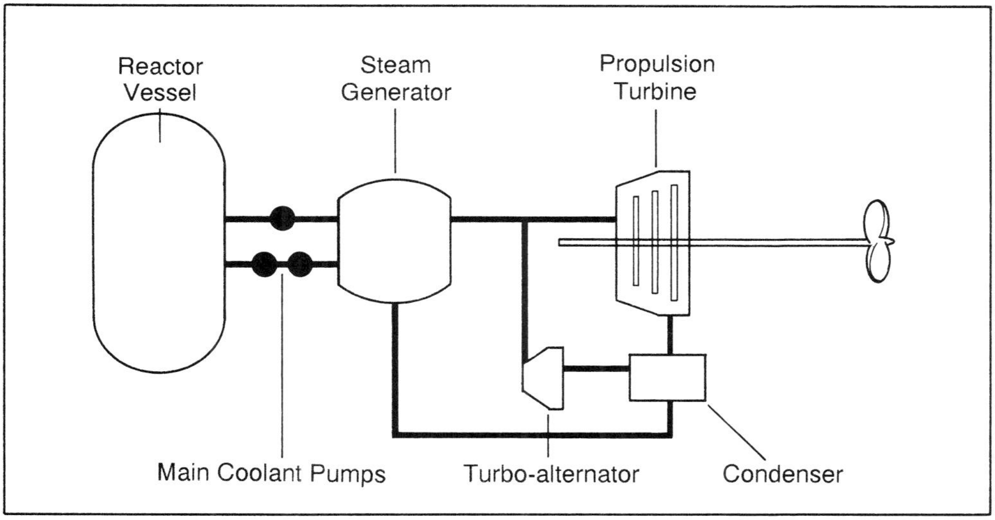

FIG. 3.2 Nuclear submarine drive train

tantly, indirect drive uses the two components (battery and motor) of the underwater propulsion system. This has proved to be an enduring and relatively cheap method of carrying out submarine operations.

The nuclear submarine uses much more exotic technology, although by the late 20th century it can hardly be considered unfamiliar. Here a nuclear reactor is usually of the pressurised water (PWR) type, although some using liquid metal coolants are also in use, and is employed as a heat generator in order to produce steam to drive a turbine. From this point power is either transmitted direct to a propulsor or else (and less commonly) indirectly by means of electric transmission. This has been used experimentally by the USA, in the Russian *Alfa* class and in French nuclear submarines.

An advantage of using a nuclear plant is relatively high power output and thus the ability to move at high speed, but a factor of perhaps even greater importance is the virtual severance of dependence on the surface.

The modern diesel-electric submarine minimises its use of the sea surface by using a schnorkel tube to run its diesels underwater and thus charge its batteries. This is a vast improvement on the submarines which began the Second World War. These had to surface fully to charge their batteries which was a lengthy process in those days; indeed as we have noticed it is often more useful to regard such submarines as submersible torpedo boats rather than true submarines. Another feature which favours the modern diesel-electric submarine is to improvements in battery technology which greatly reduce the amount of time which has to be spent 'snorting' at periscope depth in order to keep the battery at a high state of charge.

Despite these advances, the relatively low underwater speed of the diesel-electric submarine coupled with its greater dependence on the surface dictate a much lesser degree of both tactical and strategic mobility than that of the nuclear submarine. So why does every submarine operating nation not build nuclear submarines?

Firstly, many nations probably do not perceive the need for such a potent warship. Its speed and endurance endow it with great reach and this is quite simply not a quality needed by every nation in the world. Next, the technology itself is often beyond national capabilities. Of the five current nuclear submarine operators (Russia, USA, France, UK and China) the UK reactor design owes a design debt to the USA and it is possible that the Chinese design is not entirely indigenous. Some other nations such as Brazil and India may have nuclear propulsion aspirations and others, perhaps Japan, are potential operators. A capability might also be achieved without creating the ability to build seagoing nuclear power plants: India leased a *Charlie* class SSGN from the Soviet Union in 1988–91. There are no known further instances of 'rent-a-reactor', but the combination of a considerable number of nuclear submarines and urgent economic necessity must make such propositions at least potentially attractive to Russia.

It is very difficult to be clear what the true cost difference is between a diesel-electric and a nuclear submarine. It is rare for comparable costs to be available. Nuclear submarines tend to be larger, which in itself is an important cost factor. The 'ordinary' SSN, which in itself becoming more difficult to define (see later in this chapter) tends to be in the 6,000–9,000 ton bracket, although both Chinese and French SSNs are markedly smaller. Diesel-electric submarines tend to peak around 3,000 tons with many smaller than this figure. Equipment fit is also an important variable in determining price. However, one generally reliable commentator considers that American research and development on their next generation SSN, the *Seawolf* class or SSN 21, exceed a billion dollars, of which a third is on the propulsion plant alone. Such a sum could equip the entire flotilla of many submarine operating nations – this alone may explain the slow pace of nuclear propulsion proliferation.

It is also important to note that purchase of propulsion plant itself can be regarded merely as the down payment for a very large bill. Nuclear submarines require sophisticated and costly support, greatly beyond the level of the diesel-electric variety.

The example of Canada in the mid- to late-1980s is instructive. A concern with northern water sovereignty and surveillance led to consideration of a medium-sized SSN fleet. Many difficulties stood in the way of such a project, but even before the thawing of the Cold War it probably ruled out such an ambitious project. Lastly, a growing international sentiment against nuclear power in all its manifestations, especially marked since the Chernobyl disaster, can hardly aid the cause of a growing maritime nuclear propulsion industry.

Indeed, it may be argued that the threefold rationale of need, cost and technology had already limited the spread of nuclear propulsion before the last factor came into play. Even allowing for the uncertain cases, there are almost certainly more producers of nuclear weapons in the world now than operators of nuclear submarines. There are certainly more nations with access to such weapons in one way or another than deploy nuclear propulsion or are even interested in it. With the post-Cold War retrenchments in the defence budgets of the existing nuclear propulsion nations (with the exception of China), large-scale expansion in nuclear submarine fleets appear unlikely in the medium-term. This topic will be returned to in the chapter on the future of ASW.

ROLES OF SUBMARINES

Early submarines provoked much initial interest because of the one weapon which determined their role: the torpedo. Thus was born the normally underwater weapon system designed to sink ships in relatively quick order. The obvious nature of this point should not obscure its significance. Prior to the advent of the mine in the late 19th century, it was normal for ships engaged in combat to be disabled rather than sunk. Indeed, a degree of disability was often only a prelude to capture, either by boarding party or surrender, and outright and deliberate sinking was comparatively rare. This reflected two factors: the relative inability of shipborne weapons to sink similar and even smaller vessels in a reasonable time; and the economic advantages of securing a prize. The latter was not merely a matter of semi-abstract advantage to the capturing nation; it also practically benefited the crew or crews concerned who shared in the value of such a prize. This was often significant in the case of a warship capture, but was even greater if a merchant vessel carrying a valuable cargo was captured. An important element in permitting this tactic was the discretionary nature of gunfire. The mine and later the torpedo obviated the option of graduated violence: they tended only to sink or severely damage their targets. This was an important development in naval warfare and it is reflected in all submarines in service today – each one deploys torpedoes, and each is capable of destroying surface ships or causing them heavy damage.

So, first and foremost every submarine, no matter its other purposes, is capable of attacking surface ships with straight running torpedoes. It may be able to carry out many other roles, but this one is fundamental to the threat it poses to other nations. Another characteristic function of early submarines which with some modification is still important is that of scouting or reconnaissance.

Although the submarine is still an excellent platform for an underwater sensor, its performance in other media has become degraded or overtaken by other developments. Thus its already relatively poor visual observation capabilities have suffered further as it has become more a true submarine – the tower of a Second World War submarine on the surface a few feet above water had severe visual limitations; the even lower periscope is worse. It is true that advances in electro-optics such as image intensification and infra-red techniques have allowed more to be seen in poor conditions, especially at night, but these do nothing significant to improve the area of view.

Rather better results can be obtained against electronic emissions, but this is normally regarded as self-protective rather than having any greater importance. Much of what the submarine might have achieved 20 or 30 years ago is probably done better now from specialised reconnaissance vehicles, such as aircraft or satellites: these often employ passive means of information collection, but are not necessarily covert. The submarine still has advantages against those littoral targets for which a covert vehicle must be used.

However, the submarine has gained many other capabilities and roles to add to that of attacking surface ships at relatively close ranges with straight-running torpedoes. Firstly, torpedoes themselves have been greatly improved by means of homing systems, using either acoustic- or wake-homing techniques. It is not intended to consider the details of such weapons, or the counters to them, here but it should be noted that they help submarines to carry out their tasks in two ways. Firstly, they tend to remove or reduce the necessity for obtaining the extremely accurate target solutions formerly needed for a successful attack with straight-running weapons. Secondly, an associated property is that they often allow attack at greater ranges from the target. These two factors give the submarine greater flexibility as well as almost certainly reducing the risk to itself in carrying out an attack.

Wake homing weapons are a relatively recent Russian development, but the acoustic torpedo has been around for about 50 years. At the time when the latter was first introduced, submarines had virtually no realistic capability against another submarine, provided that it was fully submerged – the acoustic homing weapon together with the introduction of better sonar was to change all this. Accordingly the anti-submarine submarine evolved in the 1950s and 60s. Not all nations took immediately to this development. The leading innovators were those who saw submarines, particularly the large Soviet fleet, as a threat. Thus the Americans and British were leaders in this field. The subsequent decades were also to see a vast extension of the submarine's capability to attack shipping and an entirely new role.

Anti-Ship Missile Submarines This development and that of ballistic land attack systems were to occur almost in parallel and were to draw submarines in two important directions, but they had a common root, the missile. Practical early submarine-launched missiles for attacking ships at sea were first deployed by the Soviet Union from a variety of hulls, both diesel-electric and nuclear-powered. The earliest of such weapons, the SS-N-3 *Shaddock* system, was also deployed in surface ships and the essential nature of the two versions was the

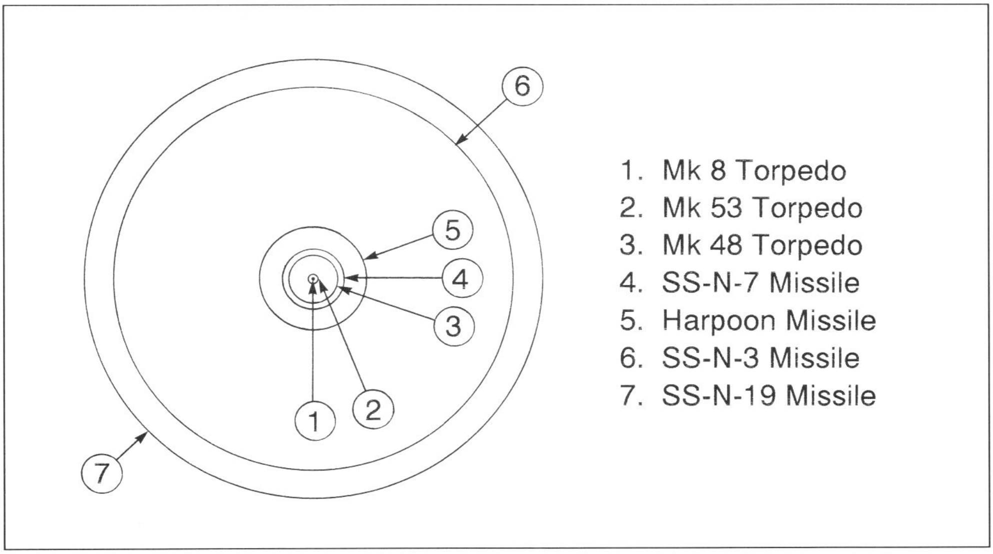

FIG. 3.3 Submarine weapon range – Mk 8 torpedo to SS-N-19

same, with the important distinction that the submarine did not have to put in an appearance on the sea surface until it was just about to fire the weapons. The missile had a range of around 250nm, needed some source of outside targeting, and as well as surfacing to fire, the submarine had to stay surfaced for part of the flight to allow missile mid-course guidance.

Although this was a considerable tactical constraint, the missile range greatly extended the reach of submarines attacking surface forces. With a maximum of eight missiles in the nuclear-powered *Echo II* class and only four in the diesel-electric *Juliett* class, and no reloads, this was obviously not a weapon which was likely to be used against stray merchant vessels or probably even convoys. Instead the target was intended to be the carrier-borne strike forces of the NATO alliance, especially those of the USA. Despite the complexities and vulnerabilities of such systems, they provided the Soviet Union with a useful capability, especially at the time when they were introduced in the early 1960s.

This development established a new type of submarine whose further evolution has continued to the present. It may be useful to sketch out a few details of this. The next innovation again came from the Soviet Union in the shape of missiles with much less range, but which could be fired from underwater and probably without any form of external targeting. This was the SS-N-7 (later SS-N-9) missile system with a range of some 30nm fitted only in the nuclear *Charlie* class of submarines and deployed since the late 1960s. Since then, the Russians have only produced one subsequent main class, the massive *Oscar* of around 13,000 tons in the early 1980s. This deploys 24 SS-N-19 missiles capable of a range of over 300nm, submerged launch, and needing no intervention from the submarine once launched. Again it would appear that major warship groups and not merchant shipping are the intended targets of such submarines.

The West has never developed the dedicated anti-ship missile-firing submarine in the same way, opting for tube-launched weapons with much shorter ranges and obviating the necessity for mid-flight guidance. Thus American and British submarines deploy the 70nm Harpoon and French the 27nm Exocet. American SSNs can also deploy the anti-ship version of the Tomahawk missile, which will be referred to later, with a range of 250nm. These systems came into service much later than the first Soviet missiles but still extend the reach of submarines from that of even the longest range torpedoes.

Land Attack Missile Submarines The early Cold War period produced a requirement for diversity in the delivery of strategic nuclear weapons and this was provided for by the development of ballistic missile-firing submarines from the late 1950s onwards. The true pioneer in this field was the American Polaris weapon system deployed in the *George Washington* class of submarines with submerged launch and carrying 16 missiles, although this was preceded by several Soviet submarines carrying only a few short-range and surface launched weapons.

PLATE 3.1 SLBM being fired *(Photo: Conway Maritime Press)*

This allowed submarines to threaten land targets far inland with weapons of massive, city destroying, capability.

Here the submarine no longer either waited in one location in the hope that the target would come to it or was more dynamic (especially in the case of the nuclear-propelled boat) looking for its targets. It could instead spend long periods at slow speeds using its inherently stealthy qualities to ensure the security of its weapon system and therefore making it very difficult for an aggressor to attempt pre-emptive action against it. Apart from a few early Soviet submarines, all of these were nuclear-powered and the speed potential was only of use for rapid deployment or escape from attack. Nuclear power's advantage in this case was to allow extended operations at sea with a minimal dependence on the surface.

In subsequent decades such submarines were to enjoy gradual improvement by means of material advances, such as those allowing quieter operation, but the greatest steps forward were to come from the increases in missile range which allowed greater flexibility in deployment area. This was to be important for the Western ballistic missile submarines of the USA, UK and France but allowed even greater changes for the Soviet Union. From the early boats which had to pass through thousands of miles of Western dominated, if not controlled, waters to reach firing positions off the American coast, successive improvements in missile range allowed first the use of much larger sea areas, then patrolling in rather safer areas without having to pass through the GRIUK gap. Later increases in range permitted both the use of home waters and, perhaps more importantly, the option of stationing SSBNs under the Arctic ice. This combination of huge areas and places impenetrable to much of Western ASW – that deployed from surface ships and aircraft – was extremely effective.

Nor was this all. The 1980s were to see the advent in both the USA and USSR of a new type of land-attack weapon, the cruise missile. To be technically correct, all this designation means is that the missile is non-ballistic in its trajectory, and flies to its target at controlled heights: thus the anti-ship missiles described earlier in this chapter are cruise missiles. However, the later development has usurped this term virtually to itself. It represented the marriage of several maturing technologies to produce a militarily useful package. Firstly, its use of small and fuel-efficient turbojet technology gave rise to the ability to project a small missile in excess of a thousand miles, albeit at subsonic speeds. Secondly, the vast increases in data processing power brought about by the microprocessor allowed the missile to find its way to its target by means of forward-looking radar being able to compare what it sees with stored digital images of land patterns, a technique known as Terrain Comparison (TERCOM). Lastly, miniaturisation of nuclear warheads allowed construction of strategic cruise missiles. The last point was to cause some political turmoil both between nations and with domestic opponents of nuclear proliferation when the weapons were under development and first deployed in the mid-1980s. But it was the combination of the ability to guide a conventional warhead to a target with great accuracy and the weapon's small size which was probably to have the greatest impact on warfare. The latter meant that not only could it be fired from road-mobile land launchers and aircraft, but it could also fit into a submarine's torpedo tube.

The *Tomahawk* cruise missile (in its land-attack version) with a range of 1,400 miles was introduced into service in submarines in the USA in the 1980s and the Russian SS-N-21, a weapon with slightly shorter range, went to sea at about the same time. The limited number of torpedo tubes available in US SSNs has led to later members of the SSN 688 class being fitted with 12 external tubes exclusively for *Tomahawk*. The Russians also have a much larger missile, the SS-N-24, in development and fitted to a converted SSBN of the *Yankee* class.

So far this class of weapons has neither been supplied to any other nations, nor are they known to be in development anywhere other than in the USA and Russia.

These weapons make many more land targets susceptible to attack from the sea, and submarine-launched cruise missiles (SLCM) were used in 1991 against targets in Iraq. Perhaps more importantly, this weapon not only adds to the capability of the submarine, but also blurs the classification of submarines by single role. Thus the American SSN 688 *Los Angeles* class is normally described as an SSN but as well as attacking surface ships with torpedoes, it can also assail them with two types of missiles, *Harpoon* and *Tomahawk*, as well as being able to engage land targets with the other variant of *Tomahawk*. Lastly, it is also a powerful ASW submarine.

This reintroduces the topic of the submarine as an ASW vehicle. Virtually all current submarines have some capability in this field, but there are enormous variations. At the high end are submarines deployed by such nations as the USA, Russia and the UK where ASW is a principal, if not the sole, role. In these not only

PLATE 3.2 USN *Los Angeles* class SSN – a powerful all-rounder
(Photo: L & L van Ginderen)

is equipment such as sonar and torpedoes fitted for ASW, but important aspects of design are also driven by this requirement.

This can have a major influence on hull structure and the detail of machinery systems and will be considered in greater detail later in the book. The other end of the scale of ASW capability is probably found in nations which deploy a few, relatively small boats.

For a submarine, as for all warships and other ASW units, ASW capability consists of more than just owning the right equipment. Two further essentials are doctrine and competence. The former is necessary to select and inform ASW strategy and tactics suited to the nation's requirements and assets: competence is needed to make the best use of equipment and doctrine. This latter facet is especially difficult to measure as it is not only difficult to observe, but also depends on essentially subjective judgements. It might be suggested that a nation deploying a small number of relatively elderly submarines remote from other submarine operating nations and having for some time rather more pressing priorities than ASW, such as South Africa, may not be too competent in this field, but it is difficult to be totally certain.

Another case which could be inferred is that of France, where despite much emphasis on defence and a good appreciation of the importance of maritime forces, SSN ownership came comparatively late with the *Rubis* class only entering service in 1983, making the French the last of five nations to own SSNs: the penultimate member of this club was China, nearly a decade earlier. Returning to the French case, it is also noteworthy that these submarines only recently had their design modified (and earlier members of the class retrofitted) to equip them with a much improved ASW capability. This suggests that their original primary role was intended as anti-surface ship and not ASW. If this is so, then no matter how good the new equipment, French submariners probably have decades less experience in nuclear submarine-based ASW than those of other similarly equipped nations.

Lastly, some mention should be made of other roles such as reconnaissance, intelligence gathering and special forces operations (such as the insertion of commandos into coastal areas). Being essentially a stealthy platform, the submarine is well suited to such work. However, as with ASW, these are difficult areas in which to measure capability and competence. Further, although these roles have been presented together there are also important differences in the preparation necessary to carry them out. Any submarine fitted with the basic sensors likely to be found in any submarine and a communications system can carry out coastal or ocean reconnaissance in at least a rudimentary fashion: intelligence gathering tends to demand more in the way of special equipment and training. In neither of the latter cases are these additions likely to be too obvious. It is thus very difficult to assess both capability in these fields and whether such tasks are being carried out by submarines. Nevertheless ASW operations may still have to attempt to counter these operations.

SUBMARINE ACTIVITIES

The description of submarine types and their roles gives an initial assessment of what these potent warships might attempt to achieve, but has not touched on how they might go about these tasks. This is a vast subject and it is covered more fully in Rear Admiral Hervey's volume, but a brief consideration is necessary here so that the potential for ASW can at least be glimpsed. Where appropriate, this will be expanded upon later in the book.

In most cases, submarines need to make passages from their base ports to their areas of operations. There is nearly always a trade-off between speed and covertness of the transit. A nuclear submarine – even the most modern – makes more noise the faster it goes, and this may make it more susceptible to ASW. Even the diesel-electric boat, which is much quieter when fully submerged, has to charge its batteries, an activity which is a great deal noisier than propulsion on battery-electric drive. A further point is that the faster the passage, the more time the submarine has to spend charging batteries. A point is quickly reached at which an unacceptable amount of time has to be spent on this activity.

Then, paradoxically, it may be faster to make the passage on the surface, despite most modern submarines having higher underwater maximum speeds than on the surface. Tactical circumstances may make a surface passage impossible, or at least highly risky. All these circumstances make the submarine vulnerable to ASW.

Submarines once in area may need to move around in order to carry out their tasks. The nature of this can be very different: SSBNs are liable to move very slowly, putting a premium on avoiding detection; SSNs or even diesel-electric powered ASW submarines (SSKs) may need to be relatively dynamic in either finding targets, tracking them or moving into an attacking position. This is particularly likely when information from outside sources is limited in quantity or imprecise in nature. Even when located, the activities of the submarine's potential target may themselves force further movement and induce activities such as excursions to periscope depth. Clearly, a slow bulk carrier as a target is probably less demanding in this respect than a large and complex task force at speed, especially when only the higher value units of the force are targets of choice. Even when the submarine has a weapon which allows a greater degree of tactical freedom, such as a long-range missile, movement may still be neces- sary in circumstances where the target(s) are highly dynamic; or an attack cannot be carried out immediately because of rules of engagement constraints; or difficulties arise in selecting which of many potential targets is the prime one. The reception of external information can involve extended periods at periscope depth, which may also have an effect on the probability of detection.

All these activities and many others afford opportunities for detection and other ASW action. It should also be remembered that not all submarines are handled with the same high degree of tactical skill at all times. For example, time spent by a submarine investigating a contact which should have been classified as spurious at an early stage may subsequently involve a high speed sprint for several hours in order to regain the vicinity of the proper target. Similarly, as with all warships, material defects such as a noisy piece of machinery may limit operational effectiveness. Excursions to periscope depth may be beneficial for ASW for three reasons. Firstly, this may limit or even curtail another submarine activity; secondly, it may make the submarine more liable to detection by ASW sensors; lastly, the process of coming to periscope depth safely and returning afterwards to depth absorbs time which might have been better spent doing other things.

CONCLUSION

The submarine is a capable and complex modern warship which is capable of carrying out a great number of roles, most of which have great value for the submarine-owning nation. Properly equipped and competently handled, the submarine poses a very considerable threat. ASW can counter or even conquer it, but the three thoughts which should always be at the forefront of any ASW practitioner's mind should be:

- What is my enemy?
- What is he doing now and what will he do next?
- How will he do it?

Unless these tenets are used to inform attitudes, knowledge and actions, practical – far less successful – ASW is unlikely to be the outcome.

4

The Spectrum of ASW

INTRODUCTION

A popular conception of ASW, nurtured by many films set in the Second World War and later, has surface escorts wheeling tightly around a cornered submarine. The hunters all 'ping' furiously and drop many depth charges which invariably explode with devastating if not fatal results around their prey. Such images have been updated somewhat by the more recent success of the book and film of *The Hunt for Red October*. Although the latter may be reasonably accurate in many ways, both representations of ASW are potentially misleading in two respects. Firstly, the dimension of time is so compressed as to introduce great distortions: in the Second World War many escorts, despite many long days, weeks and months on convoy protection duties, never gained submarine contact or participated in any action. Secondly by concentrating on the high intensity, relatively close action part of ASW, many other important activities are neglected.

Returning to the definition of ASW as 'the art and science of depriving an enemy of the effective use of his submarines', it should be evident that there is not one but very many ways to skin the ASW cat. In discussing these, it may be helpful to establish some principles for ASW as these tend to inform the decision of a nation to engage in ASW, the extent to which it participates in this type of warfare and the methods adopted. In the last chapter, stress was laid on the various types of submarine and their different roles: this is probably the most important aspect in determining an ASW policy. The types of submarines deployed by enemies, actual or likely and their roles and capabilities will always be the first and most important matters to help determine ASW policy. There is little point in pursuing some scientific development – no matter how attractive – or in declaring some new doctrine unless it relates to a potential opposing submarine force: this reactive aspect has been and is likely to remain a constant of ASW.

The mention of time brings up another important point. This is often a neglected aspect of ASW, but it is of considerable importance. This dimension will be mentioned often in this chapter, but it may be helpful to give two illustrations of its significance at the outset; one tactical, one strategic. In the Second World War, when operating in mid-Atlantic, it was important for Allied ASW forces to keep German submarines submerged as much as possible. This destroyed their surfaced speed advantage over the relatively slow convoys and made it difficult, if not impossible, for these submarines to regain an attacking position before the convoy came under the protection of stronger air cover as it approached either America or Britain. The strategic example deals with the desirability of attacking either submarine bases or building yards. Either ploy may work in itself, but it is unlikely to be of any use strategically, except in the long term. Again using an historical example, the systematic Allied attacks on German submarine-building shipyards in the latter part of the Second World War, although effective in themselves and of great importance in denying the enemy a significant capability in the future, did little to lessen the immediate availability of submarines at sea.

In many ways, the Russian approach to warfare is more helpful when considering the totality of ASW than that suggested by the examples given in the first paragraph of this chapter. Their methodical approach explores all aspects of the problem and their relatively limited experience of hot war ASW does not necessarily invalidate their theory at the higher levels of warfare. They would consider any activity which weakens a potential submarine offensive against them as ASW. Thus an attack launched from the air using cruise missiles against a land target such as King's Bay, Georgia (a *Trident* submarine operating base) or a VLF radio transmitting complex would be considered as ASW.

Such a classification would not find total acceptance in the Western nations: there, such action would be more likely to be construed as air warfare. It can, of course, be argued that what matters is the consequence and not the classification, but the Russian method allows a more comprehensive and thorough look at ASW as a whole. This approach will be used in this chapter, although many of the methods and considerations outlined here make little or no further appearance in this book. Nevertheless, it is important to bear these strategies and operational techniques in mind: ASW is much more than sinking submarines.

In order to explore this area, two main techniques will be used. The characteristics and roles of submarines discussed in the last chapter will form the essential backdrop to a consideration of ASW measures. This will be used in conjunction with the chronological progress of a mythical submarine from building to close engagement by ASW forces: from cradle to, hopefully, grave.

PHASES OF SUBMARINE LIFE

Any submarine, be it an SLBM-firing monster weighing some tens of thousands of tons, or a coastal type at a few hundred tons, has to be built. It will nearly always require specialised support in its operational life: thus it also requires a base with access to rather more than a pier and fuel. Its crew require training, both ashore and at sea. Once deployed for useful service, it will almost certainly have to make its way to an operational area. There it may not be immediately involved in action: indeed, its role may actually demand that it avoids such encounters, as in the case of SSBNs. On the other hand, it may have to search for its enemy. Then, closure of its target to weapon range may follow;

an attack on this enemy; and lastly, post-attack evasion. Broadly, the life of a submarine falls into these phases: and each of them offers opportunities for ASW.

Production Building a submarine is a long process, usually measurable in years. Even under the stimulus of war, it is still likely to be lengthy. It can also usually only be carried out in a few, normally known, locations. As far as is known, none of these are hardened sites but are clearly placed in the open. One partial exception to this was the system adopted by the Germans in the later years of the Second World War when sub-assemblies of prefabricated submarines, sometimes built in different places, were only brought together for final construction at a relatively late stage. It is possible to go even further and attack the sources and transport nodes of raw materials – by this point, the whole economy of the target country is being assailed and it is not intended to pursue this thread of warfare any further here. It is probable that the vulnerability of submarine building yards has been increased by the advent of such weapons as 'smart' bombs and land-attack cruise missiles. These make it possible to target specific parts of such facilities.

With good intelligence beforehand and satisfactory Battle Damage Assessment (BDA) after the attack, it should be possible to put submarine production facilities out of action – and keep them unproductive, should it be necessary – with a relatively small amount of effort. Such capabilities are best and most

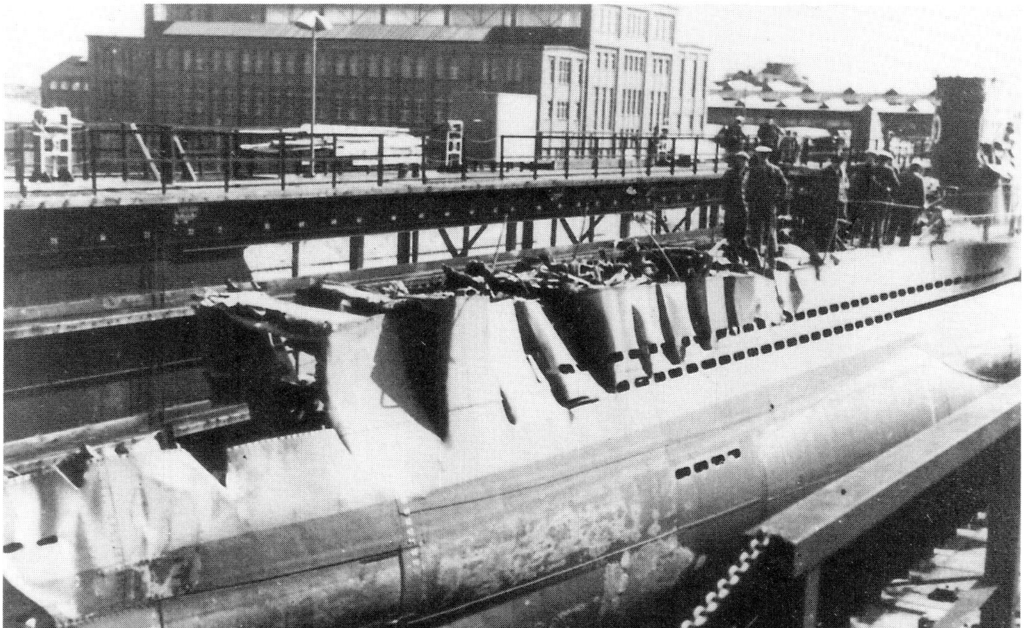

PLATE 4.1 Submarine in dock *(Photo: L & L van Ginderen)*

efficiently exercised by nations with advanced military capabilities. Nevertheless any state with reasonably modern air forces having the necessary reach ought to be able at least to attempt to destroy or disrupt submarine production facilities.

A historic example of this occurred towards the end of the Second World War. The Germans were attempting to put their more advanced submarines, the Types XXI and XXIII, into operational service. They had adopted the technique of prefabrication, only final assembly taking place in conventional shipyards. This reduced the considerable time the submarine spent in one place. But prefabrication introduced the complication and further vulnerability of having to transport sub-assemblies, themselves of significant size, to the shipyards. The Allied bombing offensive, targeted against shipyards and the transport system, was sufficiently effective to cause major delays to the programmes, and the submarines never entered productive operational service.

Although effective, there is a disadvantage to this form of attack. Attacks may be totally successful in themselves, but they will have no effect whatsoever on submarines already in service. This is therefore a technique only suited to a long war: even if carried out immediately on the outbreak of hostilities, and assuming success, the true worth will not become evident for at least a year and probably longer. As in many other aspects of ASW, time is an important factor.

PLATE 4.2 Submarine depot ship *(Photo: L & L van Ginderen)*

Bases Attacking bases may initially appear to offer a more time-efficient version of shipyard destruction, but the two cases are rather more than subtly different. Although modern submarine bases are often large and relatively easy targets for modern air attack, they may be less vulnerable in one of two ways. Firstly, some nations invest in mobile submarine depot ships. Admittedly this tends to be confined to the larger nations, such as the USA and Russia, but they also tend to have the larger submarine fleets posing the greatest possible ASW challenge. Support ships such as these are principally designed to improve reach, but their mobile nature complicates the task of attack for an aggressor. Admittedly to be fully effective, they are likely to be stationed close to land, partly re-raising the question of cruise missile attack, but they are probably easier to defend than sprawling shore bases.

The second technique is that of bunkers, sometimes known as submarine pens. Such underground works can either use existing topography, as in submarine bases in the Kola Peninsula in Russia, or else be built in the open as the Germans did in France during the Second World War. Although it is possible that such structures might be vulnerable to Precision Guided Munitions (PGMs) and cruise missiles, this has not been proved in practice. It is probably safe to say that these would be more difficult targets than facilities placed in conventional structures.

PLATE 4.3 *Conqueror* in submarine base *(Photo: DML)*

Again, the time dimension is of importance. Although likely to be less significant than with shipyards, the effect of a successful attack on bases would probably start to bite within months rather than years. However, it will be necessary to carry out effective attacks on all bases (or all in an operational theatre) to achieve the full effect. Some purpose may be served by partial attacks, leading to the overloading of the surviving facilities, but this will have to be carefully calculated if the maximum return for effort is to happen.

One facet common to both attacks on building yards and bases is that such options are more likely to be the prerogative of nations advanced in warfare skills other than pure ASW. Both cruise missiles and highly survivable bombers – a normal prerequisite for land attack – tend to belong only to the more advanced nations. A weapon such as the *Scud* short range ballistic missile (SRBM) is unlikely to be suitable for these targets: a lucky shot may land in the general area but causing the specific damage necessary to destroy the effectiveness of yards and bases is probably well beyond their current capability. The significance of such strategic ASW measures as effective land-attack systems is likely to be most effective in unequal circumstances, that is when a powerful advanced power is taking on a weaker, less developed one – even here, the caveat on time remains: attacking even such important and relevant land targets is unlikely to produce fast results.

Submarines in Transit The next chronological opportunity to take an ASW battle to the enemy is on the transit routes from a submarine base to operational areas. Sometimes, these may be very long. Germany deployed a few submarines to the Indian Ocean and even the Far East during the Second World War: more frequent deployments to the US east coast and Caribbean also took place. Such long deployment distances and times, measurable in thousands of miles and weeks, stand in stark contrast to the enormous reach given to modern SSBNs by the range of their missile systems. Often they can achieve full coverage of their potential targets without even leaving their bases. But this apparent benefit is of course eroded by the fact that this sacrifices their covertness, in which lies the whole point of deploying strategic weapons systems in submarines in the first place. Thus even this type of submarine will almost certainly have to move from a base area to a location for operations. Such movements afford opportunities for ASW; how useful these are will depend very much on several other factors, broadly described below.

Firstly, the route itself has to be considered. To what extent is it under the control of the submarine- or ASW-employing power is one very obvious factor. This will tend to determine the feasibility of ASW and the type of forces used. If much of the route is well away from areas in which the submarine-using state has control, then almost any form of ASW vehicle may be deployed. Conversely if the opposite applies, then aircraft may be the better ASW units; or if enemy control is of a higher order still, then submarines themselves might be the only type of unit capable of use without risking undue losses. If all other qualities are equal, the range of an ASW unit may allow more options in terms of choice of deployment area and, perhaps, in permitting multiple attacks on target submarines. The physical nature of the route is important, too. The extent to which deploying submarines might be constrained by land and underwater features plays a part. The way that the environment, particularly acoustic characteristics, can affect ASW sensor performance is also likely to be a prime factor.

Related to the route as well as operational considerations is the speed of deployment. Although a faster speed may minimise time to reach, and maximise time spent in, the operational area, as well as complicating the task of interception for ASW forces, it is far from being an unmixed blessing. For the diesel-electric submarine, speed is in any case a relative concept. Although short high speed underwater bursts are possible, these cannot be sustained for any significant period of time. Surfaced speeds are no more than 10-12 kts maximum, a consequence of almost all modern submarines having their hulls optimised for underwater performance. In any case, a surfaced transit may not be either desired or even feasible. The diesel-electric submarine, except when transiting friendly waters, is therefore usually constrained to underwater passages at speeds less than the surfaced speed, using batteries at a reasonably economic consumption rate and returning periodically to periscope depth. This allows

PLATE 4.4 Snort masts – a constraining factor on fast passages
(Photo: Conway Maritime Press)

recharging using snort masts. The latter process may afford ASW detection opportunities both to fixed systems such as SOSUS (see Chapters 2 and 9) and airborne radar.

In fully dived phases, the diesel-electric submarine is immune to detection other than acoustically, and even that may be very difficult.

The nuclear submarine is technically capable of very fast passages indeed, able to use high speeds at depth, free from practical cares of fuel consumption and only having to make occasional visits to periscope depth. On the other hand, nuclear submarines are very noisy at speed, with significant detectable sound coming from hull, propulsors and machinery. Provided that either fixed sensors, deployable assets such as Towed Array Ocean Surveillance Ships (T-AGOS) or large area platforms such as maritime patrol aircraft (MPA) are available, then such fast passages may be as useful to ASW forces as they are to the submarine. An option exists to make slower transits, perhaps as slow as the diesel-electric boat, but this may give the submarine operator the worst of both worlds; long operational delays and inefficient usage of resources, combined with detectability greater than that of the diesel boat.

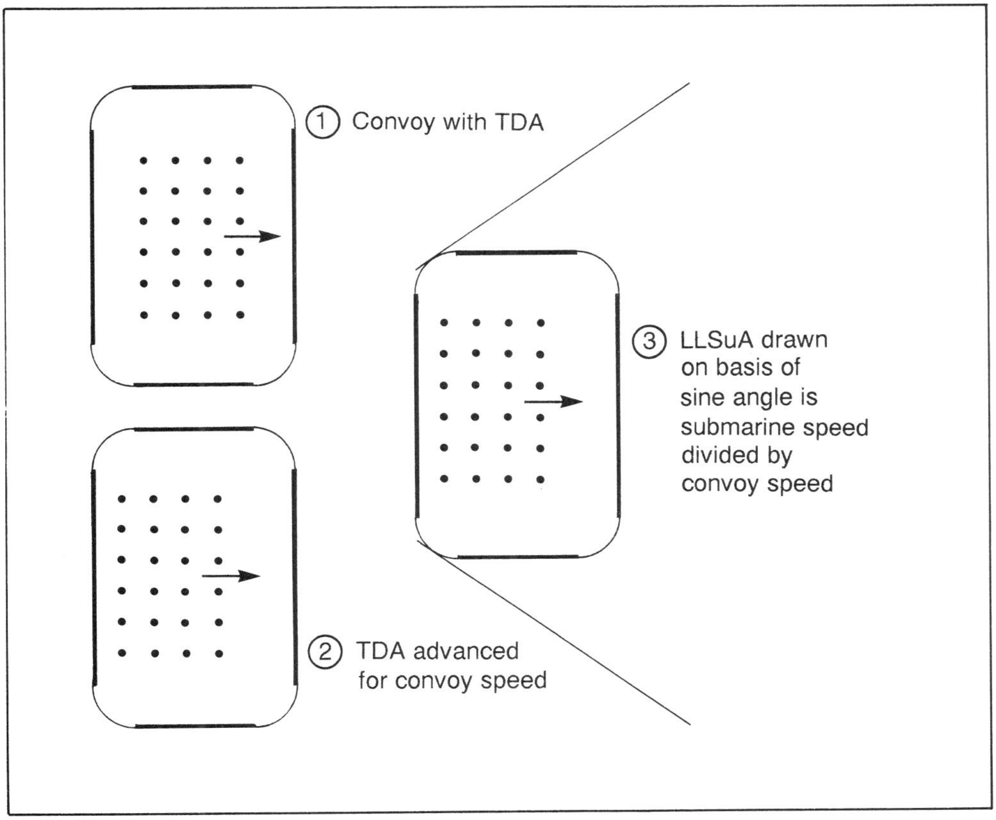

FIG. 4.1 Limiting lines of submerged approach

The Operational Area In this sequence, the last place in which ASW may be practised against a submarine is in its operational area. At one time this could be easily defined and narrowly bounded in terms of tactical geography: it was related to torpedo-firing and the processes which immediately preceded this action. Thus a circle could be drawn around a convoy or naval force, offset for the movement and speed of the formation, and this provided a good working definition of where submarines were trying to reach.

Within this area, they would be most dangerous but also perhaps most susceptible to attack. This property in two world wars enabled the convoy system to be not only the best defence for shipping, but also a very valuable means of killing submarines.

In contrast, the proliferation of roles and weapons systems has greatly increased the potential area in which submarines might be found. The most extreme example of this is probably the strategic missile firing SSBN, which will keep as far out of harm's way as possible. At the opposite end of this spectrum sits the torpedo firer whose role dictates target closure to quite short ranges. Certainly, Russian super-heavyweight wake-homing torpedoes may permit engagement at up to 35 miles, but the desirability of hitting selected targets rather than random ones may militate against the tactical use of such ranges.

For ASW, the problem becomes greater with other weapons such as missiles, whose range is often measured in hundreds rather than tens of miles. Certainly ASW sensors and weapons, too, have extended their scope and the perpetual struggle between offence and defence, at several levels from tactical to grand strategic, not to mention the difficulties of defining defence and offence in the context of ASW, have not been put to the final test in any significant manner in the last 50 years. What is clear is that a submarine in its operational area still offers significant opportunities for ASW, especially when the point is made that the submarine does not necessarily have to be sunk for ASW to be effective.

The Submarine's Purpose: the Role of Role in ASW In determining and conducting successful ASW, the stress so far has been laid on the four dimensions associated with space and time. There are further considerations to discuss, the first of which is the submarine's role: this a very important determinant of method. The subject has been touched on already in several places. A modern submarine can exercise many roles, of which perhaps the most militarily significant are:

- As a base for strategic weapons systems, such as SLBMs or SLCMs.
- Firing anti-ship cruise missiles at naval or merchant shipping.
- Attacking surface targets at sea with torpedoes.
- ASW

The topic of role has been discussed in rather greater detail in the previous chapter. A general consideration of roles suggests quite different approaches to ASW: in the first, the submarine is likely to do a great deal to keep away, or at least stay insulated from ASW forces. In the last, it has little option but to engage its enemy more closely. This alone creates a fundamental division in the strategic approach to ASW. In the first case effort, often very great effort, will have to be devoted to trying to attack, destroy or cause significant attrition to an SSBN force. The most recent (admittedly theoretical) example of this was the US Maritime Strategy of the 1980s, one facet of which was the deliberate targeting of Soviet SSBNs. It is at least theoretically possible to ignore the submarines themselves and purely to deploy countermeasures against the missiles themselves, once launched. Thus, even systems designed to oppose submarine-launched ballistic missiles can be regarded as ASW measures: a Russian strategist would certainly understand the linkage between the Strategic Defense Initiative (SDI) and ASW, even although SDI was not fully deployed.

Nor is this connection limited to the strategic case: disposing of all the missiles fired by an *Oscar* SSGN at a CVBG, either by soft (decoying the weapons or denying their effectivness) or hard (destroying the missiles themselves) kill methods could, using the broad definition adopted by this book, be construed as ASW. Certainly it meets the criteria of depriving the submarine of its effectiveness. Denying such a submarine of the information needed to both select a target in the first place and provide adequate guidance to its missiles negates its effectiveness, and this too is a form of ASW. The methods used to do this, however, are not exclusive to ASW and are discussed in detail elsewhere in the Brassey's Sea Power series.

The other submarine roles of anti-surface warfare (ASUW) and ASW tend to imply a general restriction of geographic scope, either absolutely or relatively by comparison with the use of either type of missile. This is very much the realm of aggressive, if defensive, measures such as relatively short range weapons and sensors. It is also where the influence of tactical measures such as the tactical disposition of ASW units, that is, formation design and torpedo countermeasures, both material and tactical, predominate. Submarines being used for ASW themselves pose particular problems for counter-ASW. They may well be deployed in such a way that they need not make much use of high speed, or afford other opportunities for detection: the best counter to them may well be the very submarines they are trying to attack. In a sense, role may have forced the full circle of returning to the methods needed to deal with the quietly patrolling SSBN.

The Indirect Approach: Attacking Supporting Systems The bulk of this chapter has concentrated on attacking submarines themselves from building to operational use; or their sensors and weapons systems, even after firing. There are other methods to deprive submarines of their effectiveness, but they are less directed towards submarines themselves. These exist in addition to the attacks on building facilities and bases mentioned earlier. Largely, these are concerned with attacking communications and reconnaissance systems. These may be either active or passive in their operation. Active measures might include attempts to destroy or jam either communications circuits or an active radar reconnaissance satellite. This might deny information to the submarine's command authority, or else frustrate the transmission of such data to the submarine itself. If successful, this could deprive the long-range tactical missile-firing submarine of adequate location data or reduce the efficiency of target selection. In general, the jamming of long-haul VLF and ULF communication is technically difficult and its potential benefit must be considered unproved.

Another approach to supporting systems is not to attack but to exploit them, as was done by both sides in the Battle of the Atlantic by intercepting and sometimes deciphering the enemy's signal communications. Each derived useful operational, sometimes near real-time, information that could be used either to reinforce groups or (in the Allied case) initiate diversions, often successful in avoiding submarine contact – a most useful ASW ploy. To what extent this is practised today is not easy to measure, although it would appear that some of the nations most committed to signals intelligence (SIGINT) pour large resources into this field. Even more difficult to determine are operating methods and the degree of success achieved.

The Crunch – Detection And Prosecution Despite all the ingenuity, both material and tactical, that may be devoted to frustrating the warmaking potential of enemy submarines, in the end it is often necessary to find them, and then to sink them. These related subjects of detection and destruction form the subjects of a chapter each. Although there may be many ways, not always successful, to deal with submarines these two subjects are in many ways the core of ASW. Before moving on to them, however, it is important to mention – and to some extent get rid of – one commonly used distinction in warfare: the delineation of offence and defence. Traditionally, this has caused some difficulties for many people. We all think we know the difference between the two, but do we? This is complicated by the method of dividing warfare into levels: sometimes strategic and tactical; sometimes tactical, strategic and grand strategic; and possibly adding the term operational to the mix. Convoy was described by many in both world wars as being offensive rather than defensive, as the 'defence' of convoys accounted for many submarines, which seems to be fairly 'offensive'. This is arguably the subject of a book, or at least a chapter in its own right; perhaps it can be agreed that it is rarely a useful and concise way of looking at ASW techniques. Some naval people have gone no further than defining strategy as 'tactics talked through a brass hat'. Any subdivision beyond the threefold type discussed above is probably unhelpful.

SUMMARY

There are many ways of conducting ASW and not all of them involve the destruction of submarines. Some of these involve techniques more normally considered to belong to other forms of warfare, such as attacking land targets or anti-missile defences. Although these undoubtedly form part of the spectrum of ASW, they are not described here, but in other volumes in this series. What is clear is that ASW forms an integral and important part of the sum of modern naval warfare, and indeed of the totality of warfare.

5

Everyone's Enemy and Friend – the Sheltering Sea

THE OCEAN ENVIRONMENT

Significance The environment in which ASW operations are conducted is one of the most significant factors, if not the most important of all. It dominates this aspect of warfare in a way which has few parallels in naval conflict, if indeed in any branch of warfare. Perhaps the closest analogy is with aviation; not with modern air operations, but rather with the effect weather had on the ability to operate aircraft, up until about the end of the Second World War. This chapter will indicate the ocean's importance and the ways in which it affects ASW. There will be subsequent references to this subject made in the book, where it will be specifically related to the practice of ASW, especially detection, but it is important to grasp the essential features of the subject before looking into these areas.

It is a commonplace of operations on land that two of their essential differences from sea operations are a greater concern with what is happening close to the military unit together with the necessity to take account of terrain. Despite the relatively recent practice of conducting land warfare at much greater ranges than the few miles previously of interest, the former point is largely true. The latter is literally correct but there is a maritime equivalent of terrain in the sea environment. Even in general naval warfare a competent commander has to take account of conditions above, on and under the water: high level air masses, surface meteorology and underwater environment can all exert significant effects on naval operations. In ASW, this is even more significant. Further, this is reinforced by reference to the first point about distance: he has to concern himself with this topic over hundreds of miles. There is one other extremely important difference with naval 'terrain' – despite advances in modern oceanographic science, it remains much less observable than terrestrial topography.

As in all military operations, weather plays an important part in planning and conduct. It affects the ability to carry them out at all, and may have a significant impact on mobility, reconnaissance and weapon delivery to an enemy, or deny that enemy the same. This obviously holds good for ASW with seakeeping and aircraft operations as areas of particular interest and importance. There are also other aspects of weather of especial significance to ASW brought out later.

DETECTION MECHANISMS

The modern submarine, however powered, is likely to spend most of its time underwater. It is thus essential in most circumstances to be able to detect it there. Here, a considerable difficulty arises. The normal physical means by which a surface ship or aircraft is detected at sea are either not available or else so limited as to be insignificant.

Dealing briefly with these, there are three main techniques for detecting a surface or air unit: sight, radar and emission detection. A submerged submarine is unlikely to be seen. Even when periscopes or other masts are revealed, these are deliberately designed to offer the minimum visual target. From the viewpoint of a potential detector, the best opportunity is probably offered by a submarine using snort masts to supply air and remove exhaust gases when charging batteries using its diesel engines. Despite the relatively large size of such masts and the possible presence of smoke or condensation from the diesels, this is still a difficult visual target, especially in any form of rough sea. Further, modern submarines are designed to minimise charging time: a prudent submariner will limit the time he spends doing this. Thus, four separated periods of thirty minutes charging will be preferred to one of two hours. Even in the best of circumstances for ASW forces, a range of a few miles is the best possible. At night, this is worse unless image enhancement, especially infra-red, equipment is used. Other surface penetrating devices, such as trailed aerials, are generally poor visual targets.

Similarly, radar has some difficulties, although such equipments as the UK's *Searchwater* fitted in its *Nimrod* MPA fleet does offer significant capability against periscope targets.

The main difficulty, however, is physical. Radio transmissions of radar frequency cannot penetrate water for all practical purposes. The lower part of the radio spectrum, such as VLF and below can penetrate water to significant depths, but it does involve huge aerial installations and large power requirements, both impracticable at sea. More importantly, it is thought that although suitable for one way propagation – and thus communications – both reflection from a submarine and directionality are very dubious. Thus radio frequencies can be ruled out for submarine detection.

The third area to be considered is that of emissions from the submarine, which can be divided into involuntary and voluntary releases. The former covers such as motion, water circulation, exhausts, heat, wakes, domestic effluvia and sound (also partly voluntary). The latter will be dealt with later. Most of the others have traditionally been considered difficult to detect, only limited success having been achieved. One such device was the British Autolycus fitted in maritime patrol aircraft and targeted against the exhaust of snorting diesel submarines. Basically an ion detector, it could detect the exhaust and measure its strength, but not direction. Attempts to localise or pin-point the target could then be made by weaving the aircraft upwind astride the plume towards its source. There is no doubt that it could work, but its potential effectiveness has been eroded by developments in modern submarine batteries and operational practice cutting down snorting times. At least as important in its fall from grace has been the almost universal switch to diesel propulsion in merchant fleets and the fact that the very low altitude operations needed to obtain an Autolycus intercept were at variance with the operating altitude required for the employment of other sensors. A further point concerning the involuntary case is that it is possible that recent scientific advances, mostly in remote sensing from space, allow the theoretical possibility of detecting, and possibly localising, submarines based on their emissions. Some of these techniques are discussed in Chapter 10. But such methods are not yet widespread, proven or widely discussed.

Voluntary emissions include radio transmissions, radar and active sonar. National submarine practices vary greatly, but it is probable that most submarine-operators appreciate that the advantage of using submarines is degraded by transmitting at all. Even if a more liberal regime is practised, however, detection over a wide area is not always possible.

Sound in the Sea There is one largely involuntary emission made by submarines which propagates well in the sea and which has proved to be the most useful technique for ASW detection – sound. This can be used passively by listening for the sounds made by a submarine over considerable distances. Alternatively it can be used actively when sound is transmitted from a ship, helicopter sonar or sonobuoy, reflects from the submarine hull and is then received back at its transmitting unit, providing data concerning the presence and position of a submarine.

Frequency ranges of interest stretch from a few Hertz (Hz) for long range passive detection of submarines' own noise, through a few kiloHertz (kHz) for medium range active detection to a few hundreds of kHz for torpedo homing and minewarfare purposes. These applications arise from the increasing

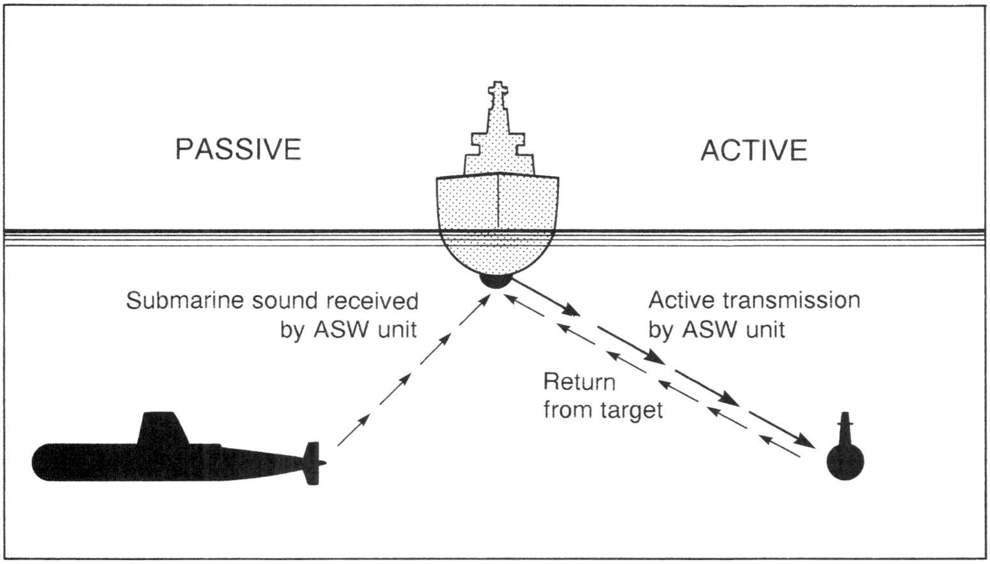

FIG. 5.1 Active/passive sonars

attenuation (ie. shorter ranges) as frequency increases, and the increasing requirement and ability to determine bearing more accurately with rising frequency. In addition to attenuation, which is explained in greater detail on page 53, the underwater environment dictates all aspects of sound propagation between target and sensor, and one of the skills in ASW is to understand and exploit these mechanisms.

Detection and its subsequent processes are discussed in the next chapter. What is common to active and passive uses is the way sound moves in the sea, and the essential matter is to determine the wanted signal against background noise. In order to understand this phenomenon fully, it is first necessary to look at the sea as a whole.

THE SEA AS INNER SPACE

In human organisations, it has become common to use the terms top-down and bottom-up. Although intended as alternatives, it is helpful to consider the marine environment from both these perspectives. At the same time their inter-relationship should always be borne in mind. For example, the water mass influences the weather, and vice versa. These connections are often complex and go through many changing iterations. It is not possible here to do more than hint at the extent of these. For ease a mathematical approach has been avoided except where necessary.

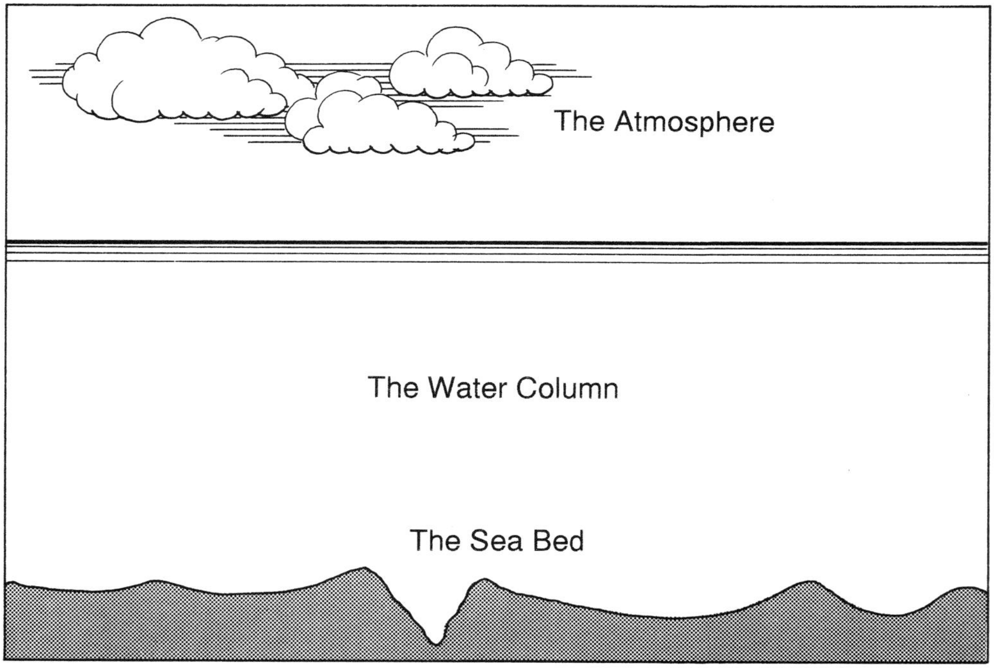

FIG. 5.2 Atmosphere/water column/seabed

The Atmosphere and Weather Taking a top-down approach, the earth's atmosphere and its weather forms an important, if not obvious, part in determining propagation of sound in the sea. One way in which this has an impact is the weather's contribution, largely from wind, to the background noise of the sea itself. The noise created is spread about a wide frequency band, ranging from about 100 Hz to about 100 kHz and peaking around 1 kHz. The intensity difference from Beaufort wind-scale Force 1 to Force 10 can be as much as 17dB (around 50 times as much) at a few kHz – that of a fairly normal hull-mounted active sonar. It is obvious that strong prolonged winds result in high seas; what may be less evident is that this generates significant noise, and that this will persist some considerable time after the wind has dropped. The visual manifestation of this is swell remaining after the evidence of high winds (breaking seas) has gone. Nor need this weather effect have to occur in the immediate vicinity of either the noise-making submarine or the detecting unit for it to be significant. To increase the background noise at the detecting sensor, the noise only has to be on the same bearing as the prospective target. Indeed, with sensors which do not produce a single unambiguous bearing, such as towed arrays (see next chapter), the noise source may not even be on the target bearing but that of the bearing pair, that is, at the same relative angle on the other side of the line array.

It is not only wind that can make noise. Precipitation of any form creates marked noise where it falls. If this occurs outside visual range of the detecting unit, it may not even be aware of this happening. Clues may exist such as general weather forecasting or the presence of clouds on radar but there is no certainty

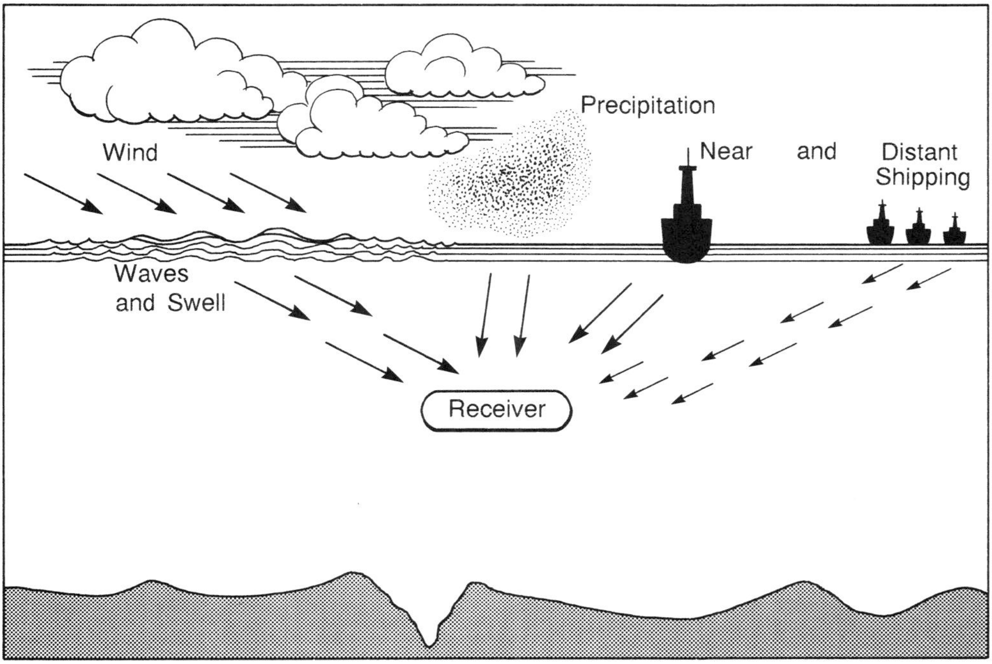

FIG. 5.3 Wind/precipitation/near and distant shipping as noise sources

that this is happening (or conversely that it is not). Even the absence of winds or precipitation can adversely affect the paths of sound in the sea. The subject of sound channels will be addressed later when looking at the water column, but one particular, weather-induced phenomenon is known to several generations of ASW practitioners as 'afternoon effect'. This is caused in conditions of light wind and marked solar heating, leading to relatively warm sea surface layers. The sea temperature then drops off rapidly with depth, refracting any sound transmitted from a surface active sonar sharply downwards. The result of this in sonars (largely hull mounted) operating in this layer is markedly reduced ranges against submarines.

Wind is not merely a noise-producing hindrance: it also mixes surface water with deeper water creating a deeper layer at a relatively homogenous temperature. Wind, along with thermal influences (partly weather induced) is also the main engine of the complex system of ocean currents which are an important part of the ocean environment. Again a fuller examination follows. It is worth noting as an example the close relationship of both the prevailing winds and the current flow system in the northern and southern parts of both the Atlantic and Pacific Oceans.

THE WATER COLUMN

Between the atmosphere and the sea bottom lies what is best described as the water column. This not only exhibits properties derived from the other places, but also has important characteristics of its own However, before describing the effects the column has on sonar operations, a consideration of the propagation of sound is most important.

Sound Speed in Water An important part of how sound moves in the sea is the speed of sound in water. Three factors influence the speed of sound: temperature, salinity and pressure. An increase in any of these results in an increase in the speed of sound which tends to be around 4,900 feet per second. The importance of variations at different depths are the consequent effects on sound paths, both through the water column itself and sometimes through the seabed, which under some conditions may act as a fluid. For example, this may occur with low frequencies in thick sediment. These paths have a crucial impact on the ability to detect a submarine, and on the problem of placing a sensor in the water column to achieve best results against the target.

Generally, pressure increases uniformly with depth. Unless the ASW unit is operating in an area in which differential salinity is significant, such as the Grand Banks, where strongly saline Gulf Stream water mixes with the colder, less saline Labrador current, salinity is unlikely to be important. Mostly, therefore, temperature or more precisely its change with depth (or gradient) is the dominant factor in determining the variation of sound speed from a steady increase with depth caused by a steadily increasing pressure, which dominates in the deepest water.

A representative volume of oceanic water is likely to demonstrate three main characteristics:

- ► A volume of water extending down from sea level called the Surface Layer (caused by wind mixing) in which temperature decay, if present, is relatively mild. Thus increasing pressure dominates, and leads to the refracting of the sonar beam back towards the surface where it is reflected, refracted back, and thus trapped, making for good ranges in that duct. From now on the term 'duct' means a relatively constricted part of the water structure which tends to have acoustic properties markedly different from those surrounding it.

- ► The next layer down, showing a markedly rapid decline in temperature, known as the 'thermocline', causing a decrease in sound speed, thus sharp downward refraction and poor ranges.

- ► The deepest layer, relatively stable, in which the decline continues but at a slow rate. Here the increase in sound speed due to increasing depth – and threfore pressure – overcomes the decline of sound speed caused by the now slowly decreasing temperature, again causing upward refraction with sound re-appearing near the surface at ranges (in the North Atlantic) of about 30nm (at the so-called Convergence Zone (CZ)).

This is a generalised representation of what can occur. Many variations are possible. For example, earlier in the chapter mention was made of 'the afternoon effect' where a marked secondary thermocline occurs close to the surface leading to strong downward refraction and very short sonar ranges. The depth of the surface layer varies with season and location as well as other shorter term factors such as wind and solar heating. Broadly the deeper the layer, the better the ranges.

As well as the general structure, less significant changes can trigger quite large effects on sonar performance. The vertical angle at which an active sonar beam is projected is also important here. A number of things may happen when this beam interacts with the thermal (and thus sound speed) structure actually encountered. Reflection and refraction both within the water column and from the sea surface may take place. Shallow water introduces some other factors, discussed later. Some illustrative examples are:

- ► Part of the sonar beam propagates to good ranges in a relatively shallow surface duct, and part turns rapidly downwards resulting in short ranges against a target below the duct.

- ► There is a deep isothermal layer giving good ranges to all practical depths.

- ► A sound channel may form between the thermocline and the next increasing sound speed layer causing sound to be trapped within it giving good ranges for a target and sensor in this channel.

- ► There is no significant near-surface duct and thus little chance of detection at medium range, but the beam is subsequently bent upwards to allow long-range detection (again usually known as Convergence Zone or CZ).

The monitoring of actual conditions is dealt with in Chapter 8 and there are techniques available which may be able to alleviate some of the limitations of operating a hull-mounted active sonar in adverse conditions. These include the use of: lower frequency equipments less affected by the thermal structure; variable depth sonars, deployed by ships or helicopters, placed at an optimal or at least better depth; and sonobuoys which can also place their sensors at more useful depths. Another possible technique is 'bottom bounce' (BB) in which a sonar transmission tilted downwards further than normal can fill water with sound after being reflected from the bottom. This usually requires high transmitted power, advanced signal processing and, most importantly, a suitable bottom type. None of these provides a complete answer but it is important for planning purposes that ASW commanders know the size of their problem.

Currents and Fronts We have so far considered variation in the vertical dimension only of sound speed. The ocean structure also varies horizontally. This is partly controlled by the depth of water, but is also a function of ocean currents. The general oceanic system of currents in the world's oceans is, at sea level at least, well known. Water movements such as the Gulf Stream, moving from the Gulf of Mexico up the USA's east coast, then passing across the Atlantic and dissipating its strength west of the UK is a considerable conduit of water movement. Its warm water has profound climatic effects, but there are other consequences for ASW. Off the American coast, the stream has significant width and depth. Its boundaries, often referred to as walls, create difficulties for sound transmission, leading to short and variable ranges which are difficult to predict with any degree of certainty. A further characteristic is that such boundaries may either be strong and clear-cut, or they may be less distinct with swirls and eddies.

Lastly, boundaries may move on a short- or long-term basis. Wind is the most important driving factor for currents; however, the interplay of the current with the ocean bed topography is also an important factor limiting the variability of the current boundaries markedly. The meeting region of different currents will frequently lead to a rapid variation of sound speed profile with distance, from one water mass to the next. This boundary is an ocean front. These resemble the better-known weather fronts, but are less easy observeable, although this has been much improved by satellite sensing of sea temperatures.

There are also sub-surface currents which, being less easy to measure, are more difficult to take account of. Many of these are at great depths, but there may be underwater currents shallow enough for submarines to make use of, such as those used by German submarines to penetrate the Straits of Gibraltar during the Second World War. In any area of frontal activity, be it at the surface or submerged, with marked differences in the composition of the water masses sound propagation is likely be affected (particularly at higher frequencies) and the prediction of the boundary structure and its effect on propagation can be difficult.

Nor are movements confined to the horizontal. There can be marked vertical movements of water within the first 1,000 feet, the general area of submarine operations, as well as elsewhere. The phenomenon of upwelling will be described later in this chapter. In shallow water, currents are often dominated by tidal

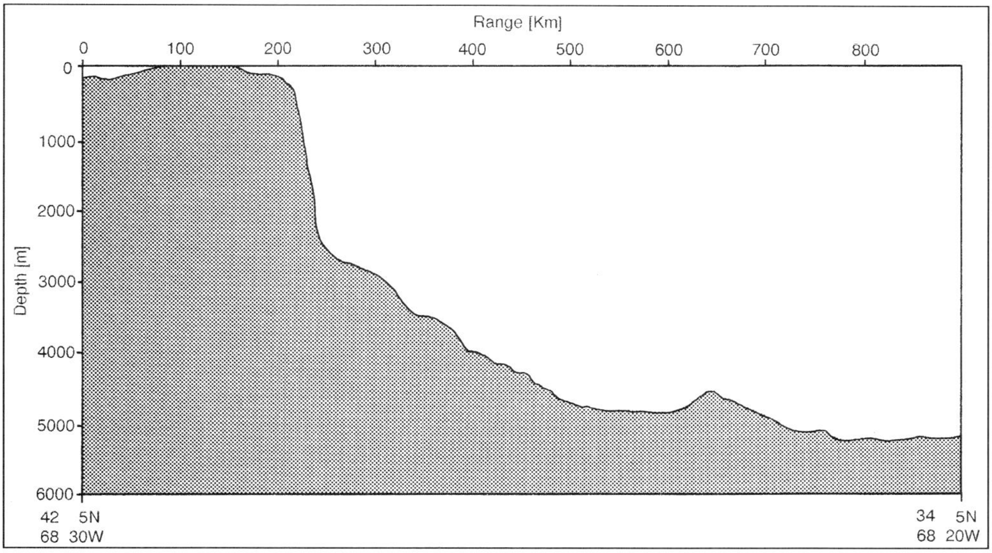

FIG. 5.4 Continental Shelf

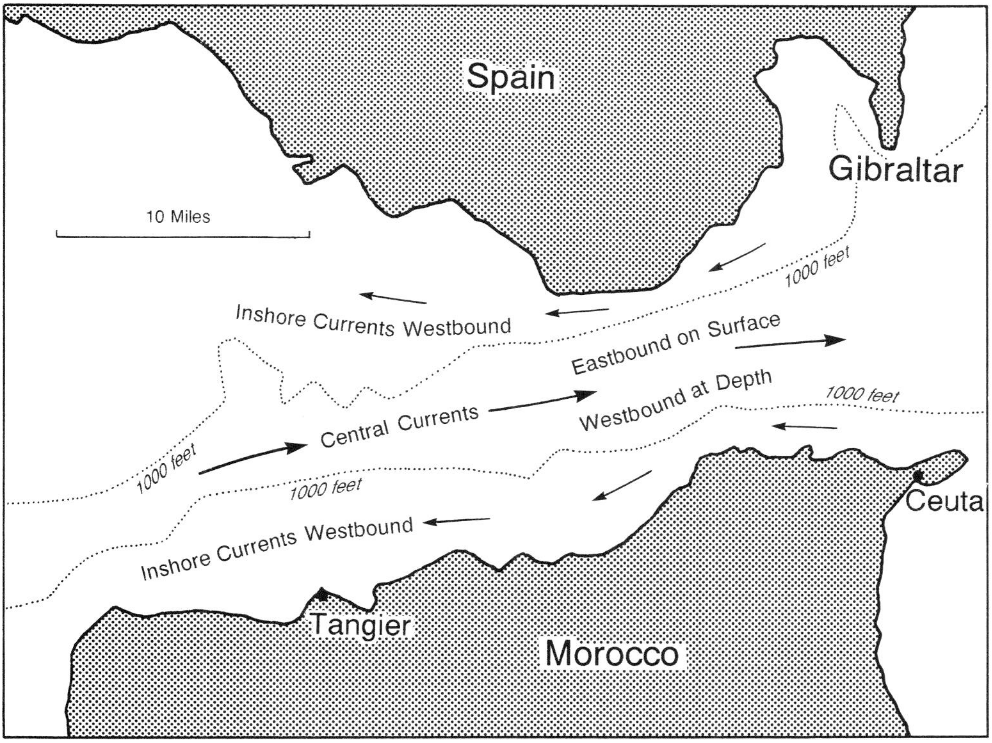

FIG. 5.5 Gibraltar currents

events, but rivers and topography also exert a strong influence. The particular effect of such water motion in restricted depths is to give other objects on the seabed apparent motion, complicating the ASW task.

THE SEA BOTTOM

The sea bottom too has a significant influence on sound in the sea This is an area with which no human has had more than fragmentary contact or seen directly, unlike the atmosphere and above. It is inimical to human activities: cold, wet and under intense pressure.

Not only does the seabed play a determining factor in ocean circulation, but it can also dominate sound propagation where it intersects important sound paths between target and sensor. The underwater topography in general is characterised by a continental shelf of about 200m depth at the ocean margin (of varying width) falling relatively rapidly at the continental slope down to the continental rise and abyssal plains. The deep ocean is punctuated, particularly in areas of volcanic activity, by ridges and seamounts.

The effect of the bottom on sound propagation can be to reflect sound or to scatter it, to pass sound through it with little loss or to absorb sound. These effects are both frequency- and bottom constitution-dependent. For example, a typical shelf bottom of sand overlying rock can give good propagation at high frequencies via bottom reflection but high loss at low frequencies due to sound coupling into the rock with consequent loss of energy. However, in medium depth water where there is a deep sedimentary layer of mud, low frequencies will propagate satisfactorily to several kilometres into the bottom, be refracted and emerge further down range with little loss; high frequencies will be totally absorbed in this same bottom.

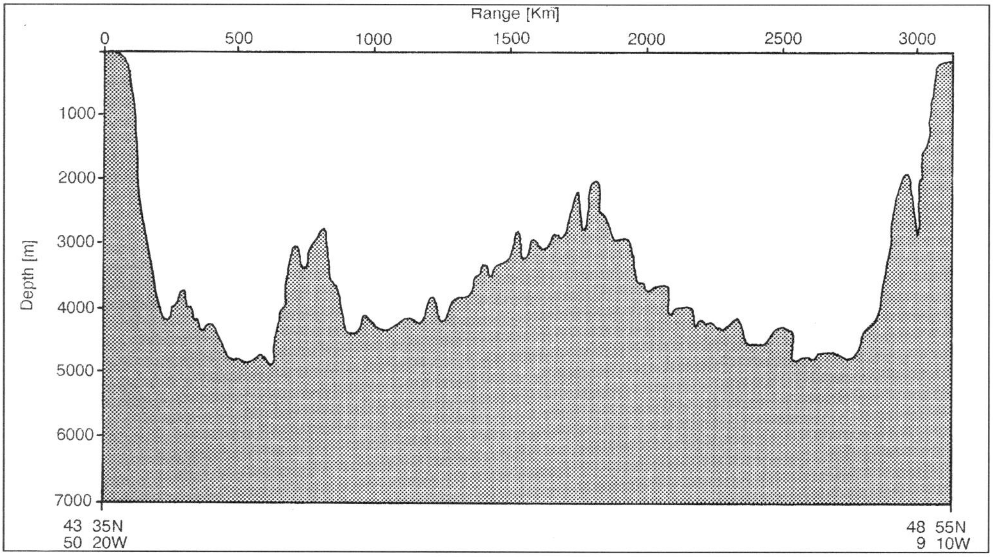

FIG. 5.6 N Atlantic cross section – points and depths

Like the water column, the bottom shows obvious variation with distance. The exploitation of this variation is a key skill in ASW. For example, the bottom can be used to mask the effects of ambient noise originating from a shipping lane by placing a listening submarine in the acoustic lee of a seamount, or the focusing effects of the continental slope can be exploited to improve the received signal. In all cases the object of the ASW unit is to improve the local signal-to-noise ratio to increase the probability of detection.

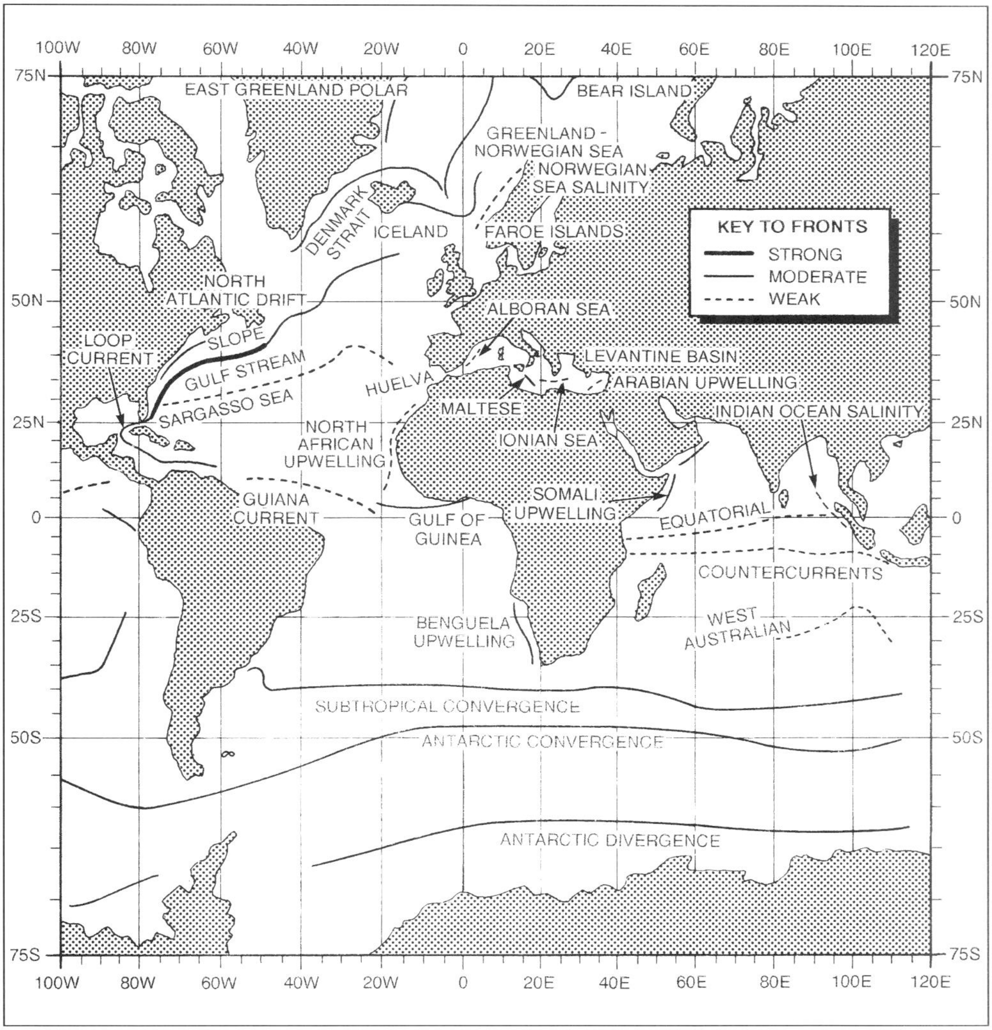

FIG. 5.7 Frontal regions of the world

Reflection and attenuation characteristics may be greatly changed by depth, topography and nature of the bottom. There may be deep layers of sediment, originating either from land sources – usually major river systems or from fault zones. These might take the form of mud, sand, rock or a combination of any of these. Sound may not only be absorbed or reflected by the bottom: it may also be refracted or indeed the sound may be reflected back towards its source. The latter is known as reverberation.

In the passive case this results in less sound reaching a potential detector. Reflection usually results in some loss of sound intensity but it may also form part of a longer-lasting (and thence persisting for a greater distance) sound path than that taken directly. When more than one sound path from source to receiver is evident, a phenomenon known as multi-path propagation exists. This may increase or diminish sound, usually depending on the phase of the components: it can also suggest that the sound is coming from a direction which is not the source's true bearing.

Lastly, in this account of bottom effects, topography may affect water flows and the consequent effects. Examples of this occur on the Pacific coasts of North and South America, where there is a very much steeper Continental Slope than in much of the Atlantic Ocean. Combined with currents this converts horizontal water mass movement into strong upward movements known as upwelling, bringing much biological material towards the surface and producing marked

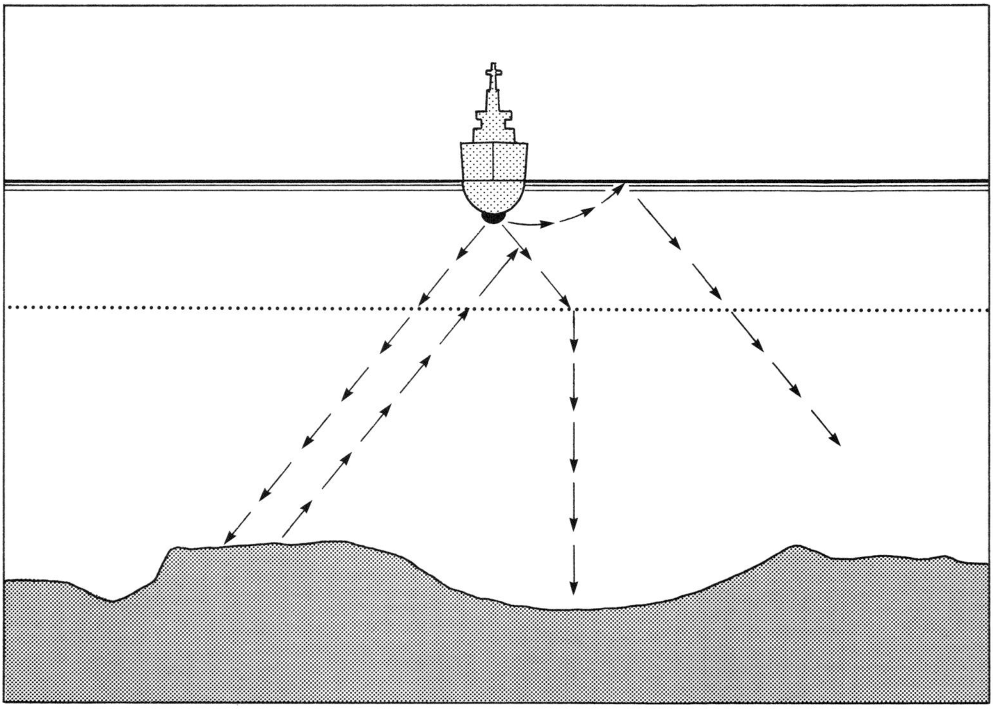

FIG. 5.8 Reflection/refraction/absorption

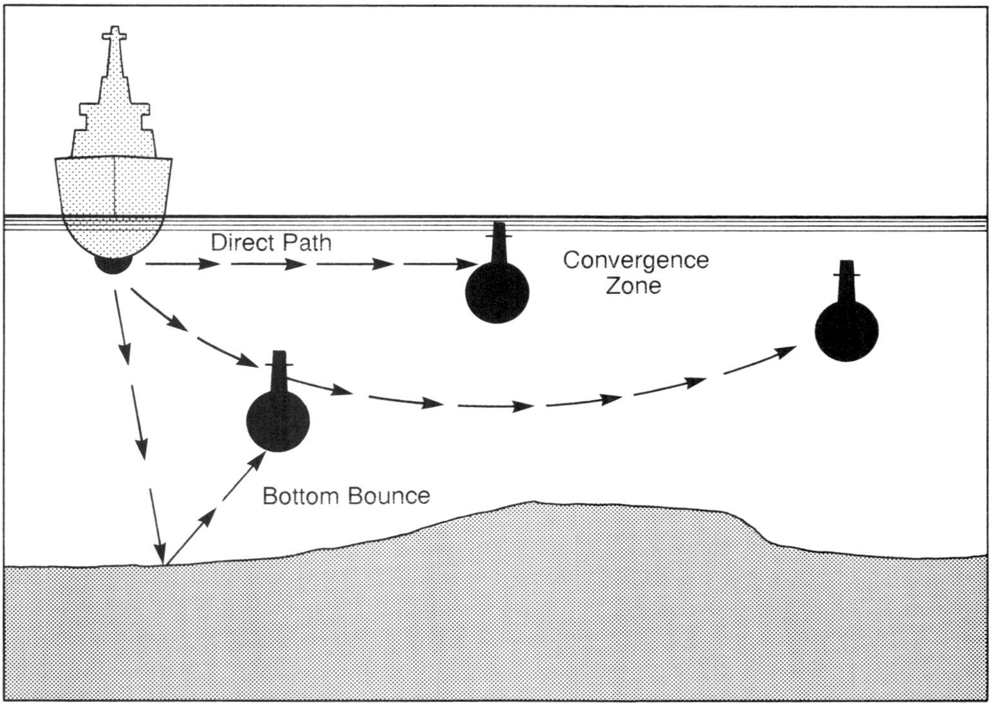

FIG. 5.9 Direct Path/Bottom Bounce/Convergence Zone

climatic phenomena. Perhaps it as well that this has never been one of the great ASW battlegrounds, for it is difficult water.

This section of the chapter has done little more than provide a very sketchy overview of a little-known but important subject. Much of what we know of the ocean bottom has only come to light in the last two decades. Before that, most data gathering concentrated on rudimentary bathymetry: technology was simply too inadequate to do very much more. It would be foolish to consider that enough is known about this dark, cold hostile environment to be totally certain of the theories which are currently accepted: listen to this space.

Biological Life The oceans contain a great deal of animal and vegetable life. It would be fair to say that despite much recent research work that the subject is still not fully understood. However, since the beginning of ASW, it was evident that marine life has an effect on ASW that is often difficult to measure and to take into account. Life on earth began in the sea and some of the most primitive forms of life are still to be found there. Size can vary from the microscopic forms known as plankton to the largest creatures on the planet, the great whales. These and many other intermediately sized organisms can all affect ASW, if in different ways.

Plankton exists in layers of millions of creatures. These move vertically in the course of the day, shunning daylight and lying around 350m, returning close to the surface by night. They probably have the effect of attenuating sound at the expense of ASW. These creatures do not exist in isolation; they attract larger sea creatures. These too complicate ASW, sometimes producing noise and often acting as alternative targets for active sonar systems. In the case of smaller fishes this is probably manifested mostly as micro reflection or refraction, impairing the transmitted sonar's power, absorbing the radiated noise of submarines and causing reverberation. Nor is marine life entirely acoustically passive. Although it usually moves through the water with greater efficiency than most man-made devices, it is not silent.

Concentrations of creatures indulging in vigorous activities, such as feeding, may generate significant amounts of noise. Some, particularly whales and dolphins, deliberately transmit signal-like noise. Snapping shrimp can generate large amounts of interfering noise at active and the higher passive sonar frequencies. The purpose of this is not entirely understood. Whatever its reasons, it may interfere with ASW.

The larger fishes and more often whales will actually generate false sonar targets. A blue whale may be up to 100 feet long and although this is shorter than most submarines, sonar may have difficulty making this distinction. Whales are also highly mobile with sustained speeds of 10 knots being common and the ability to move at 20 knots for short periods well known. The most recent sustained ASW campaign, fought by the British against the Argentines in the South Atlantic in 1982, involved a high expenditure of ASW ordnance. With the exception of one submarine attacked on the surface, none was sunk or damaged. But it has been reported that a number of whales were attacked by torpedoes and depth charges.

Sound Paths and Loss Modes Having now introduced the elements that effect sound propagation, it is a good point at which to synthesise their overall effect, as none can be considered in isolation in ASW. Although the three-part model of water structure – surface duct, thermocline and deep layer – is probably rather simplistic, it does provide a useful starting point. When conditions are good for a surface sonar, that is with a deep surface duct present typically in winter, it is possible that all practical submarine operating depths can be covered easily. But as the start of the thermocline rises in the water column with the onset of summer, surface sonars become more limited; for example the only detection gained at any worthwhile range may happen with a submarine at periscope depth. The only solution is to use a variable depth sonar, either towed by a surface ship, dipped by a helicopter or deployed by a sonobuoy.

In the first case, unless the tow cable is very long, radiated noise from the towing ship may limit performance. It may also not be possible to lower the body as deeply as desired. But sound is not only constrained to certain paths (two-dimensional (range/depth) or three dimensional (area/depth)) but in any given path it will also decay with increasing range. This does not exclude the case of the apparent augmentation with range of multi-path effects: each individual path is still subject to loss. Moreover, both passive and active systems are subject to such losses, the latter doubly so.

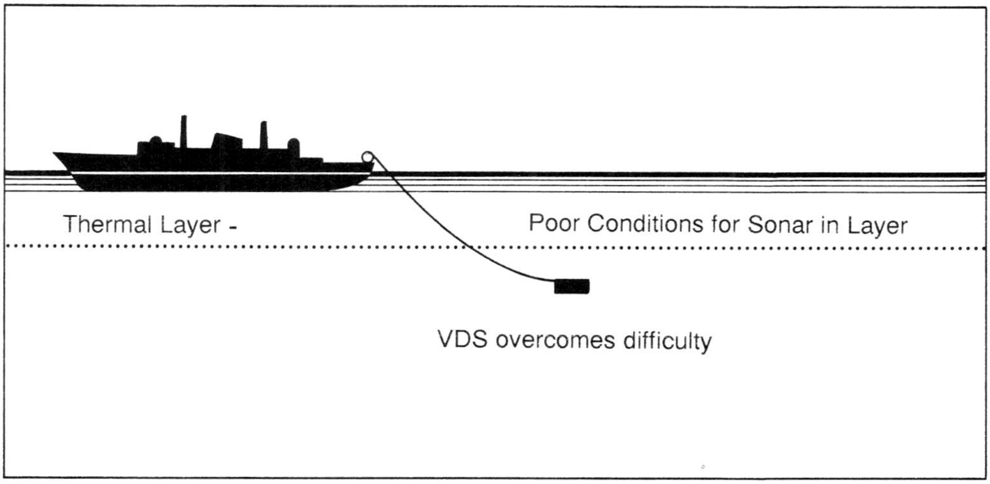

FIG. 5.10 VDS overcoming effect of layer

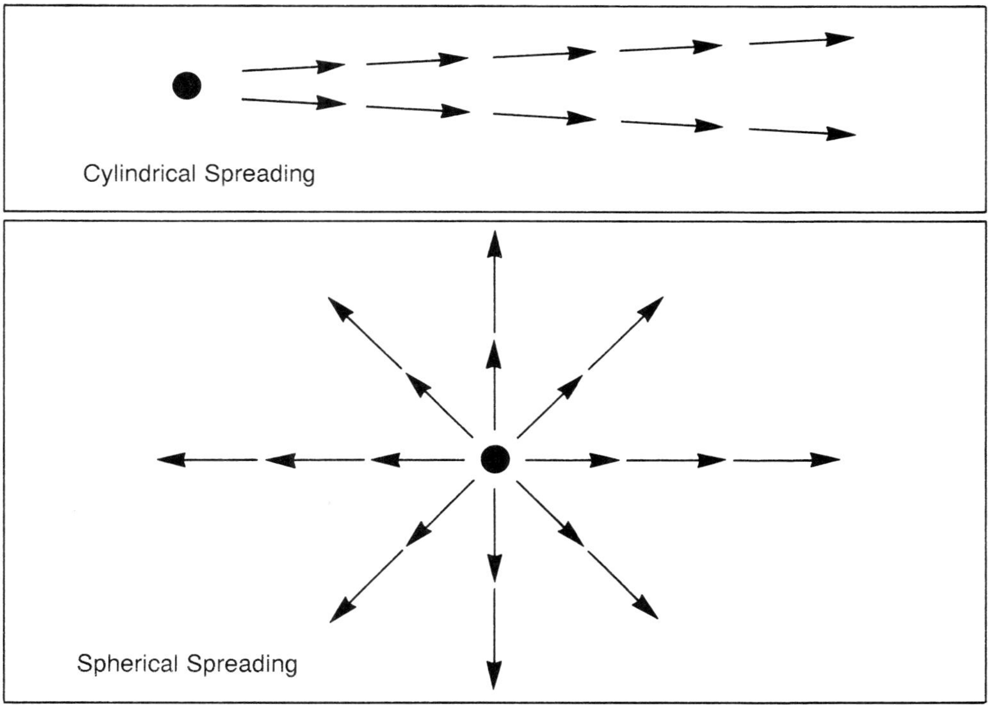

FIG. 5.11 Spherical/cylindrical spreading

This loss, often called attenuation, may be caused by a number of factors. Firstly, the way in which sound spreads is of primary importance. In deep water and unconstrained, sound will spread spherically. When it is constrained, it may spread cylindrically. In many circumstances spreading may be a compound of these modes. Clearly, the former will lead to intrinsically higher losses.

The next element is the medium itself. Perfectly isothermal and pure sea water is likely to lead to an ideally low loss regime, but oceanic water is rarely pure and never simple. Three main mechanisms dominate such loss: reflection, refraction and absorption. Reflection occurs when a sound wave meets an abrupt change in the medium, such as the sea surface, the bottom or a target. For active sonar, reflections that return to the sensing unit may either be wanted, from the target, or unwanted, by scattering from the sea surface, bottom or other phenomena within the water column (such as fish). This latter phenomenon as noted earlier is known as reverberation.

Refraction occurs when the direction of propagation of the sound wave is bent by less than 90 degrees by a change of sound speed along the path. This could be, as discussed previously, as the sound speed changes with depth within the water column, or for a sound beam penetrating the bottom at the interface with the bottom, where this is of a sedimentary type or deep within this same sedimentary bottom. Lastly, in addition to these two, sound energy will be absorbed by its passage through the transmitting medium. This will depend largely on the frequency of the signal and the nature of the water or bottom through which it propagates.

It is important to note that the relative importance of these properties varies with circumstance. All are likely to be present to some extent most of the time, but their significance can veer wildly from marginal importance to great significance over small changes of water volume and short periods of time. The effects of refraction have already been noted in its effects on sound path and the bottom.

The Significance of Frequency It has already been noted that the frequency of sound transmitted – involuntary or deliberate – has a very important effect on propagation. Lower frequencies (say below 1 kHz) are, on the whole, less affected by the loss modes referred to above. The relationship, however, is complex. The dominating factor at low frequency is often attenuation: when this is low the ranges are much greater. Low frequencies are less likely to be transmitted in ducts than higher frequency sounds, leaking out of the duct with range. This is good for detecting targets below layer which would otherwise be in an acoustic shadow, but worse for the case when the target is in layer when the benefits of cylindrical spreading within a duct are reduced. However, in general terms, very long acoustic ranges are only achievable at low frequency. However, determination of direction is more difficult. It is not impossible to use very large receivers to deal with this problem, but until the advent of the towed array, this was rarely practicable. Even with long arrays, and sophisticated and powerful signal processing, some difficulties remain. Direct Path (DP) reception, subject to least distortion, is obviously to be preferred, but others such as BB and CZ may also be present. If all exist, DP can often be distinguished, but in other circumstances problems of selection may hamper subsequent exploitation. A further practical difficulty exists: exploiting the benefits of long range active sonar at low frequencies requires very large and heavy transmitting transducers, which are not necessarily compatible with a fast moving warship.

TWO SPECIAL CASES - SHALLOW WATER AND THE ARCTIC

Shallow Water The shallow water environment (in which the interaction of sound with the bottom dominates, but practically can be considered as the Continental Shelf) poses particular difficulties for ASW. At the same time, it can also aid it and pose difficulties for the opposing submarine. Shallow water ASW is addressed in greater detail in the following chapter, but there are general environmental features worth noting. Firstly, the influence of local features may be important over a much smaller area than in oceanic ASW. The effect of rivers, rapidly changing bottom and coastal topography, and differences in salinity may all occur very suddenly. Secondly, the bottom type is liable to have a marked – and on the whole greater – influence on ASW.

Not only is the bottom a close and therefore often large contributor to reflected noise – reverberation – but the influence of bottom objects as false active sonar targets is often significant. This is partly a problem of vertical proximity: wrecks in deep oceanic water rarely pose false-target problems, but this is a considerable problem in shallower water. It is compounded by the density of false targets: shallow water is also often constrained water, leading to more ships becoming grounding casualties. Even when an initial grounding has not been fatal, the consequent damage has often resulted in a nearby sinking. Thus the English Channel, for example, is littered with wrecks.

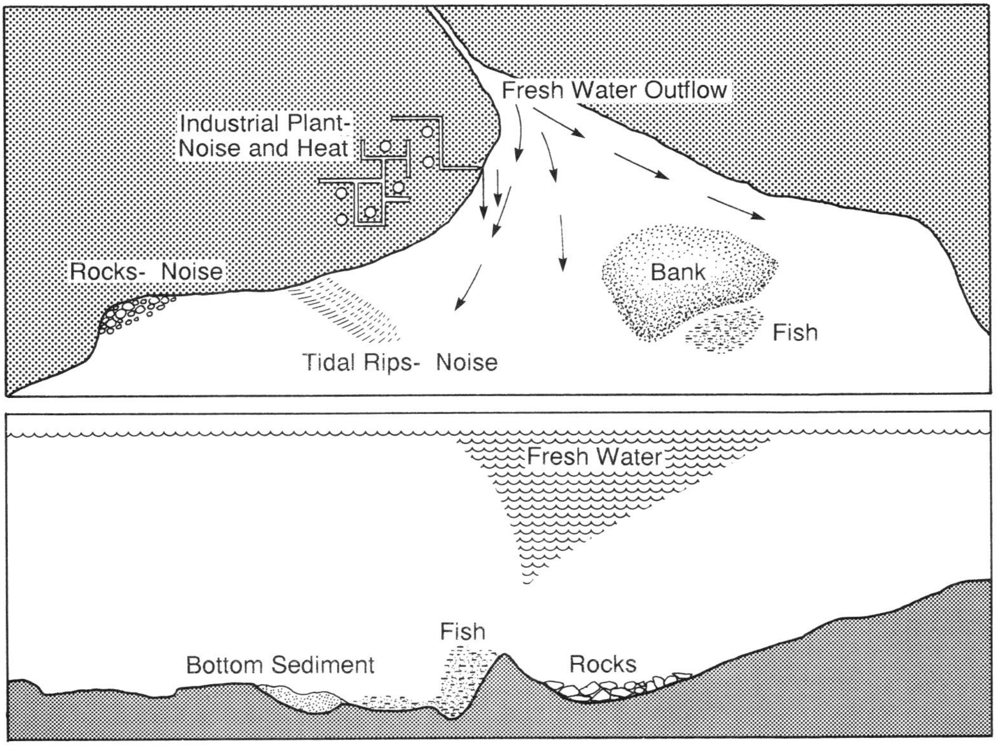

FIG. 5.12 Particular properties of shallow water

A further difficulty that may arise is that the nearness of land leads to a great deal of terrestrially-based noise from large industrial plants, as well as that from the rapid growth of offshore facilities, such as oil-rigs, in the last three decades. Although ocean technology now permits these installations to operate in deeper water too, the economic imperative biases these installations towards shallower water. However, all is not bad for ASW in shallow water. Water condition may often be isothermal leading to long and reliable sonar ranges for active sensors, particularly over low loss bottoms, and less need for investment in exotic technologies. Similarly, it may often be possible to put some reliance on relatively short-range but cheap shore installations, both sonar and radar.

There are clearly advantages and disadvantages of shallow water ASW: a balance of opinion might suggest that it is inherently a more difficult place to conduct ASW, but that the need for it will vary greatly. What is clear is that it poses different environmental challenges than the open ocean.

The Arctic The Arctic is a very special case. Its ASW significance rests on its use by the Russians as an operating area for submarines, particularly SSBNs. For some time now, they have used this as an operating area noting its proximity to their bases in the Kola Peninsula and the many advantages inherent in the environment. Not least is ice cover, protecting them from the attention of Western ASW surface ships and aircraft.

But the Arctic environment, despite this fundamental advantage, is not without its own difficulties for submarine operations and ASW alike. As the only ASW vehicle that can operate under the ice is a submarine, many of these characteristics apply equally to hunter and hunted. Broadly speaking the region has two main divisions. The first, the Marginal Ice Zone (MIZ) at the circumference of the core area is where open sea gives way passing through drift ice, then pack ice, before the nucleus of solid ice is reached, the whole extending for about 1,000 miles (depending on season). The main points to note about the MIZ are the likelihood of local temperature anomalies and the mixing of water densities dependent on the state of freezing or melt of the ice; together with considerable noise generated by the friction of ice clashing with ice, as well as a certain amount of biological noise. This noise makes the MIZ a rather difficult area for passive sonars.

Underneath the polar ice cap proper, conditions tend to stabilise somewhat, at least in terms of time. Ice characteristics, although longer-lasting, may nevertheless have marked variations in their underwater shape. Underwater, there may be marked variation with very large ice keels, presenting considerable problems to navigation. On the other hand, there may be lakes of relatively thin ice or *polyni* which permit surfacing or at least mast penetration for communication and other purposes. The water mass is relatively stable and the environment quiet, however. A last point to note about this region is the relative difficulty of obtaining observations about it – many methods routinely used in the open ocean have no validity here for obvious reasons. It is well-known that only three nations operate in this difficult domain: Russia, the USA and UK. It can also be conjectured that data collected here is unlikely to be shared with others, and even within this club (and allowing for the recent warming in international relations) only the UK and USA are likely to collaborate extensively.

PROBLEMS OF PREDICTION

Returning to the broader scene, an ASW commander (afloat or ashore) has more than a scientific interest in the environment. It is also necessary to consider parameters for some time ahead – hours, days or even weeks – for the conduct of present operations and the planning of future ones. In doing this it is necessary to produce a synthesis from three sources: historical data, scientific modelling and present observations. Historical data can render a general picture of the areas of interest related to their known characteristics and their variability with the seasons and other factors. For many of the areas of greatest interest, much data has been amassed over time. Further, remote sensing has also allowed access to a vast amount of pertinent data, but mainly concerning the sea surface itself with little detailed indication of what happens at greater depths. It has often been possible to divide the oceans into a number of domains of varying sizes. Here bodies of water and/or bottoms which have generally similar characteristics can be delineated and this alone can be a considerable aid in planning operations.

Scientific and mathematical models can also contribute to prediction, but as in weather forecasting only a certain degree of trust can be applied to any particular outcome. It may also be the case that different models produce widely differing outcomes and a degree of subjectivity may thus inform any result. In any case, even a thoroughly trustworthy model is only as good as its data and, especially when factors such as weather or shipping noise change rapidly, unstable or unreliable inputs may well result in uncertain outputs. Models are, however, a very good way of synthesising observations from many sources (eg. sea surface temperatures from satellites and single-point ocean thermal/depth measurements from ships) often not available at the same time.

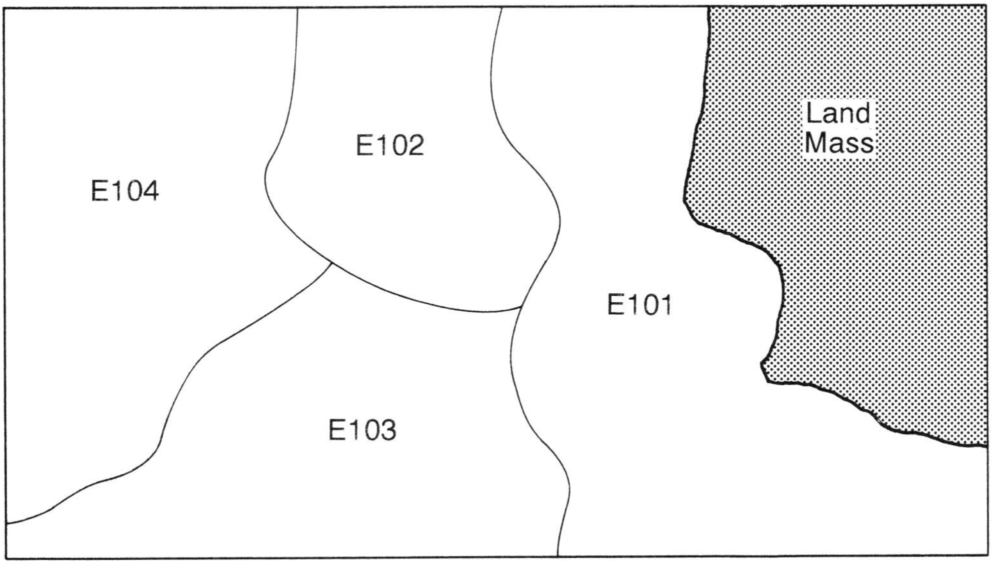

FIG. 5.13 Domain map

This all emphasises the importance of making good and plentiful observations of those quantities that can be measured. Although space systems have improved this capability enormously, there is still a need for information directly from the sea. Even here, there is probably much less real time data available than required. An analogy might be drawn with horse racing: historical data is the form book; models the computational system adopted by a gambler taking into account form and his own method of assessing a horse's potential. Contemporary observation can be compared to looking at the track in the weather conditions on the day concerned and visually assessing the horse and its competitors at that time. But what if the only picture presented was a very partial one, only being able to see part of the course (and not knowing which part); only being able to see one snapshot of one part of the race (and not knowing where or when)? Who would pick a winner in these circumstances? Despite modern science and sensing, this is the difficult problem of the modern ASW commander. Oceanographic models can often explain what happened afterwards, but the science and art of this field is to be able to say what might be happening now and, more usefully, what could happen in the near future, and at other places which may be of interest, at some distance from the ASW unit itself. Oceanographic models thus also have a key role to play, having assimilated the wide area satellite data and the individual point bathythermal data, and with the atmospheric driving forces, to try to predict the future state of the ocean for some days and over a wide area. However, many will say that ASW will require as much art as science for some time to come.

TWO LAST POINTS

In other parts of this book, it will be made clear that modern submarines are becoming quieter and that modern passive acoustic sensors are becoming more powerful. Looking at the latter first, the worth of such a sensor can be measured by its ability to detect target sound which is quieter than the background environment in which the submarine is operating: without using figures, there are physical limits to the degree to which this can be done. Turning to the submarines themselves, it has long been generally agreed that Western submarines for many years enjoyed a considerable advantage in terms of noise emissions over their Russian counterparts. In the heyday of powerful passive sensors – the 1970s and 80s – this was converted into a considerable detection range benefit. On the assumption that Russian submarines have closed this gap, then the conclusion reached by some that both sides will enjoy long-range detection is fallacious. This is because the submarine-radiated noise has to be compared not with that made by its adversary, but rather with the environmental background – a parameter that neither side can control. Good passive sonars are capable of detecting radiated noise at levels well below that of background noise – but only to a certain extent. The consequence of this – at least for submarine versus submarine encounters – is that future meetings may take place at short ranges in quick time, unless the return to active sonar, but at lower frequencies, is adopted. This might be attractive to the surface ASW unit, but will many submarine commanders really wish to make a beacon out of their vessel?

Although important, this is merely one particular facet of a much broader and more significant point. In present and future ASW, unless forces are grossly unequal, then success in the long-running (approaching a century now) battle between submarines and ASW forces will not go to the side which does not understand, far less exploit, the oceanic environment.

6

Detection and Sensors

INTRODUCTION

Although effective ASW can be practised without knowing where opposing submarines are, either in general or more specifically, success is unlikely in the long term if submarines cannot be detected. In technical terms detection is usually taken to mean that the relevant sensor has achieved the appropriate signal strength so that the target is displayed on the appropriate apparatus. Despite the utility of such a concept for system design, it is probably more helpful to draw a broader definition which takes in the ideas of recognition by an operator (or even the command), classification and, to some extent, localisation. The definition can stop at the point at which a decision is made to attack, and the processes which follow that point will be described in the next chapter. Nevertheless such processes may recur, but their general principles are described here and not later.

Detection can happen in many ways and submarines by their nature, construction and modes of operation offer different opportunities to different systems. Earlier in the book, mention was made of many of these characteristics and in a wide survey of this nature they cannot be listed exhaustively, but some of the most important may be indicated:

PRINCIPLES OF DETECTION

Although the nature and details of methods of detection vary, certain principles apply to all detectors. Full details of the theoretical derivation of these are available in publications noted in the Further Reading section at the end of this book. It is important, however, to recognise the operation of these principles as it helps to understand the performance and limitations of active and passive sensors and also the comparative worth of different models of what are ostensibly the same sensor. As an example, the working of passive sonar is considered.

In basic form, this can be considered as a simple model with three boxes – Submarine Noise, Propagation Loss and Receiver Characteristics. Obviously, each of those is a gross simplification and some of the complications will be discussed shortly. But for now there is a very easy set of three numbers to consider. A (the submarine noise) may be anything from the submarine's total noise to a particular piece of machinery emitting a very narrow frequency band;

TABLE 6.1
Sensor Opportunities

SM Activity/ Opportunity	*Sensor*	*Products*	*Remarks*
Hull	Active Sonar	D, L, C	
	Radar	D, L	If SM surfaced
	MAD	D, L, C poss	
	Space	D, L, C poss	Unproven
Propulsion	Passive sonar	D, C	L in time
	Exhaust sensor	D, C	Obsolescent
Use of Radar	ESM	D, C	
Use of Masts	Radar	D, L, C	
Weapon Discharge	Passive Sonar	D, L, C	
	Radar	D, L, C	If missile
	ESM	D, C	fired *

Key:
C Classification
D Detection
ESM Electronic Support Measures – detecting electronic emissions
L Localisation
MAD Magnetic Anomaly Detection
poss Possibly
SM Submarine
* Applies to both Radar and ESM

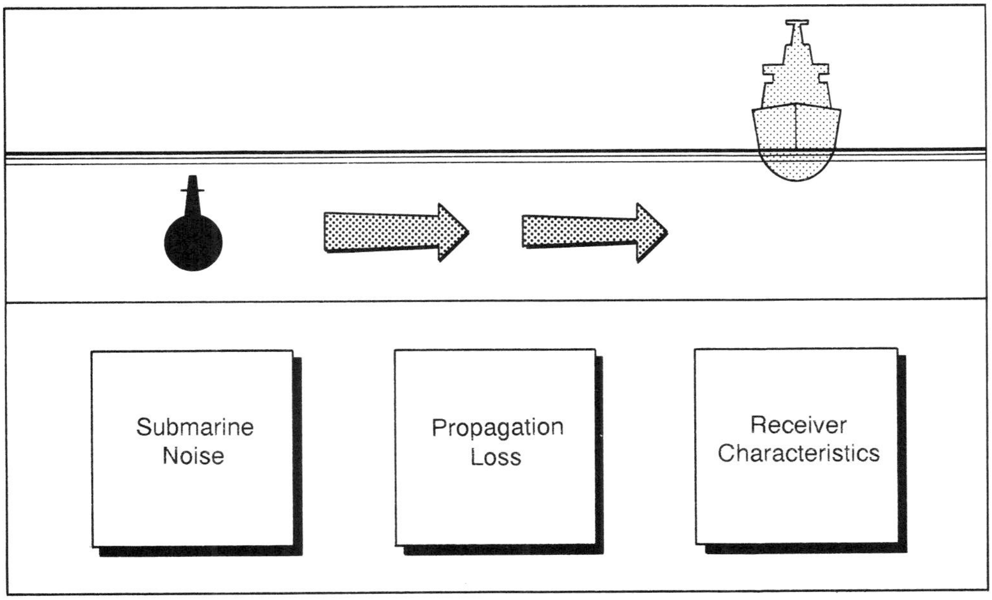

FIG. 6.1 Three box model

B is the propagation loss, that is the rate at which noise of this particular type will decay with distance in the existing environment; and C is, simply said, the ability or otherwise of the receiver in distinguishing this type of noise from unwanted background noise. For an active system, such as radar or active sonar, for A read transmitted power. On reaching the target, the signal is bounced off the submarine and the quality of bounce is usually referred to as Target Strength. Returning to the original source, the sensitivity of the receiver again comes into play. There is a significant difference this time with Propagation Loss, because it has to be considered twice – once on the way to the target and once on the way back. For this reason, amongst others, active systems tend to have shorter potential ranges than passive ones.

Real life at sea is never quite as simple as the last paragraph has implied. Looking first of all at the passive case and taking the components one at a time, complications arise readily. No well-designed submarine operated competently is going to make any more noise than it has to. But a nuclear submarine has a complicated propulsion system with much auxiliary machinery, some of it quite powerful, as well as the necessity to transmit main propulsive power into the sea. It will not, however, always sound exactly the same, depending on such variables as propulsive mode and speed. Thus there may be a quite considerable noise to detect, or hardly any. It may also vary greatly in frequency, bandwidth and other important characteristics. Here it may be best to jump to the receiver at the other end (Box C). The concept of receiver sensitivity was introduced earlier, but there are many problems facing the designer of such a system. Firstly, the nature of the target or noise signature has to be considered. This will be known to a greater or lesser extent by means of intelligence data, and assumptions made by the designer of the passive system, or will be built-in in the active case. Almost certainly, however, the passive sonar equipment will have to cover the characteristics of more than one class, propulsion type and nationality of submarine. There will also be physical constraints placed on the system. Generally, very low frequencies may present some difficulties, particularly as regards the size of the receiver array. It is also likely that optimum coverage of particular target emissions may have to be sacrificed to obtain a broad spread of capabilities, as well as such factors as background noise. This can originate from sources including shipping noise, biological activity, rain and sea state. Lastly, physical limitations in the host platform can impose restrictions. Examples of this can be found by considering towed passive arrays in T-AGOS ships, surface warships and SSNs. In the first, as the ships concerned are used largely in relatively static areas, array length is very long. Surface warships have limited space for array stowage and may have to move at speed with the array streamed, limiting its length. In at least the early SSN designs, it was not possible for the submarine to recover the array itself, and thus a fairly short array was necessary.

There are huge variables implicit in the two words, propagation loss (Box B). Some of these were discussed at greater length in the previous chapter on the environment. Broadly, losses caused by distance vary with frequency. The water structure is important: variations in temperature and salinity, together with different water masses, can produce losses which are difficult to measure and predict. Paradoxically, multipath propagation of some sounds may be stronger at greater distance from their source than at intermediate distances. Lastly the nature of the bottom may affect losses.

NEXT STEPS – CLASSIFICATION AND LOCALISATION

In order to make practical use of a detection, it is necessary to carry out two further stages. Classification may precede localisation, or vice versa; quite commonly, the two processes are carried out simultaneously and may even be interrelated. We shall consider classification first. Usually, detection has done little more than tell the operator of a sensor, be it active or passive, that there is something there. The process of classification can be quite complex, but it is essential to determine which detections originate from a submarine and which from other sources. The range of classification problems may be indicated by considering two examples:

► A submarine towed array detects a single narrow band tonal with some submarine characteristics. Over several hours its bearing does not shift.

> *Classification* – possibly a submarine, but really too little information to say. It could be a piece of machinery on an oil rig. It is probably some distance away.

► A frigate on passage in water of 60 metres depth detects a contact on active sonar at a range of two miles. It moves rapidly down the ship's side, passing one mile off. Plotting and sonar information suggests a target speed of four knots. There is excellent visibility and nothing can be seen on the bearing and range of the contact.

> *Classification* – possibly a submarine. The lack of surface contact is highly suggestive, but in water of this depth it is necessary to check whether it is not a wreck and strong tidal stream is not inducing the 'target speed'.

These examples only touch on some of the facets to be considered in reaching a classification of a sonar target. The nature of the contact, its movement and behaviour all have to be considered. Classification may also be able to go beyond the basic in concept, but complex in practice, decision of submarine or non-submarine. Passive sonar particularly may gain information which allows more detailed categorisation into type or class, or even an individual submarine.

This advantage is largely balanced by active sonar, when it comes to localisation. Active has one important advantage, that of instantaneous range information. Such information may or may not be immediately useful for the purpose of attacking the submarine, but it is certainly helpful, providing an immediate answer to one of the most important aspects of tactical decision-making. However, to further balance the situation, the submarine will almost certainly know of the active sonar's presence (and range via bottom bounce), whereas knowledge of a passive sonar and its attached vehicle may be denied him. Classification may be a long drawn out process, particularly in the case of a passive sensor with long range potential.

Moving on to localisation, the merits of active sensors have already been mentioned. With passive sensors, localisation tends to be more difficult. To take the most difficult case, that of a non-directional passive sonobuoy – as early narrow band buoys were and some still are – it is usually necessary to drop extra buoys in the vicinity of the buoy(s) in contact. After this, it is necessary to use complex techniques to plot and track a submarine. A towed array, whether surface ship or submarine mounted, should be considered next. This is inherently a much more powerful sensor and it is directional; however, there are a few problems. Firstly, being linear it produces not a single bearing but a pair; the true bearing and its mirror on the other side of the array. There is no way that an operator can tell immediately which is which. To do this, it is necessary to manoeuvre the array, altering its heading. This produces a second bearing pair of which only one, of course, corresponds to one of the previous pair; the ambiguity is thus resolved.

The process of course alteration and the array resettling – especially with very long arrays – can take some time. Also, the amount of bearing accuracy can vary greatly, depending on such variables as the acoustic frequency of the contact, the beam of the array in which contact is held (a function of frequency and array design) and the ability to measure the array heading. As this latter function is generally gauged by small compasses which are cold and under pressure inside the array, the theoretical accuracy potential of many designs may not be realised. Furthermore, the very power of such a sensor, which may be capable of detecting a submarine at ranges in excess of 100nm may work against it when it comes to localisation. Such a sensor produces two types of information: not very accurate bearing and very accurate frequency. The latter may be the subject of Doppler calculation techniques which can be very helpful in terms of esti-

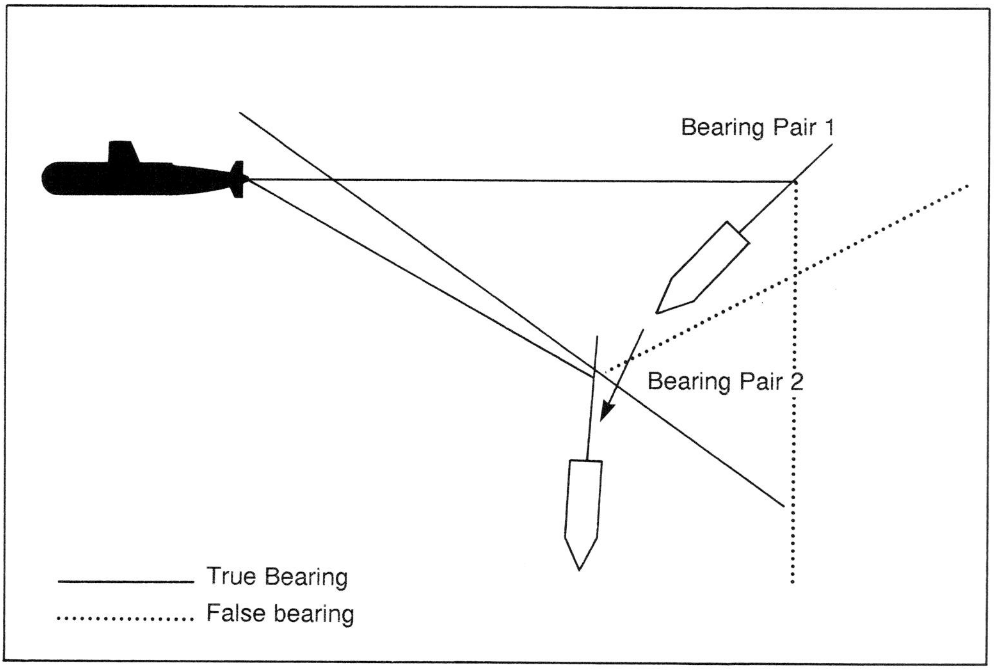

FIG. 6.2 Resolution of bearing ambiguity

mating target speed and course, but of no use whatsoever in determining range from the sensor. For this, bearing movement is required – a quantity at a premium at long range – and which can come from one of three sources;

- Substantial sensor movement.
- Substantial target movement.
- Time.

The first will almost certainly involve speed leading to loss of contact which may not be regained on subsequent slowing. The second is beyond the control of the detecting unit, so in most cases it comes down to time. Even when some estimate of range can be made, there are still likely to be considerable uncertainties. Resolving these means either putting the sensor much closer to the submarine, or the use of another vehicle for further localisation. In the case of a submarine locating another submarine, it may be possible for it to call in an aircraft to localise the target submarine, but this may also involve the submarine having to sit at periscope depth for some time to facilitate communication. In the process, the submarine may lose contact. More often the ASW submarine itself may have to close with the target submarine itself to localise and ultimately attack the target. In that sense – that of being able to do every task from detection to attack autonomously – the submarine itself may be the best single platform for ASW.

A surface ship needing to localise is much better placed to employ aircraft, either MPA or ASW helicopters, for this purpose. It always has a radio aerial in the air, and communicating with aircraft has no adverse effect on sensor performance. Aircraft can come from land, aircraft carriers, auxiliary tankers, or even the detecting unit itself: the later British Type 22 frigates and all the successor Type 23s can carry a fully ASW-capable helicopter: the combination is powerful.

SENSOR CATEGORIES

Although several types of sensor have been alluded to and, in some cases, their principles described in some detail, it is now intended to describe these sensors more extensively. In doing so, a preponderance in favour of acoustic sensors will be noted. It is understandable that this should be so; the tendency has grown for the 20th century submarine to be more and more at home underwater. Since the Second World War, nuclear propulsion has allowed extended underwater excursions, and the 'Albacore' hull form has resulted in a ship which is physically capable of greater underwater speed than that on the surface. Even the diesel-electric submarine only partially penetrates the atmosphere to recharge batteries by way of a schnorkel. As noted in the previous chapter, most forms of detection which work well in the atmosphere are poor performers underwater, although this may be changing (see Chapter 10). Sound remains most certain for medium and long distance underwater travel: therefore the methods of exploiting this phenomenon would still seem to have some life left in them. There are challenges to the dominance of acoustic systems: against active sonars, the techniques of reducing submarine's target strength, such as anechoic coating; against passive sonars, the reduction of submarine noise signatures. But despite these challenges and the possible rise of other means of detection, acoustic systems will still probably dominate detection for some time. In the succeeding sections active and passive sonar systems will be discussed together with other ways of detecting a submarine.

PLATE 6.1 Bow sonar dome *(Photo: C & S Taylor)*

ACTIVE SONAR

Active sonar is fitted to a very large number of ASW platforms, ranging from sonobuoys through helicopter dipping sonars to large ship and submarine installations. Its basic principle has remained the same since the pioneering Asdic days: a sound pulse transmitted and an echo received, but modern sets are very much more powerful and sophisticated than those of the early days. The more challenging nature of targets and the opportunities offered by modern electronics have led sonar in this direction. The nuclear propulsion challenge took sonar away from the narrow beam, medium frequency equipment through broadbeam to simultaneous all-round coverage using lower frequencies to obtain longer ranges. This in turn imposed some constraints on ship design. Not only was a large sonar transducer required to be mounted in an optimal space, but considerable volume was required for electronics, cooling and operators. The latter considerations have tended to shrink again recently, due to advances in electronics, but the transducer tends still to be an important factor in ship design. Historically, that is since the Second World War, this has tended to be a feature dictating the minimum size of ASW surface ship, which is now around 1,500 tons; no more 900 ton *Flower* Class corvettes. In surface ships, the positions favoured are either in a retractable dome (also known as a hull outfit) under the forward part of the ship or in a fixed position. This location is dictated by the necessity of ensuring separation from the ship's own machinery noise. The usual alternative location, which has been the US Navy's solution for some time, is that of placing the sonar in a bulbous bow.

This is a good location, obviating the need for retraction and usually improving seakeeping. In a submarine, main active sonars are likely to be found either built into the rounded bow, the preferred solution for most nuclear submarines, or in a separate dome mounted on the bow, often used in diesel-electric boats.

Examples of modern surface-ship sonars are Type 2050 (British) and SQS-53 (American). As well as the features mentioned above of all-azimuth performance and medium frequency, usually of the order of a few kilohertz, there are other characteristics often found in a modern active sonar. Firstly, there is a great deal of use made of acoustic and electronic technology. Carefully designed signal shapes are used to make detection more certain and at longer ranges; receiver signal processing has also received much attention to optimise the probability of detection; techniques to minimise the detrimental effects of high bottom reverberations in shallow water are employed and perhaps most importantly methods of automatic detection have come into common use. Furthermore, the increased geographical scope of contemporary active sonars has also led to the potential of more candidate targets being presented to the operator, so system autotracking is commonly employed, but with the ability to look at a few targets in greater detail. Passing of likely targets into AIO/CIC systems is usually carried out automatically.

Nor does this end the scope of active sonars in large platforms: a major source of performance limitation in hull-mounted active sonars is their inability to realise their range potential in conditions of marked thermal layers (see Chapter 5). When these are especially pronounced, sonars may not be able to make

PLATE 6.2 VDS at stern *(Photo: C & S Taylor)*

detections beyond a few hundred metres, except when the target is in a shallow surface duct. A solution to this is the use of variable depth sonar (VDS). Here a transducer, usually stern-mounted, is lowered by means of a gantry into the water abaft the towing ship, thus penetrating the layer. Some examples of this can be found in Canadian (SQS-505) and Russian (*Mare Tail* and *Horse Tail*) service. Often such sets are partially or fully integrated into the hull-mounted sonar set, sharing electronics and display facilities.

A further variation is the use of propagation modes other than Direct Path (DP). Those most commonly used are Convergence Zone (CZ) and Bottom Bounce (BB) For a full explanation of these terms, see the previous chapter. Both require particular seabottom characteristics to be effective: in the former case, sufficient depth of water; in the latter, a sufficiently reflective bottom type. Operating in either of these modes may increase range performance, but nearly always at the cost of accuracy, at least compared with that normally available in the DP mode. Clearly, this has implications for prosecution of any targets identified in CZ and BB modes. Normally, this implies relocation by some other method or sensor.

Similar considerations apply to active sonars in submarines, except that as a sonar transmission is usually detectable at ranges well in excess of those at which returns can come, submarines may be loath to use an active sensor unless absolutely necessary and operational need overrides the requirement for covertness. As a surface ship is more vulnerable to detection by other means, such a consideration may carry less weight. One occasion on which a submarine might use active sonar is to confirm a target's range just before firing a weapon when its fire control solution is slightly dubious.

There is one other point about active sonars, which is their use for functions other than their main one of surveillance. Previously, ships would carry separate specialised sonars for such work as torpedo detection. Now this is commonly a subsidiary mode of the main sonar, often using autodetection techniques, and making significant economies in equipment and operators. It is, of course, a reflection on the absence of hot war over the last 40 years that such a philosophy has not apparently been put to the test fully.

Active sonars can also be deployed from aircraft, either in the dipping form from helicopters, or else sonobuoys from both helicopters and fixed-wing aircraft. Dipping sonar complements ship-mounted sets well. Although for many reasons, such as space and weight, it cannot have the same capability, it does possess some important advantages. Firstly, it is by definition VDS, control of its winch permitting optimum depth deployment, providing there is sufficient cable available. Earlier sets were somewhat limited, but a modern one such as Marconi's *Cormorant* can be lowered to more than 450m. Relatively low frequencies can now be used, as can panoramic display, and combination with passive sensing. The ability to vary depth with virtually infinite choice makes dipping sonar attractive and the ability to use more power than an active sonobuoy can also be of use, but its greatest tactical asset in comparison to surface ship sonar must be its unpredictability and speed of deployment.

Active sonobuoys, despite their longer heritage than dipping sonar, could be regarded as expendable dipping sonars. Battery life usually limits them to a

PLATE 6.3 Helicopter with dipping sonar *(Photo: USN)*

certain time or number of pings. Further, as suggested above, they can usually only be set for a particular depth. It is normally feasible to lower them further, but not to return them to shallow depth settings, as this would not only use up the limited amount of power available but also complicate buoy design. Nevertheless, they have advanced greatly since their original conception as final localisers, prior to weapon release. A modern active buoy, such as SSQ-963B Command Active Multi-Beam Sonobuoy (CAMBS) can be switched on and off, as well as being able to vary its depth downward.

Another interesting concept not in operational service, open only to sonobuoy or fixed sensors, and then only in deep oceanic water is ERAPS (Expendable Reliable Acoustic Path Sonobuoy). In this an active, very deep-laid buoy – up to 5000m – can exploit the ability for all sound to be present at great depths, currently unexploitable by submarine hulls themselves, or even current towed arrays.

Some other applications of active sonar are considered in other chapters – those dealing with prosecution, supporting systems and the future – but it is clear that active sonar still plays an important part in modern ASW.

PASSIVE SONARS

Passive sonar can take a variety of forms and also be deployed from most platforms ranging from surface ships to sonobuoys. The advantages of longer range and exploitation of a wide part of the acoustic spectrum is, as has been pointed out, partially offset by the necessity to carry out further processing over time to localise any contact.

Early passive sonars largely used the versatile medium of the human ear to detect and classify underwater sound. Skilled as a trained operator was, it became increasingly difficult to deal with the vast amounts of data which became available as firstly improved hydrophone design and then large hull arrays became available. The advent of more sophisticated signal processing increased the problem further by focusing on narrow band noise rather than traditional sources such as the overall output of a noisy propeller. This led to reliance on visual displays, usually of a frequency against time nature. Further complication was introduced by the towed array, whose lengthy arrangement of single and simple hydrophones was not only powerful, but when combined with electronic beamformers allowed the splitting of the azimuth into 30 or more beam pairs. Thus, in designing a modern passive sonar, care has to be paid to hydrophone and mechanical design, as well as processing architecture and design engineering.

In a surface ship design, such as the American AN/SQR-19, the 'wet end' consists of an 82mm diameter array of hydrophones towed by a 1700m cable, which permits operation down to 365m. This is widely fitted in US warships from *Aegis* cruisers to *Oliver Hazard Perry* class frigates, and claims the ability to detect submarines at 'tactically significant ship speeds'. Such a statement implies a reasonably quiet towing ship, in itself a useful attribute for ASW. Without knowing some of the presumably classified details of its operational performance, it is impossible to comment directly on its effectiveness, but its widespread fitting tends to suggest that it is at least competent against current generations of nuclear submarines. It was designed for operations in support of US CVBGs against Soviet operations using both SSNs and SSGNs. Allowing for forward deployment of US units and the missile range of the Soviet *Oscar* SSGN, AN/SQR-19 might be capable of achieving detection ranges in the order of 100nm or so.

In submarines, internal configuration and size limits towed arrays to somewhat less ambitious dimensions, but the submarine's quietness and ability to change depths compensates to an extent for this disadvantage. An example of this would be the British 2026 system built by Marconi. Further, the submarine hull itself, totally immersed and usually working in a quieter environment than a surface ship in the relatively turbulent surface water, can be used for the optimum placing of acoustic sensors. As well as the obvious bow area, linear arrays of significant length can be placed along the hull, generally avoiding the noisier machinery areas. Again Marconi has produced a system which has been supplied to the Swedish Navy.

Attempts have been made to overcome the ranging difficulty inherent in passive sonar by such systems as the Unisys Corporation's MicroPUFFS (Passive Underwater Fire control Feasibility Study), which is apparently capable of producing instantaneous range information on targets. The system appears to work by using three arrays on each side of the submarine and cross-correlating data received at these, and making use of time differentials. The relatively limited fit of this equipment – to Australian *Oberon* class submarines but hardly at all within the USN – suggests either that the concept was more promising than the reality, or that subsequent other developments have rendered MicroPUFFS already outmoded.

Although applicable elsewhere, it is probably best to mention sonar intercept in the context of submarines. This is the technique of detecting active sonars which may be a threat to the detector, in sufficient time to be useful. Although almost any passive sonar is capable of detecting an active one – underwater telephones have for many years done well at this – it is also useful to know some less readily extractable details of the signals, such as frequency, bandwidth and pulse length to aid identification. It may also be possible to indicate what mode the active sonar is in: searching or immediately prior to weapon release. Under some circumstances of multipath reception of a sonar signal transmitted by an opponent, it may be possible to calculate the range of the transmitter. An example of specialist equipment in this field would be BAeSema Marine's SPRINT system.

Helicopters, too, can deploy passive sonars, although these are obviously relatively limited in size by comparison with those that ships and submarines are capable of carrying. It is also becoming more common for some passive capability to be built into what are primarily active dipping sonars.

The sonobuoy, however, is the main way in which passive sonar is employed by both fixed- and rotary-wing aircraft. Such techniques have been around for many years, initially working on broad band detection, but now more often based on narrow band systems. These can also use such methods as summing inputs from more than one buoy to enhance information, directional passive buoys and narrow band analysis. In some instances, radio frequency (RF) relay is used, so that processing takes place elsewhere than on board the launching aircraft, an example being the US LAMPS I system now going out of service.

Modern passive sonobuoys are versatile and powerful – although their range performance is usually inferior to that of a good passive sensor mounted on a surface ship or submarine. On the other hand, most aircraft can deploy a number of them, and with the advent of small (F-size) buoys, even a medium-sized helicopter can carry a reasonable number of these. In such aircraft, the effective limit is imposed not so much by buoy stowage – previously of importance – as by the ability to process the output of several buoys simultaneously. Such a constraint is imposed both by equipment, such as the number of RF receivers or the storage facilities within the processor, and by the ability of a human operator to scan and use a great deal of information: this is especially marked in helicopters where there is likely to be only one sonar operator at most.

Nevertheless the capability of a modern passive sonobuoy such as BARRA (a British-Australian system) or AN-SSQ-53D (US/Canadian under licence) is considerable, especially against a nuclear submarine or a diesel-electric one engaged in noisy activity, such as snorting.

PLATE 6.4 Sonobuoys – available in various sizes *(Photo: Dowty)*

OTHER SENSORS

It was noted earlier that acoustic sensors are the principal ones involved in finding and localising submarines: this remains so, but some others should be mentioned. Firstly, certain methods whose potential for submarine detection relies on space-mounted sensors should be noted; these will be discussed in the chapter on the future. Environmental reasons for this dominance were stated in the last chapter, but further consideration of radar, electronic support measures (ESM) and magnetic anomaly detection (MAD) are given here.

Radar, largely when aircraft mounted, continues to be of use in ASW. Although modern radar, such as *Searchwater* fitted in the *Nimrod* MPA, is a very capable piece of equipment and easily able to detect submarines or their masts and snorts, the value of radar lies probably as much now as ever in its power to deter submarines from making use of the surface. This is probably less likely now, with modern submarines being underwater vessels more than hitherto, but an effective radar does deny a submarine this option.

Similarly, ESM depends for its efficacy on a submarine choosing to make use of radar. Although western submariners are brought up in a tactical culture which has a strong aversion to using radar, this does not necessarily apply to everyone else. Again, despite the unlikeliness of a submarine transmitting, ESM is a relatively cheap form of insurance against this contingency.

MAD takes advantage of an involuntary property of a submarine, namely that it is a large lump of ferrous metal against a relatively weak magnetic background.

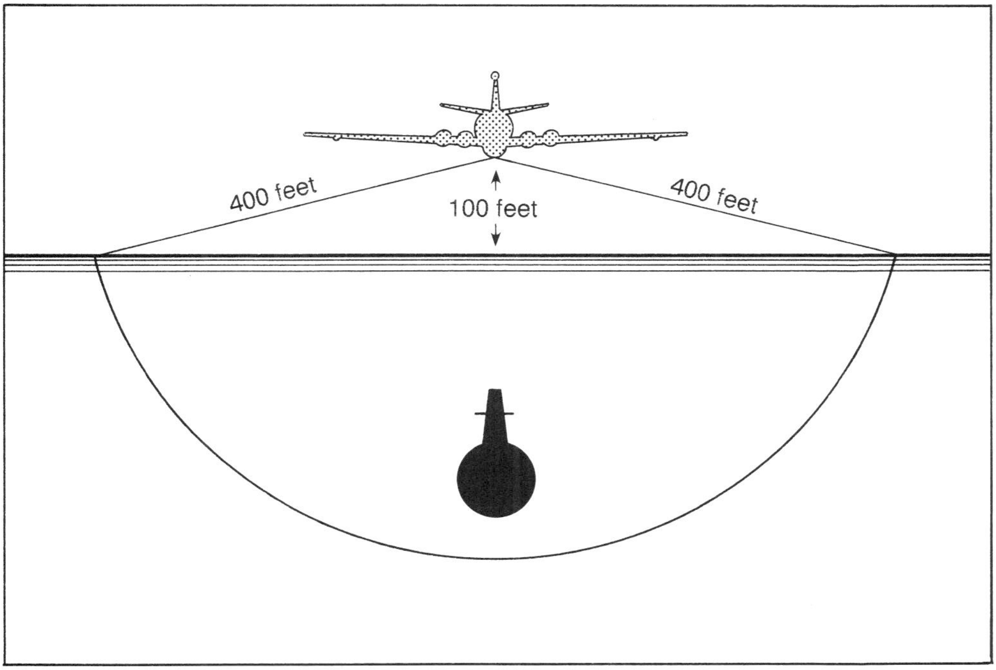

FIG. 6.3 MAD swept path

This is helpful, because of the lack of a corresponding visual or radar contact on the surface. However, despite modern technology, the slant range capability of such a system is usually less than 1,000 yards. Further the requirement to provide some magnetic separation between sensor and platform demands airborne deployment, either in the form of a tail boom (MPA) or towed 'bird' (helicopter). This means that some of even this limited range potential is absorbed by the safety requirement of the aircraft having to fly at a minimum height. When the depth potential of the submarine is added to this, the tactical swept width of MAD is reduced further.

For this reason, MAD can normally only be considered as a localisation or confirmatory sensor prior to attack; one historical exception to this was MAD being used against German submarines in the Strait of Gibraltar during the Second World War. Commonly fitted systems are AN/ASQ-504(V) (Canada) and AN/ASQ-81(V) (USA).

Thus it can be seen that acoustic methods still dominate the spectrum of detection and its associated sensors. The topic of what might happen in the future in this field will be looked at in more detail in Chapter 10. However, it is useful to sum up the general position on detection as it appears in the late years of the 20th century. The nuclear submarine, although much quieter than in its original form, still probably produces sufficient noise to offer significant detection opportunities to passive acoustic systems. Active detection, the counter to the quieter diesel-electric submarine similarly has worthwhile, if slightly less spectacular, potential. But nothing necessarily stands still, and research continues into quietening and anti-active measures such as hull coating, which may make future acoustic detection more difficult, if not impossible.

But what may have changed over the last few years are two linked factors. Firstly, the end of the Cold War has removed, or at least vastly reduced, the submarine/ASW dynamic, which has produced such stunning technological developments. The USA and the USSR were undoubtedly the two big league players: is there still a game to watch? Related to this is the likelihood of altered defence spending profiles. Even where expenditure remains high, priorities may well be altered. High-technology air-launched systems as in Iraq in 1991, or relatively low-tech infantrymen on the ground – Bosnia in the mid 1990s – could well figure higher on the agenda than ASW. These topics will be addressed towards the end of the book.

7

Prosecution and Weapons

INTRODUCTION

An earlier suggestion was made that ASW could be carried out without detection, far less sinking, of submarines. Although this has some historical precedent, it has rarely been the case that any significant ASW campaign has been fought without resort to destroying submarines. In the Battle of the Atlantic in the latter part of 1941 submarines were robbed of their effectiveness by being denied contact with convoys, but in the middle of 1943 it was the Allied ability to sink submarines which was crucial. Thus, both skills are needed and this chapter will concentrate on weaponry and the business of attacking submarines. Further, it will do this largely at the level of one ASW unit attacking one submarine. The matter of more than one unit or type of unit working together will be dealt with later. The approach taken here is firstly to consider the general principles of attacking a submarine, the types of weapon needed to implement these principles and some aspects of their use. Then the applications of these weapons to attack from particular platforms will be considered.

The submarine has always been, is presently, and is likely to continue to be a tough nut to crack. Firstly, it is immensely strong. Designed to deal with physical pressures with which no other warfighting vehicle has to deal merely in order to carry out its normal business in the ocean depths, it is very robustly built. Secondly, it has less in the way of externally mounted systems, such as radars in surface ships. Damage to these could neutralise if not destroy the unit. Certainly, it has its weak spots such as periscope mechanisms and towed arrays, but attempting to damage these is both more difficult and probably less productive for an opponent. Thirdly, the submarine is probably more difficult to detect – or at least to localise – than enemies on the surface and in the atmosphere. It is perhaps the original, and still one of the best, stealth vehicles. Lastly, the modern submarine is both fast and highly manoeuvrable. Its speed may not seem particularly significant, but a nuclear submarine can out-pace most surface vessels and is often little slower than some of the underwater weapons ranged against it.

FIRST ATTEMPTS

There is only one basic way to harm or sink a submarine and that is to place a charge of explosive close enough to it to cause damage to the hull by significantly breaching its watertight integrity, or put its control mechanisms or propulsion out of order. Apparently simple, the realisation of such an aim poses many problems in practice. Early ASW technology dealt with the issue by using the detecting platform itself as what might be termed a semi-guided missile. An attacking ship, holding contact with a submerged submarine, would over-run its target, dropping depth charges at an estimated time to explode at set depths. There were many inaccuracies inherent in this, not least those involved in over-running and thus losing contact. Once dropped or thrown, the weapon received no further guidance. As its lethal radius could be measured in feet, even against the submarines of the Second World War, a degree of luck and the ability to repeat attacks was needed. Advances were made in the ability to deliver multiple charges simultaneously, but submarines also learned the value of a drastic manoeuvre at the moment of or just before being over-run. The system was adequate rather than consistently successful.

Nor was the depth charge much more effective when dropped from the air. There were errors inherent in aiming by eye and the selection of the correct depth was often critical. This finding was one of the early successes of operational research, a subject described in the next chapter. Until reliable methods of locating a submerged submarine from an aircraft were deployed, visual aiming was the only way of attacking a submarine with such a weapon.

PLATE 7.1 Mortar Mk 10 – projecting aimed explosives *(Photo: C & S Taylor)*

Returning to the surface ship case, it was recognised that the errors generated just by losing contact were probably sufficient in themselves to lessen the impact of even quite a heavy depth charge attack. Although there were tactical solutions such as creeping attacks, where one escort remained in contact and directed a second as weapon carrier to a firing point, inaccuracies remained and the use of a second vessel was usually uneconomical in terms of time and force. What was really needed was a weapon which could be projected ahead of the attacking ship so that sonar contact could be maintained to the last moment. Early systems using explosive propulsion and ranges of a few hundred metres enjoyed some success against relatively slow submarines. Depth determination of the target remained a problem, requiring the design of special sonar types in the first instance; an alternative was to make warhead explosion conditional on either contact or magnetic triggering.

Such systems, although over 50 years old in concept, are still being manufactured and fitted. They are especially useful in coastal waters where target speed is unlikely to be high and a consequent degree of inaccuracy is more acceptable than in the high speed case likely to be encountered in deep water. Not surprisingly Baltic countries are leaders in this field with Sweden being particularly prominent. Not only is there a long-established family of Bofors 375mm systems, but ELMA-SAAB have a smaller light ASW-600 system suitable for small craft such as fast attack craft (FACs) and corvettes. The Russians too have made use of this technique for many years with the RBU series of multi-barrel launchers. The majority of systems now extant use rocket rather than explosive propulsion, cutting down time of flight and thus time to attack. Although often effective in being able to deploy explosive weapons in a short time to ranges of several kilometres, the problem of accurate delivery remains.

ASW MINES

Before moving to the preferred modern solution of homing weapons, there is one other class of weapons to be considered, the ASW mine. This is a rather specialised weapon as specific targeting of submarines is not easy and a degree of unwitting co-operation on the submarine's part in putting itself in the proximity of the mine is needed. In designing an anti-surface ship mine, it is relatively easy to deal with target depth. Clearly, the target is on the surface and can be attacked either by ground or moored mines in relatively shallow water and by moored mines in deeper water. Various methods, such as rising mines, can be used to increase the effective radius of the mine. Submarines pose difficult challenges to the mine designer. They are inherently quiet and their depth needs to be determined to maximise explosive efficiency. It is important to note that any ASW mining strategy is likely to be limited to areas of particular depths and geographic limits.

This has not stopped attempts to design ASW mines. Perhaps the leading example of this is the American CAPTOR (for enCAPsulated TORpedo) system. There are two main components to such a system: a Detection and Control Unit which detects and classifies the target as an enemy submarine before releasing the weapon, a Mk46 ASW torpedo. The project has enjoyed somewhat stop-start progress since the 1970s, suggesting possible difficulties with the technical realisation of the concept, or alternatively that CAPTOR is operationally too limited to have more than a marginal effect on any likely ASW campaign.

BIGGER BANGS AND PRECISION DELIVERY

The main ASW weapon now and in the foreseeable future is the homing torpedo. It has many forms and delivery systems, which are outlined below. It was the inherent inaccuracies of dropped and projected weapons which led designers in this direction some decades ago. Underlying their ineffectiveness was a very simple physical law on explosions, namely that of spherical spreading. Put simply, the effective radius of effect of an explosion is proportional to the cube root of its power. Another way of expressing this is to note that a desired doubling of lethal radius requires an eightfold increase of explosive power. This usually implies eight times the weight of the same explosive mixture. Whilst the first 50 years of the 20th century saw considerable progress in the chemical composition of explosives, none of these were sufficient to keep pace with the demands of ASW. The advent of the nuclear submarine, an even stronger and much more dynamic target, put paid to any lingering hope that more efficient explosives by themselves could solve the ASW attack problem.

At the same time nuclear science also allowed the possibility of the ultimate explosive solution, compensating for the cube root law in the crudest way possible: the nuclear depth bomb (NDB). This weapon has now largely gone out of use in most countries. Although no doubt technically effective, there were many disputable implications, political and ecological, as well as tactical difficulties, such as keeping friendly units well clear of the impact point.

The real solution to the practical explosive load and realistic delivery accuracy conundrum lay in a system which was capable of reaching its target by means of guidance received after launch to compensate either for unknowns at that time, or for target motion after weapon discharge. This suggested a weapon with the ability to guide itself to the target with no further assistance coming from the launching unit. The obvious vehicle for this was the torpedo, already a locomotive device. This was to see its first realisation in the Second World War with an acoustic homing torpedo, introduced by the Americans in 1943, for air dropped use against submerged submarines. These relied on the target making a certain amount of noise on which to home, and enjoyed some success, not least because the Germans were slow to appreciate their introduction. If they worked, they were effective and sank submarines, usually leaving no survivors to tell tales.

But such early devices were relatively crude, and were only really suitable for air drop, because of the risk of friendly surface ships' noise seducing the torpedo away from its proper target. Further, the torpedo on-board sonar was relatively insensitive, it being severely constrained by size and power as well as being affected by the torpedo's own noise. In the postwar period, a series of developments were to greatly improve the homing torpedo as an ASW weapon. The main advances were:

- Adoption of more versatile acoustic tracking methods.
- Improved automotive performance.
- Better warhead design.
- Faster, longer and more accurate delivery methods.

Improved Tracking Methods A typical modern ASW torpedo is capable of using either passive or active homing techniques of considerable sophistication. It may be possible for it to switch between active and passive modes either using external commands or on board logic. This is likely to depend on tactical circumstances. For example, a heavyweight submarine torpedo may well make use of initial guidance provided from the firing submarine using a wire guidance link. This allows the torpedo to be steered towards the target at a quiet speed, optimising the performance of the torpedo sonar whilst minimising the chance of the target being alerted. Once the torpedo has made valid passive acoustic contact its wire guidance can be cut, returning fuller tactical freedom to the firing submarine. Subsequent loss of contact by the torpedo can be allowed for by reversion to other acoustic modes, initiation of search patterns and the use of variable speed to make the best use of the previous two measures.

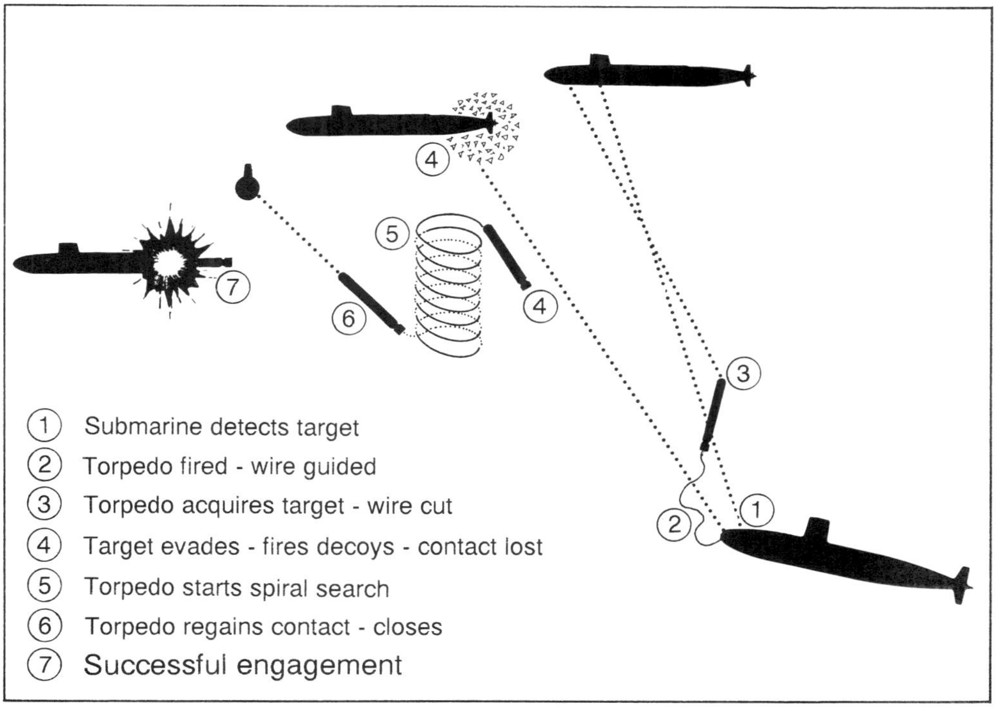

FIG. 7.1 Heavyweight torpedo homing phase

Improved Automotive Performance Early torpedoes, dating from the late 19th century and designed for use against surface vessels, could only obtain the desired automotive performance by means of piston engines using hydrocarbon fuels. These could perform well for their size, but nearly always left trails of exhaust bubbles which could betray the attack in suitable water conditions. This was not

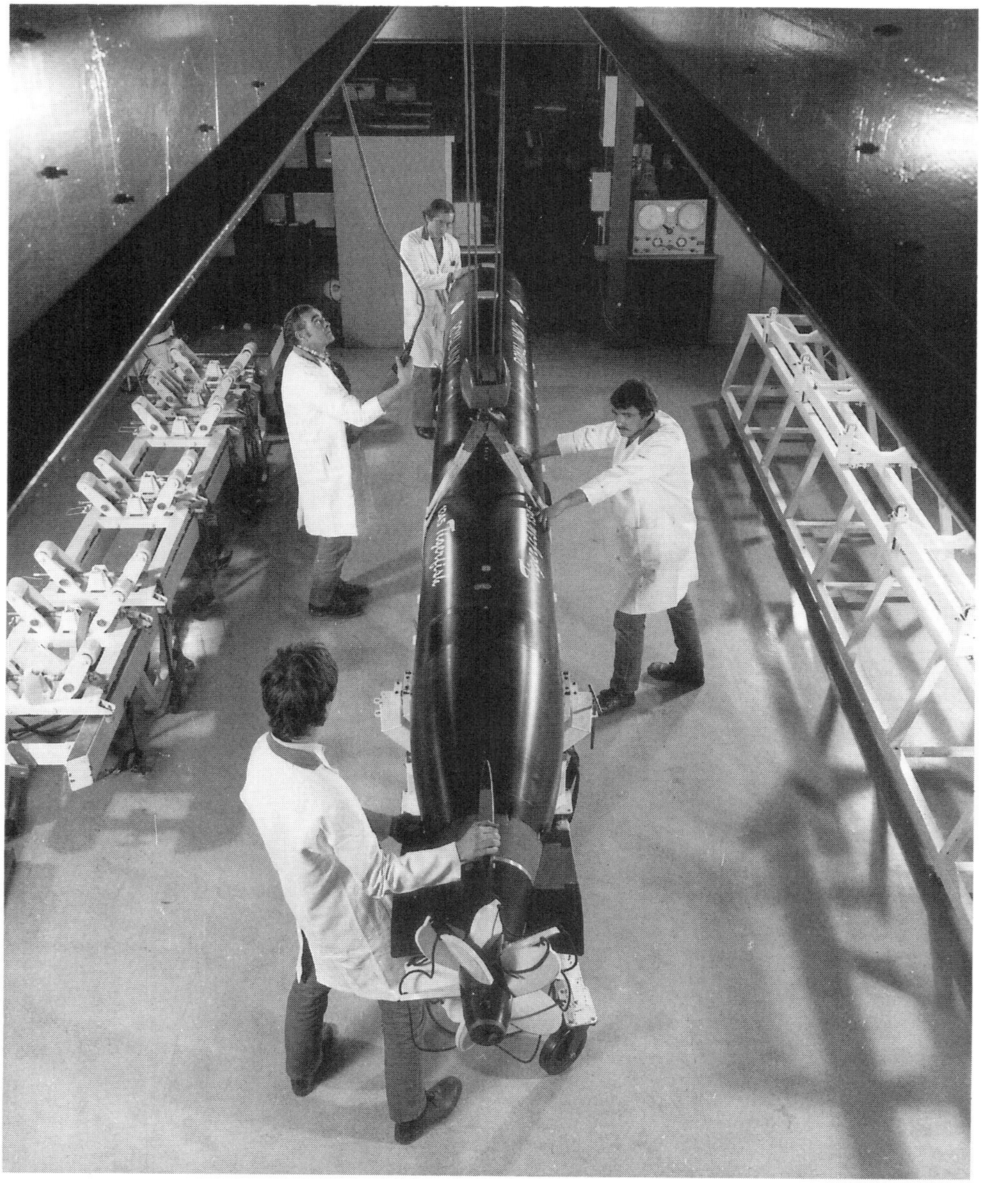

PLATE 7.2 Tigerfish torpedo *(Photo: Marconi)*

a desperate disadvantage with surface launched torpedoes as the manoeuvres of their launching ships was an earlier indicator of attack. But for submarines this was a greater drawback. By the Second World War, the Germans were deploying electric torpedoes which obviated the bubble trail problem. These were generally of lesser performance than fossil-fuelled torpedoes, but electro-chemical improvements had lessened the disadvantage to acceptable levels. Ironically electric torpedoes were initially more suitable for ASW work because they were quieter and their targets, submerged submarines, were not very fast.

Subsequent developments were to allow both automotive approaches. The faster, deeper diving, nuclear submarine target demanded more of automotive performance but both methods rose to the dual challenges of performance and quietness. There is, however, a trend noticeable towards the thermally-propelled weapon often utilising such techniques as closed-cycle propulsion, turbines rather than pistons and monopropellant fuels which contain their own oxygen and need no separate supply for combustion. Thus the American Mk 48 ADCAP (heavyweight), Mk 50 (lightweight) and British *Spearfish* (heavyweight) use thermal propulsion whilst the British *Tigerfish* (heavyweight) and *Stingray* (lightweight) use seawater battery electrical propulsion. All of these torpedoes apparently operate in the 40-55 kts speed range.

Better Warhead Design With early submarines the attack problem was to place a practicable explosive charge close enough to the hull to either penetrate it or else cause sufficient damage to vulnerable areas such as control surfaces or important internal fittings such as periscopes, propulsion or air systems. The homing weapon appeared to obviate the inaccuracies of thrown systems at least for a while, but further problems arose with the development of the fast, deep diving, strong nuclear submarine. The first two attributes could largely be countered by the automotive improvements described above. As demonstrated, torpedo speeds are now usually sufficient to overhaul even the fastest submarines; however, there was another consequence which will be returned to: the tendency for all engagements to end up as stern chases. Deep diving tended to place strains on thermal propulsion systems which exhausted into the sea, but this problem too was solvable, not least by the employment of closed-cycle or electric systems.

But a more insidious and possibly unintended counter to the homing weapon was the growing strength of submarines. The earliest American and Soviet nuclear submarines had used hulls which were essentially little different from those of their diesel-electric contemporaries. But once the Albacore or tear-drop hull form had been adopted, leading to improved hulls, a problem was also created for the homing weapon. As these submarines were intended for greater depths and higher speeds, their construction both in terms of structure and material strength was considerably greater. There was also a tendency for them to become physically bigger at the same time, which in itself introduced features, such as double pressure hulls – one inside the other – which made them structurally a more difficult proposition for weapons with relatively small warheads. The requirement to let the submarine operate at deeper depths also introduced thicker, stronger materials in the hulls themselves making the task of weapons even harder.

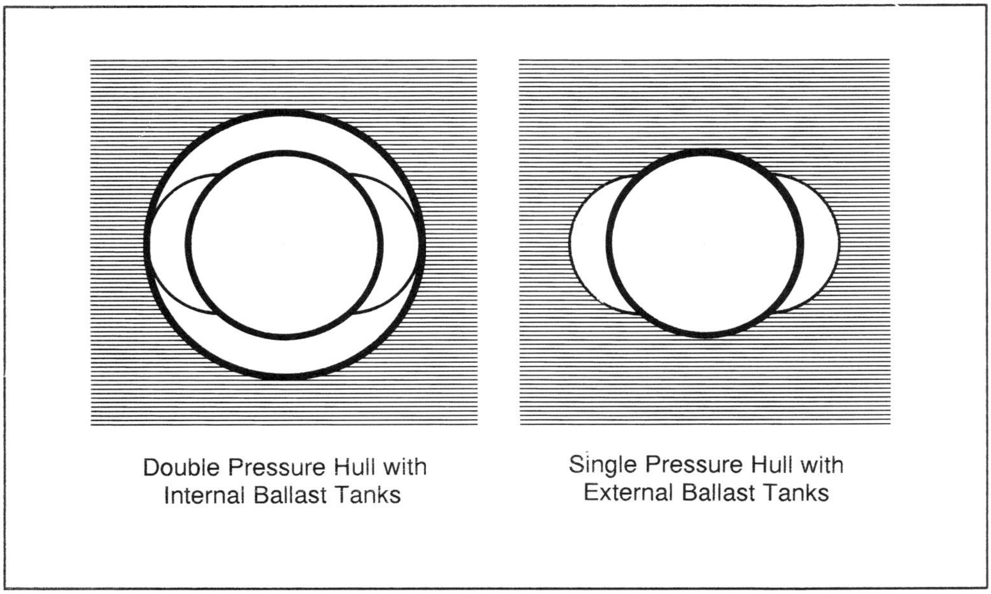

FIG. 7.2 Submarine double hull

As a result vulnerability, especially to lightweight torpedoes, was probably much reduced. At this point it is useful to digress on the classification of torpedoes by weight. There are two main categories and these have been mentioned briefly earlier. Lightweight torpedoes weigh between 200 and 350 kg and are generally of about 300–400 mm diameter. They are suitable for discharge by surface ships and air vehicles. Because of their limited size and weight warheads are usually of no more than 60 kg weight. The Russian definition of lightweight is slightly stretched to include somewhat bigger weapons which can accommodate 100 kg of explosive. On the other hand heavyweights measure around 530 mm and weigh in at 900–1,600 kg with warheads of 100–300 kg. Again the Russians manage to overtop this range with both 650 mm super-heavyweight torpedoes with 900 kg warheads (probably intended for anti-surface use) and a nuclear tipped weapon, which again is almost certainly not exclusively for ASW.

The size and weight of the true heavyweight preclude its use from aircraft of any type as well as imposing severe design constraints on surface warships. Nevertheless the Soviets persisted with this design feature in many of their surface warships. The submarine, therefore, is the true home of the heavyweight torpedo with its specialist handling facilities and the ship being designed to some extent around the tubes.

The significance of the smaller explosive charge of lightweight torpedoes came home in the west with the realisation that Soviet submarines were constructed with double hulls and free flood spaces in between. The significance of this was the appreciable stand-off distance between the likely point of impact of an ASW torpedo and the true pressure hull, reducing the chance of a complete and tactically significant hull penetration.

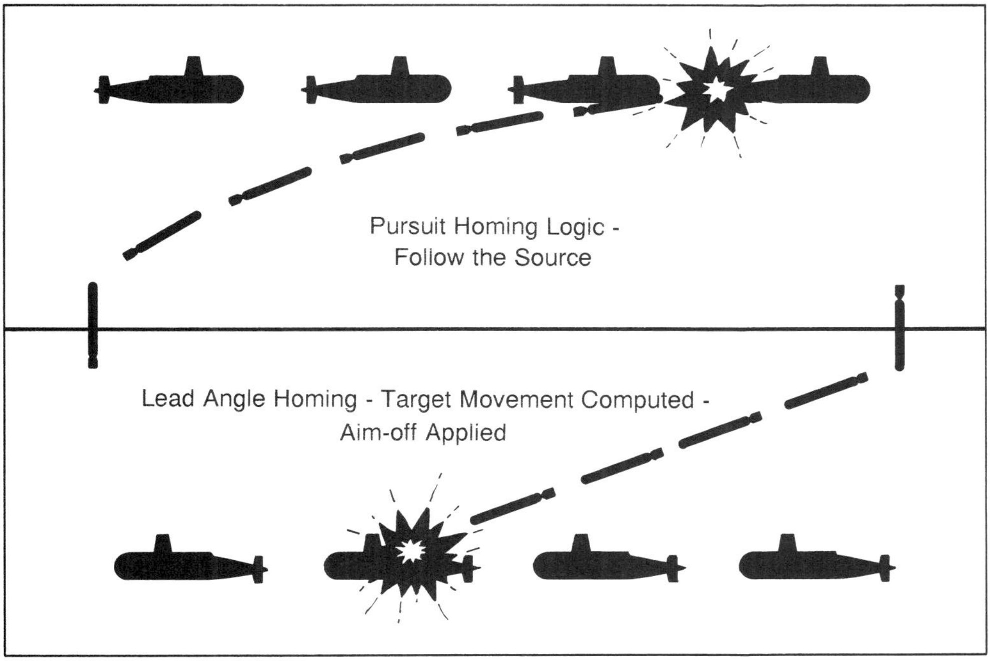

FIG. 7.3 Lead and pursuit closure

Earlier it was mentioned that many ASW torpedo versus submarine encounters were likely to end in a stern chase. This was certainly likely to be the consequence of a nuclear submarine detecting a torpedo in time to increase to full speed and place the weapon astern. Such a problem could be overcome by employing sophisticated homing techniques, such as algorithms which could 'sense' target shape and movement, and thus direct the torpedo into a lead rather than pursuit intercept.

This would allow an approach from directions, other than astern, possibly even allowing selection of an area especially vulnerable to attack. An example of such a technique is the British *Stingray* lightweight torpedo. However, even with such helpful sophistication, it is possible that the sheer limitation on warhead size employed by the lightweight torpedo imposes severe constraints on effectiveness against modern submarines. Thus shaped charge technology, used for many years in anti-tank weapons has now been employed in torpedoes such as the Italian A244/S and the American Mk 50 lightweight weapons.

The technique has even been extended to the British heavyweight *Spearfish* torpedo. It is important to remember that such theoretical justifications for developments have never been put to the test in 50 years, either in terms of demonstrating the futility of light, simple charges or of indicating that the heavier more complex warhead will be effective.

Better Delivery Methods The traditional method of delivering a torpedo for many years was from a tube, either integral with the hull in the case of submarines or in swivelling tubes in the case of surface ships. Lightweight torpedoes were

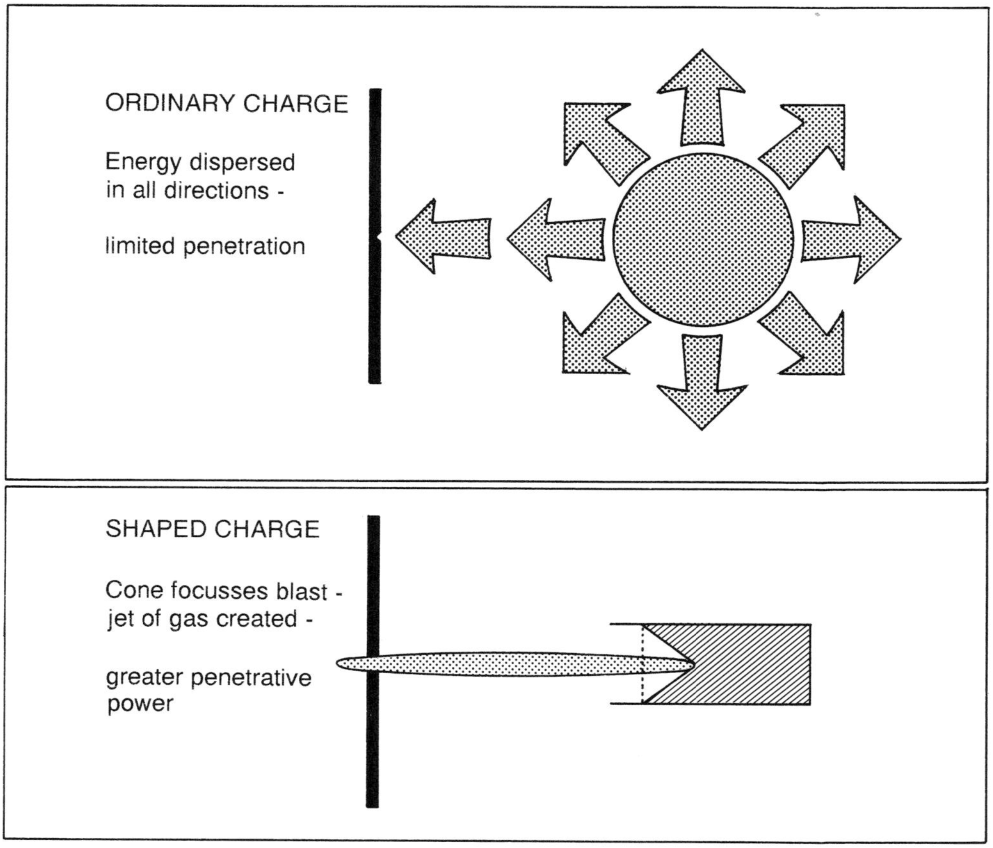

FIG. 7.4 Shaped charge principle

carried by aircraft, either underwing or in internal bomb bays. With submarines and surface ships, this implied putting the ship or submarine itself within torpedo range of the submarine target. If the torpedo itself had a short range or made use of an initial circle search – which occurred in some instances where lightweight torpedoes originally designed for air drop were adapted for surface launch – this required an uncomfortable and dangerous closeness to the target. There were a number of ways in which the problem could be overcome, some simple and some much more complex.

One relatively easy way in the lightweight modification case is to change the torpedo search pattern from circular to a variant on straight running. In this, the torpedo is programmed to carry out a weaving search based on a preset course, calculated using the last known or best predicted position of the submarine before torpedo launch. The weave is necessary to extend the torpedo's search front.

Such a system, however, effects only marginally the tactical requirement of keeping the ASW firer at arm's length from the target: the likely maximum range of a lightweight torpedo is liable to be much less than that of the submarine-

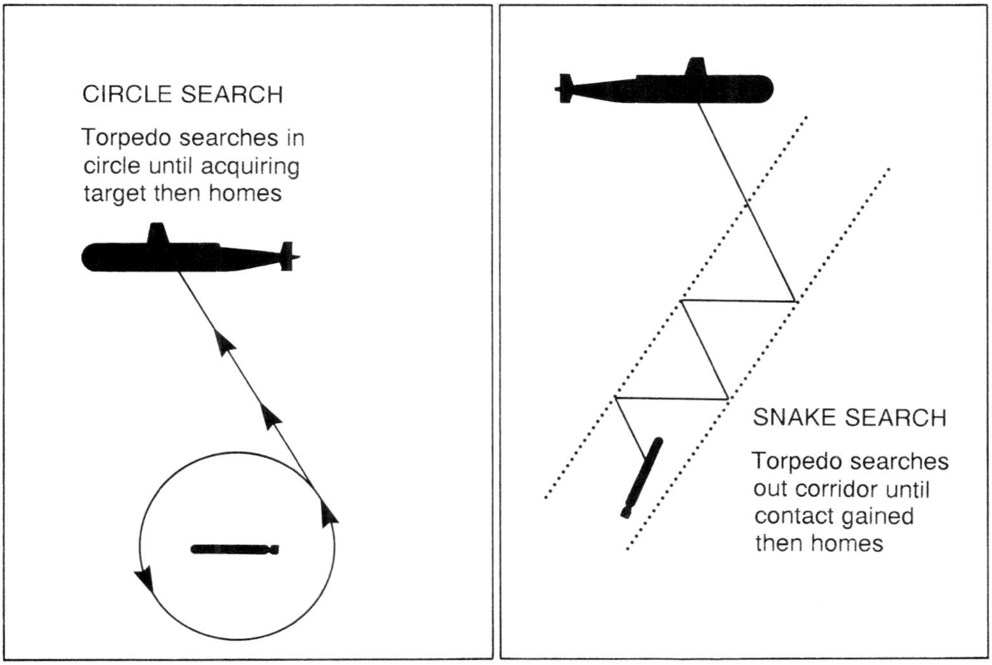

FIG. 7.5 Circle search and snake search

launched heavyweight torpedo or other weapon aimed at the ASW vessel. What is needed therefore is some kind of intermediate delivery vehicle, whose main characteristics are speed, accuracy and reliability of delivery. The speed requirement effectively means an air vehicle of some description and there are two main approaches, helicopters and missile systems.

Ignoring what might be termed the prehistoric helicopter solution of DASH – a drone deployed by the USA in the 1950s and 60s whose innovative design was not matched by sufficient maturity of radio control systems of the time, the first helicopter-based solution was probably a British one.

All British frigates which came into service from the early 1960s onwards had accommodation for a Westland *Wasp* light helicopter. Although subsequently used in other roles as well, the helicopter was designed to carry one or two lightweight torpedoes. With the target tracked by the medium range sonar of the frigate and the helicopter by means of a radar enhancer and later a transponder, the aircraft was guided by a human controller to an optimum drop point. This had not been designed as a system from the outset and it suffered from many sloppy links, but it was capable of putting a torpedo in the right place, whilst minimising the risks to the launching ship. On the other hand, it was weather-limited as well as being unavailable around the clock because of maintenance requirements and crew limitations. Nevertheless, this was a step in the right direction and the helicopter solution will be returned to later.

The other alternative was to use some form of missile as the intermediate delivery vehicle. This was less likely to constrain ship design and operation to

PLATE 7.3 Lightweight torpedo launcher – a short range expedient
(Photo: C & S Taylor)

the extent that a helicopter did on a frigate sized ship. Round the clock availability was also likely to be better as were weather constraints. Perhaps more importantly, a system design could be used rather than the somewhat improvised British helicopter solution.

The first such system in the field was the American ASROC in 1961. It is still used today although the original weapon has been updated to allow vertical launch and integration into the USN's multiple-weapon launcher systems. Payloads have been updated to permit deployment of weapons more advanced than the original, now obsolescent, Mk 44 lightweight torpedo. The system is linked to ship's sonar and launches a ballistic rocket over ranges reported to be about 10,000 yards, although this may be greater. Having a ballistic trajectory, the time of flight is very short, compensating for the lack of mid-flight guidance. At the end of the rocket's flight, the torpedo is released to attack its target.

Another similar weapon is the Australian developed *Ikara*. This, however, uses a cruise profile and mid-flight guidance. It is now only in service with the Brazilian Navy, is more sophisticated and complex than ASROC, and has a range of some 20,000 yards. An improved version, *Super Ikara*, has been proposed by the Australians in conjunction with British Aerospace. The range of the weapon would be 60,000 yards and there would be other improvements, but this project has apparently attracted little interest. The reason for this may lie partly in the rise and increasing capabilities of shipboard ASW aviation.

The Russians, too, deploy similar weapons in the form of the ship-mounted SS-N-14 *Silex* system which can carry either a NDB or a torpedo to ranges of 55,000 yards. That nation also has underwater launched systems: SS-N-15 *Starfish* and SS-N-16 *Stallion* deploying NDB and torpedo respectively to ranges of about 50,000 yards.

US submarines previously deployed SUBROC, a similar system, using a nuclear warhead. The US withdrawal of all tactical nuclear weapons has left their submarines with no ASW weapon of longer range than the Mk 48 torpedo. A successor system, SEA LANCE, has been developed but not deployed. It would also be suitable for use from surface ships, and uses as payload the Mk 50 lightweight torpedo. Whether this will be fitted depends on the future of new US programmes in the future defence economic climate. A French system, *Malafon*, broadly similar to *Ikara*, is now ageing and may be replaced by a joint French/Italian project, *Milas*, carrying a torpedo to ranges of 55,000 yards.

Aircraft, either fixed- or rotary-wing, do not have quite the same concerns about the speed of delivery or the vulnerability of the firer. On the latter subject, reports persist of deployments of submarine-launched surface to air missile (SAM) systems, but these seem to be based largely on manufacturers' optimism and intelligence analysts' worst case analyses rather than reality. Improvements in aircraft delivery stem therefore more from the spread and qualitative advances

PLATE 7.4 *Sea King* helicopter deployed from a Canadian destoyer
(Photo: L & L van Ginderen)

in ASW aircraft than from anything else. Shore-based aircraft have continued to advance, but perhaps the biggest moves forward have come at sea with the deployment of such advanced fixed-wing aircraft as the S-3 *Viking* in the USN and, even more significantly, the medium helicopter in relatively small ships.

The latter was pioneered by such nations as Canada, but has been exploited by most major marine powers including the USA, Russia, UK, India, Japan, France and the Netherlands. Although the medium helicopter, with radar and MAD, such as the Sikorsky/Westland *Sea King* is the most significant and useful, types of aircraft start from relatively small ones which can do little more than launch a torpedo.

In future, helicopters such as the Anglo-Italian EH-101 will be deployed which are capable of autonomous search, location and attack at significant distances away from their parents, which can now be as small as a frigate.

SUMMING UP

When a number of specialised and marginal cases (shallow water and ASW mining) are excluded, the dominant weapon in ASW is the homing torpedo, which can take a number of forms such as active and passive homing, heavy-weight or lightweight, thermal or electric propulsion. Delivery can be achieved either directly from an ASW platform or by means of intermediate launch vehicles. The latter have become an almost compulsory adjunct to the longer-range sensors that are now available. The lack of a hot ASW war over the past 50 years has prevented a demonstration of whether present weapons could pass the final test of effectiveness: whether they can sink or severely damage the modern submarine.

8

Supporting Equipment, Skills and Techniques

INTRODUCTION

The core skills of ASW, detection and attack, have been described in previous chapters. Before moving on to the way in which these are tied together in a large scale way to produce ASW organisations, it is useful to consider some of the ancillary equipments and skills which complete the lower level picture. Of necessity, these do not always link directly with each other but an understanding of such subjects is necessary to appreciate fully the central techniques as well as to connect to the larger picture.

As the environment chapter indicated, as full an understanding as possible of the area in which ASW forces are working is essential to success. In circumstances in which submarines and ASW forces are finely balanced against each other, the better knowledge and exploitation of the underwater environment will be the crucial factor which tips the balance. Coupled with this to some extent is the subject of signature control. This takes in much more than ASW measures, as the recent interest in general stealth technology has indicated. But the measurement and reduction of acoustic signatures is central to ASW, both as an aid to improved performance, a preventive against counterdetection and in the last resort a means of avoiding attack. A further subject linked to this last point is countermeasures to attack.

Two facets of ASW which are often overlooked are training and assessment. Both of these were amongst the most important lessons learned from the 1939-45 war. All participants saw the value of training and, sooner or later, carried it out to the necessary depth. Some, such as the Canadians, were greatly constrained by lack of facilities and the problems of over-expansion. The British were probably the nation who were best trained in terms of depth from junior seamen to escort group commanders, and in breadth by joint training of ships and aircraft. They and the Americans virtually invented operational analysis, using it to great effect to improve the use of existing sensors and weapons, together with suggesting the direction for new systems. This was one of the great areas of advantage which the Allies enjoyed over the Germans, whose effort is summarised as too little, too late, too unco-ordinated.

ENVIRONMENTAL MEASUREMENT AND PREDICTION

The extent to which the complex oceanic environment can affect ASW has been discussed earlier. The ocean is both intricate and dynamic; even if its mechanisms are understood as fully as is possible, there is still a need to measure key variables in real time, so as to be able to use the derived picture fully. This can indicate present conditions as well as showing likely near-term future trends with important consequences for operational planning.

The influence of weather and the ability to forecast its changes are well known and will not be repeated here. It is sufficient to say that ASW forces cannot only reap the benefits of meteorological products designed for other uses, but can contribute to them as well, often being geographically well placed to make and transmit observations.

Reaching down from the water surface, it is possible to measure sound velocity, which has a key effect on sound propagation, either directly or through the intermediary of depth-temperature profiles. This can be done either by means of expendable probes linked by thin wire to ship launchers or by buoys. The former are relatively cheap, sink at a known rate and transmit temperatures back to a recorder on their launching ship.

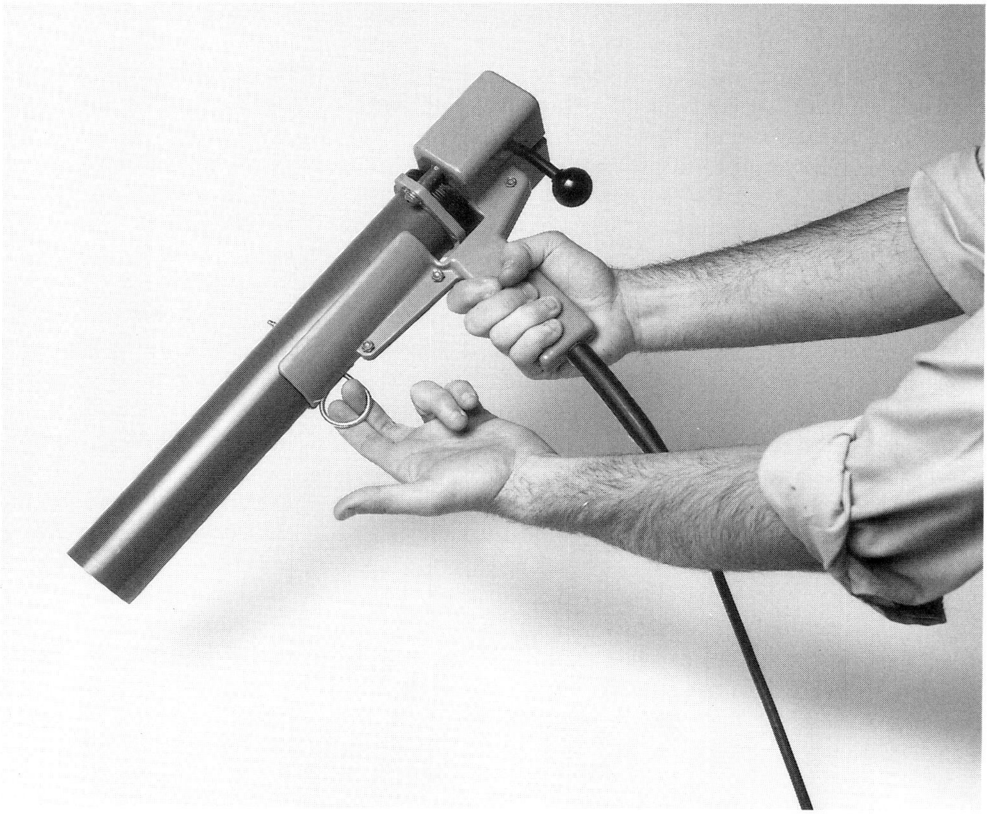

PLATE 8.1 Expendable bathythermograph launcher *(Photo: Sippican)*

The latter, incorporating radio components, are more expensive but necessary for operations from aircraft. A more complex probe or buoy will measure actual sound speed, or allow its computation from direct measurement of temperature and salinity, which may be of more use in complex water structures, especially where the latter is highly variable. All these equipments are manufactured by companies such as Sparton of Canada, and Sippican in the USA. It is not unknown for submarines to use such equipments, with the additional complication that they may have to go up as well as down. Thus it is more normal to use a hull-mounted velocimeter and move the submarine itself in depth. This has the disadvantage of being time consuming as well as possibly putting the submarine itself in undesirable water, either because it lends the ASW submarine's opponent a counterdetection opportunity or because it takes up time better spent on other important tasks.

Once such data has been obtained, it is combined with some broader but coarser knowledge obtained from external sources. This may be nothing more than an oceanographic atlas giving very general data, but is likely to be a more sophisticated product, supplied by the ASW unit's shore command authority. Such information is likely to draw on a wealth of historic data obtained over many years of observations and specific surveys. Further, it may make use of high-speed computing facilities, drawing on a number of advanced oceanographic forecasting models, not directly accessible to the forecaster at sea.

The ability to draw on such products, together with instantaneous observations at sea, allows the production of predictions which are as accurate as possible.

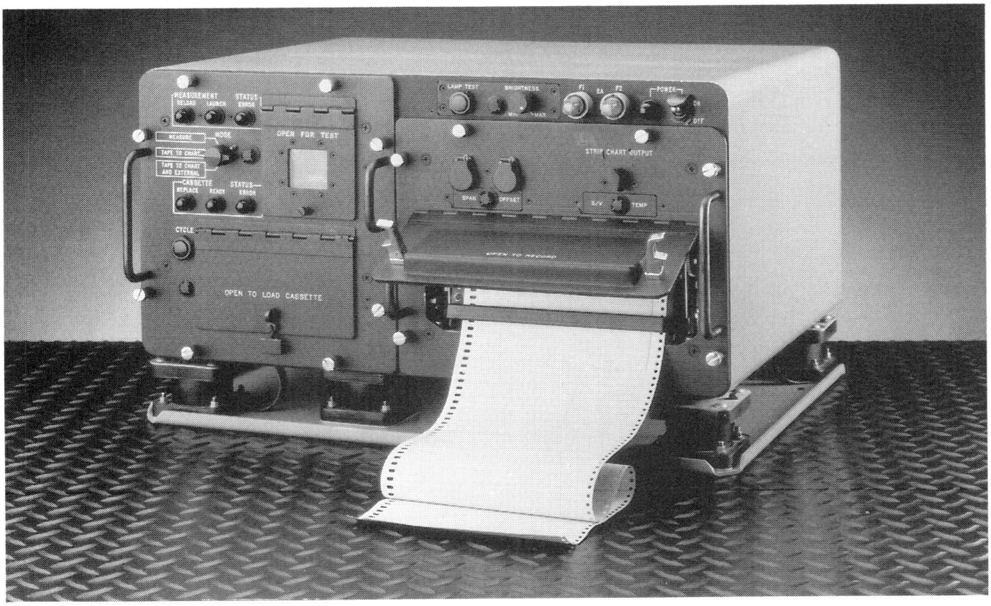

PLATE 8.2 Expendable bathythermograph recorder *(Photo: Sippican)*

These may well be presented with respect to a particular target, details of which will be known from intelligence, either historic or current. The predictions are likely to be expressed as probable ranges against likely targets. Such processes, either derived by calculation or using computer systems such as the British SEPADS developed by Dowty-Sema, can then be used in the design of search plans, to ensure an optimal chance of detecting a likely target using particular sensors.

Further uses of prediction systems are by taking data from the ASW platform itself to work out such essential information as the range at which a target submarine might counterdetect the ASW unit. A great number of separate predictions may be needed to deal with different sensor/target depth configurations, varying speed cases and the use of active or passive sonar.

Further, variables will need to be considered such as bottom depth and type. It is a commonplace of soldiers when talking of war at sea that sailors do not have to deal with terrain. This is literally true, but it may be useful to meditate on the fact that the sailor does have 'terrain' to deal with, and that it is largely invisible. The ocean environment is incompletely understood and difficult to measure completely or accurately, but if all other factors cancel out, then success in the submarine versus ASW struggle is likely to go to the side with the best understanding of the environment.

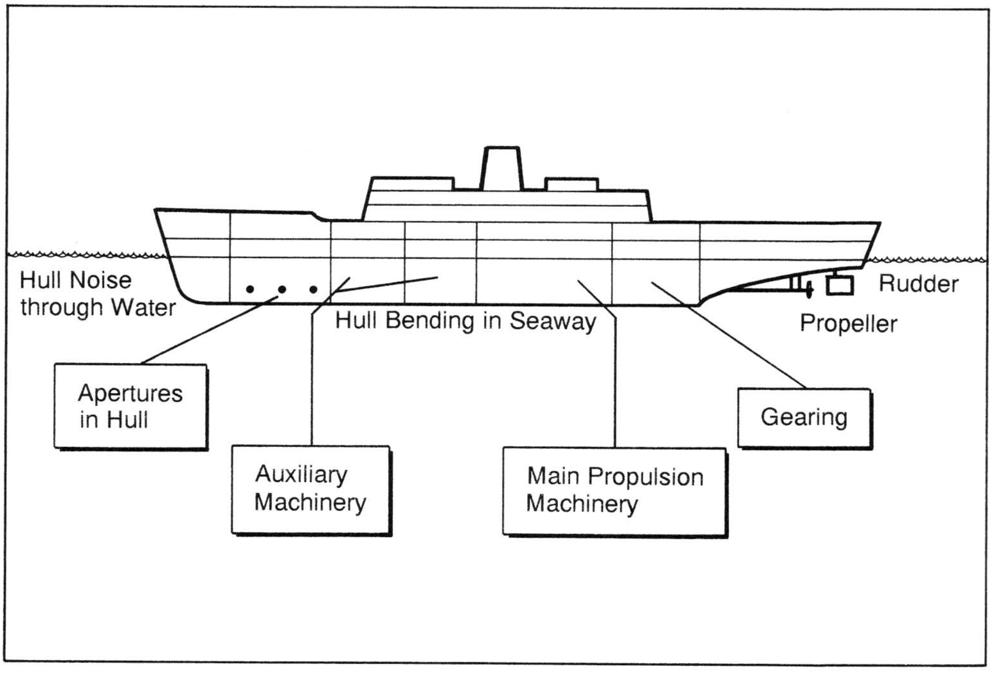

FIG. 8.1 Ship noise sources

SIGNATURE MEASUREMENT AND CONTROL

In the 1980s, the word 'stealth' became a defence buzzword. It has been largely used in the context of a number of aircraft projects, mostly American, but its application rapidly moved to any system where the techniques of any form of signature reduction were employed. Thus stealth covered radar, magnetic and infra-red emissions. None of these are irrelevant to ASW, but the most important aspect of this subject is acoustic signature control. Before departing from stealth, however, it is worth re-noting that the submarine is the original and still probably the best stealth vehicle.

A low and controlled acoustic signature is of help to all ASW vehicles, but especially benefits the two moving in the water, surface ships and submarines. Its advantages are:

- Improved performance of underwater sensors.
- Lessened susceptibility to counterdetection.
- Smaller chance of successful attack by acoustic homing weapons.

There is a large range of techniques built up over decades by the nations which are in what might be called the ASW premier league. Broadly speaking, there are two primary types of noise in signature control. These are self noise, which might affect the ASW vehicle's own sensors and weapons, and radiated noise which has more impact on counterdetection and opposing acoustically based weapons.

Sources of Noise Both types of noise emanate from different sources on board the relevant ship. In this section, ship is taken to mean both surface ship or submarine, unless one of these vessels is specifically mentioned.

The first source is the hull itself. Obviously, a major consideration in its design if it is an ASW ship is low noise production and transmission. It is entirely possible, indeed quite easy, to construct a very quiet hull – but it may not be of much use for its intended purpose. This is because the 'perfect quiet hull' is likely to be compromised by other important requirements. A Royal Naval joke of the early 1980s when towed arrays were being introduced was to illustrate the ideal towing vessel – a sailing ship.

Virtually all surface ASW ships are required to have top speeds in the range of the high twenties of knots, or even faster. They also need to be both seaworthy and stable. These three constraints alone will compromise the ideal low noise hull. A further practical problem arises with hull openings. The apertures are necessary for the purposes of supplying seawater for cooling main and auxiliary machinery, electronics and domestic systems, either directly or indirectly. A hull packed with powerful machinery, heat-producing electrical systems and human beings generates significant fluid flows. It is possible to streamline and fair these inlets and outlets, but this has to be done carefully and with regard to the whole hull layout.

Before leaving the hull itself, it is important to note too that a hull 100m or more in length cannot be considered merely as a simple girder. It is strong, but it will also have to bend when subject to stress. This is particularly so in the case of a surface ship operating at the wild interface of sea and air. Such bending and working is itself likely to be a source of noise. In fairness, this may be the type of noise which is likely to be the most difficult to detect and classify, being not only low frequency, possibly not discrete, but also hard to classify.

The next major source to consider is the propulsion machinery of the ship. This has three major sub-sources: main machinery, gearing and the propulsor system. Main machinery comes in several forms, each with different noise characteristics. One thing is clear: with the exception of specialist classes of ship, naval machinery is distinct from merchant propulsion. There are a number of reasons for this but they can be briefly summed up thus: naval requirement is generally for very high performance and flexibility with space at a premium, whilst the merchant case stresses utmost economy without space being such a major constraint.

Naval vessels tend to use:

- Diesels with either electric or direct final drive.
- Steam turbines with geared final drive, stoked by fossil fuel boilers or nuclear reactors.
- Gas turbines with geared final drive (surface ships only).
- Electric drive from batteries (submarines only).

Diesel direct drive by itself is virtually never used in modern major warships. It is vulnerable to damage and noisy; perhaps more importantly it is unlikely to deliver sufficient power to meet the speed requirements of a warship. There is, however, some utility in diesel-electric propulsion for both submarines and to some extent, surface ships. Diesel-electric has been the preferred option for non-nuclear submarines almost from the outset of that ship type. Petrol and to a lesser extent steam had some currency in early days and air independent propulsion (AIP) systems may have some future application, but arguably these are merely an extension of the same principle. The train of diesel engine–generator–motor is efficient, reasonably compact and controllable. From the submarine viewpoint, it also ideally adaptable for air-free underwater propulsion with batteries substituting for the diesel driven generator. It also works well for schnorkelling. With the diesels running, despite the percussive potential of a repeating internal combustion system, it is fairly quiet provided that adequate noise precautions are taken and the engines are not yoked to the hull structure by the curse of direct drive – the ideal mechanism for transmitting propulsive percussion to the sea. In surface ships, diesel-electric drive is less common, but it is to be found in the Royal Navy's Type 23 frigates, where diesel-electric drive is used for slow, quiet ASW search. In these gas turbines are used for speed.

The use of steam turbine propulsion for warships extends back nearly a century leading from *Turbinia* to *Dreadnought* and beyond. It gave relatively high power with finely engineered but relatively simple and compact machinery. Having dominated surface fleets for many decades, it is now being supplanted by gas

PLATE 8.3 Type 23 frigate – using diesel-electric propulsion for lower noise
(Photo: L & L van Ginderen)

turbines. In the 1950s it gained a new lease of life becoming the medium of transmission of thermal energy from a nuclear reactor. Steam turbines are universally used in nuclear plants. The nuclear reactor itself involves multiple heat exchange loops, often with considerable fluid flows; such movements together with the associated powerful pumps (often multiplied for safety reasons) add considerably to the potential noise bill of a nuclear plant.

There are rare examples in the Russian Navy of hybrid machinery plants using both nuclear and fossil fuel stoked turbine systems in the *Kirov* class battle cruisers.

Steam turbine systems can be relatively quiet, although not as much as electric drive because the turbine and gearbox are all mechanically linked to the propulsor, providing a longish chain of machinery, with abundant opportunities for noise generation and transmission. Final electric drive, which obviates many of these disadvantages is used in the Russian *Alfa* class submarine, as well as in the nuclear submarines of France and China.

Gas turbines are a relatively recent addition to propulsive history, but they have made great inroads in the field of frigate- and destroyer-sized warships. The reason for their adoption has little to do with noise reduction, but they offer significant advantages in fuel economy, flexibility and relatively small manpower bills. Early versions used Controllable Pitch Propellers (CPP) to make use of the relatively narrow useful speed range of the gas turbine, not always to the advantage of noise reduction. However, some recent ships have since abandoned this feature.

PLATE 8.4 *Kirov* class cruiser – a rare nuclear/fossil fuel hybrid ship
(Photo: Conway Maritime Press)

Electric battery drive is the quietest of all propulsion methods. It is flexible, needs virtually no auxiliaries but cannot practically deliver the high power outputs demanded of surface warships and realise the power potential of nuclear systems. Its natural home is as the completely submerged propulsion system of the diesel-electric submarine. The inherent quietness of such systems accounts for the impotence of passive systems in dealing with such submarines.

The general nature of noise from propulsion machinery is related to its rotary nature, and the frequency of such noise is a function of its speed. Thus a shaft moving at 60 rpm generates a 1 Hz frequency. A five-bladed propellor attached to the same shaft would produce a noise at five times this frequency, that is 5 Hz. Whether such a noise is detectable is a function of its being significantly loud, its finding an acoustic path to the sea and ultimately its transmission in the sea (see Chapter 5). Prevention of the first two of these are functions of design and engineering observation. The techniques of noise reduction, however, often involve expensive, space-consuming techniques such as rafting in which the machinery is mounted on complex resilient mountings in addition to those necessary for shock insulation.

Moving to propulsors, one basic system is employed, the screw propeller. This has been in use since the mid-19th century in a form remarkably similar to that used today. Indeed one of the ironies of time is to stroll through the ship galleries of the Science Museum in London and look at the many propeller models on show. In the 19th century, the aim was to ensure maximum propulsive efficiency and many empirical designs were tried. What is surprising is that some of these have a distinct resemblance to late 20th century noise reduction designs. What goes around, comes around.

It is not easy to design a propulsive system which is quiet and efficient, especially within the constraints of warship design. The general hull form will limit size; the amount of power to be dealt with at speed is high and many solutions to these problems are noisy. This has tended to lead in the direction of a complex propeller which has multiple skewed blades.

One of the principal sources of noise, especially in surface ships, is cavitation. Operating in near-surface water which contains a lot of air, it is easy for unstable air bubbles to form around propellors, particularly as speed is increased. Their subsequent collapse is very noisy. One way of overcoming, or at least delaying, this problem is to provide compressed air at the blades to improve bubble stability. This not only quietens the system, but also increases the service life of the blade. The cost here is that of extra machinery: obviously the solution is not available to submerged submarines. Similar techniques may also be used on surface ships' hulls. At high speeds, propulsor silence is not practically attainable, but good noise reduction measures can increase the size of the quiet operating envelope. One recent innovation is the pump jet, a system of rotors and stators, simply described as a turbine in reverse. This has produced significant decreases in noise, but has adverse manoeuvring characteristics.

Other machinery also transmits significant amounts of noise into the sea. Some of this may be only transient, such as reloading mechanisms of weapons systems, but in other cases it may arise more frequently. An example of this would be electrical generating machinery. Only the fully-submerged diesel-electric submarine does not have a significant requirement for generating electricity. In most steam systems turbo-generators are used, with diesel machines generally being used in others. As the need for electricity is quite large, so too are the machines. They can produce noise capable of being detected by a passive sonar system. Just as with main machinery it is possible to counter this problem, but again often at the cost of complication, space and money.

Nor does the problem stop there. Any motor or other piece of machinery, fluid system and even human activity can produce significant noise. There is also a diminishing return law in force where noise reduction is concerned. Deal with the major sources and the medium-intensity ones become important: rectify these and reveal others. Overall noise characteristics will diminish, but the totally silent platform appears to be wishful thinking.

As overall noise levels reduce too, the demands of reducing self noise – what the ship's own sensors hear – may conflict with those of radiated noise. An example of this would be sonar hull outfits, projecting below the normal bottom of the ship. These may provide a good way of putting the sonar in a relatively quiet place to do its work, but at the expense of making the hydrodynamic flow over the whole hull noisier, even after considerable attention has been paid to fairing.

COUNTERMEASURES TO UNDERWATER WEAPONS

Earlier in this book, the point was made that ASW is involved in denying an enemy the effective use of his submarines. Ideally, this should be achieved without putting the ASW platform itself at risk, but submarines and especially surface ships, whether engaged on ASW operations or other activities are susceptible to attack by submarine. Aircraft are less at risk from submarines.

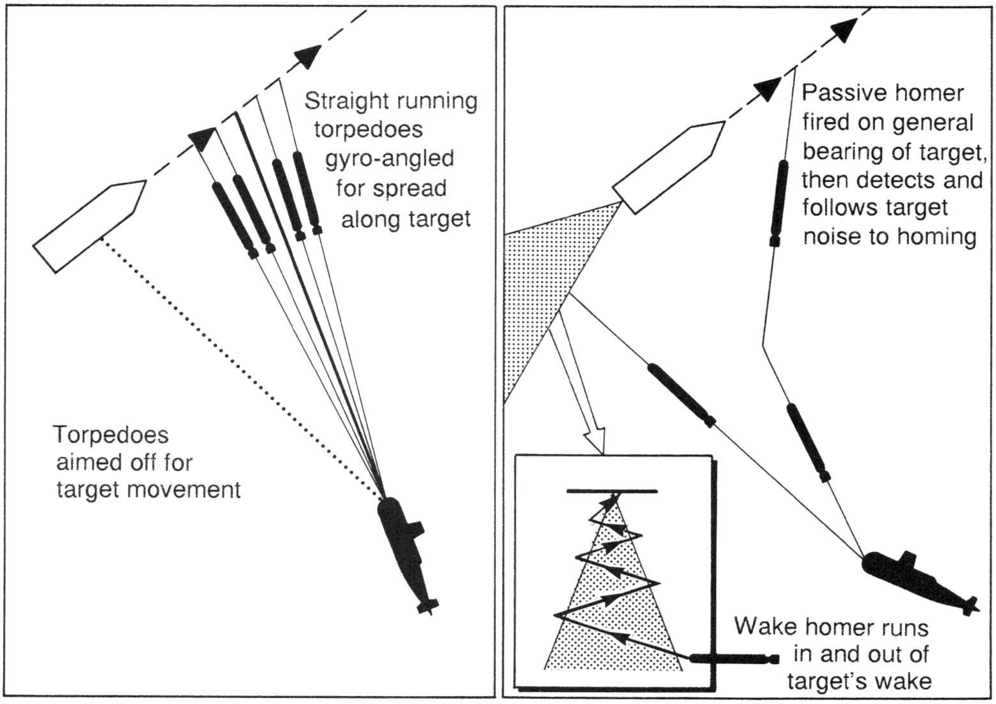

FIG. 8.2 Straight running and homing torpedoes.

The danger may come about inadvertently because the ASW unit is disadvantaged – say by having to use speed – and an aggressor submarine is well placed to attack. Alternatively, ASW attack other than with long-range stand-off weapons is risky for the ASW unit. It is not intended to discuss those submarine-launched weapons such as SM 39 *Exocet* whose terminal homing phase is conducted above water. This is a matter for another volume of this series. The use of such weapons, however, indicates both the breadth of submarine warfare and the blurring of categories.

The underwater weapons of which an ASW unit has to take account are therefore torpedoes utilising various forms of guidance. These can be categorised as straight-running and homing. The latter break down further into the acoustic homing variety (active or passive) and wake homing.

The straight running torpedo has a long pedigree. The earliest challenges of torpedo engineers were to make it run straight at the right depth. Once this obstacle was overcome, several variations were introduced. Perhaps the most important grew out of the use of gyroscopes in torpedoes as a device for ensuring straight running. It then became possible to make the torpedo run at an angle to its original launch heading. Although this introduced a slight degree of unpredictability into torpedo aiming, it had the tactical advantage of allowing a firing submarine to maintain a minimum profile for sonar detection – pointing directly towards its target – whilst being able to aim with a lead angle to hit. The technique also allows salvo spread to take account of aiming errors.

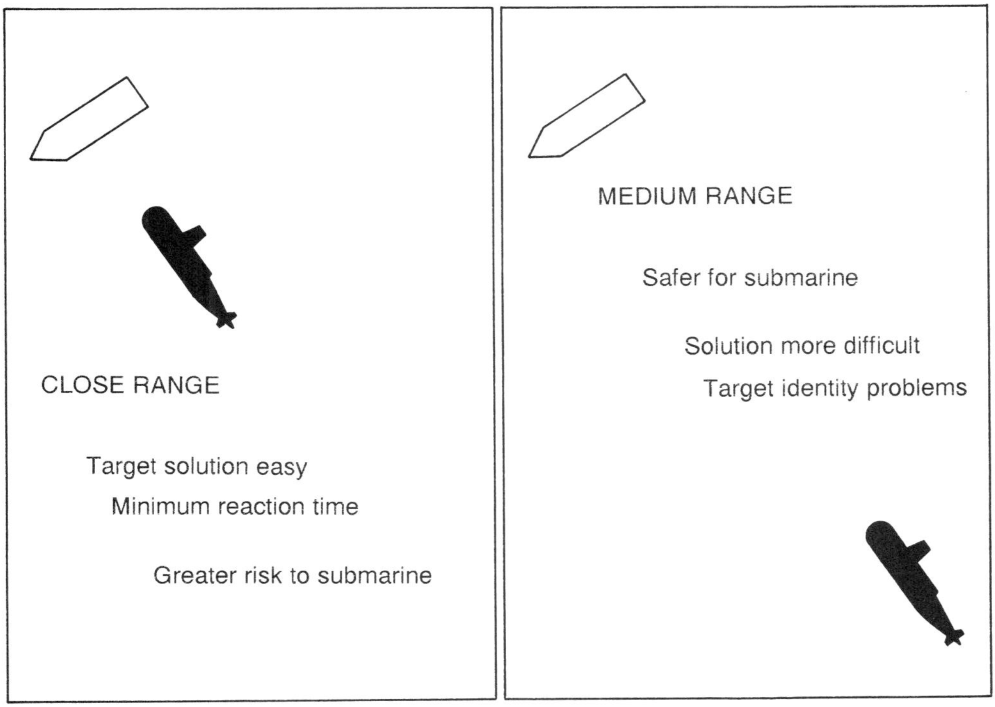

FIG. 8.3 Close versus medium range torpedo attack

It is now necessary to digress into torpedo firing tactics to consider countermeasures. There are two fundamental approaches to firing straight running weapons. The first, most daring and difficult involves closure to relatively close range to the target before firing. The advantages of this are that it usually possible to resolve problems of target selection and movement to best advantage. Further, the target is given the least possible time in which to react to the torpedo salvo, and thus the best guarantee of success in what may be the first and only attack allowed. Such an attack by the British submarine *Conqueror* sank the Argentine cruiser, *General Belgrano* at a range of 1,800 yards in 1982. There is a fairly important disadvantage in that proximity to the target will often imply a greatly increased risk of counterdetection. For example, it may be necessary to penetrate a screen of escorts around a high-value unit.

The second approach involves firing from greater range, often of the order of several times that used in the close attack. This obviates the difficulty about screen penetration of the close attack. However, with modern escort sonar operating in good conditions, this may put torpedo attack out of practical range. Assuming this not to be so, the residual difficulties are often those of determining target track, range and – at such distances – even identity. One way to compensate for the longer torpedo running time implied in such an attack and the resultant risk of target manoeuvre is to space the torpedoes to run further apart than in the close attack. In order to ensure that this does not vary with range (complicating aiming even further) double gyro angling may be adopted. The first angle lets the torpedoes fan out until the desired inter-track spacing is achieved and the second angle brings the torpedoes back onto parallel courses. From the submarine's point of view, a disadvantage is that only one hit may be obtained.

The problems of fire control and, above all, of depth determination mean that the surface ASW unit is the only one likely to be subjected to straight running attack. No matter how aimed, and from what distance fired, the problem for such a unit is knowing that such a weapon is about to be fired, or has been discharged. Particularly in the longer range attack, such knowledge is unlikely to be freely available. It is therefore important to make the task of the submarine as difficult as possible, at least complicating and hopefully frustrating his attacking intent. This is accomplished by means of tactical countermeasures in the form of evasive steering or zig-zag. In order not to lose too much of speed made good, a precautionary zig-zag, that is one made without having some good indication of a submarine in the immediate vicinity, would probably not deviate very much from a base course, and have relatively long legs, of several minutes' duration. The aim here is not so much to avoid a torpedo, which cannot be achieved by such means, but rather to deny a submarine good enough data for a firing solution. Such zig-zags can be used by all types of ship and when synchronised form the basis of evasive steering for whole groups of warships or merchant ships in convoy.

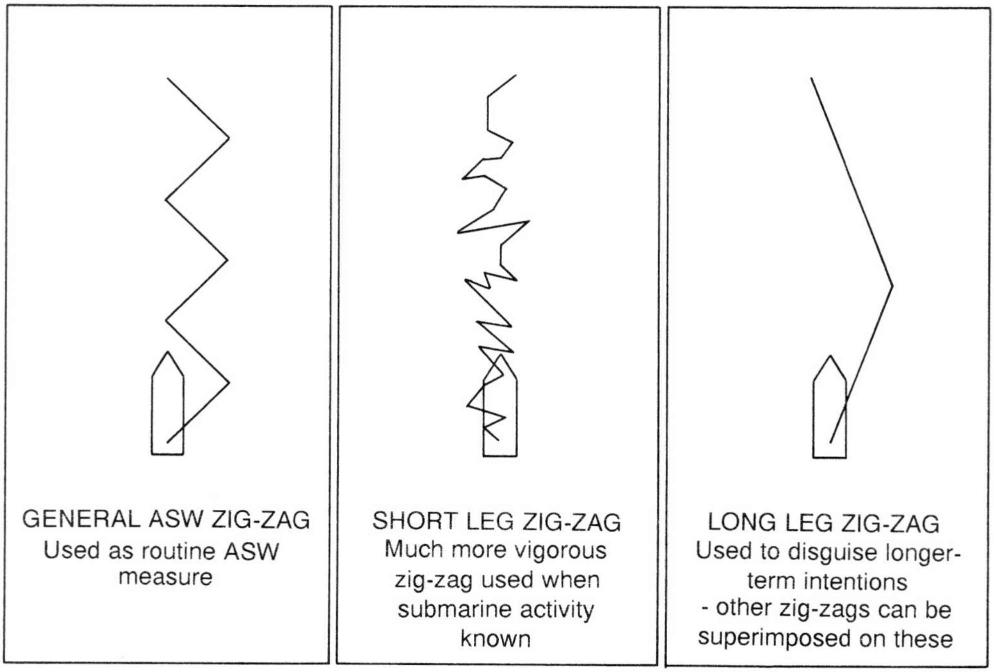

FIG. 8.4 Types of zig zag

When more definite information of a submarine's whereabouts is known, such as approaching its last known position, then a more vigorous pattern is likely to be used, with radical, more frequent alterations of course. If a torpedo is detected closing the ASW ship, then more radical action is required. Against the straight running weapon, the only countermeasure worth employing is combing the tracks. In this the aim is make the weapon or weapons pass harmlessly down the side of the ship by paralleling its track or the reciprocal. In order to execute this manoeuvre successfully good information is needed together with the correct and rapid reaction from the ship.

The problems of submarine fire control mentioned earlier led to the innovation of the homing torpedo, effective against both surface ship and submarine. Passive homing weapons are normally used against surface ships and these pose a difficult threat, which is not easy to counter. The normal approach has been to deploy towed noisemakers which hopefully will seduce the weapon away from its target. Mechanical variants of this device have been around since shortly after the first acoustic torpedoes entered service. More usually, an electrically driven system such as the Graseby G738 is used. There are two tactical aspects. Firstly, although capable of performing without warning it can be helpful to know the direction of approach of the torpedo. This can ensure that the torpedo hears the decoy rather than the towing ship.

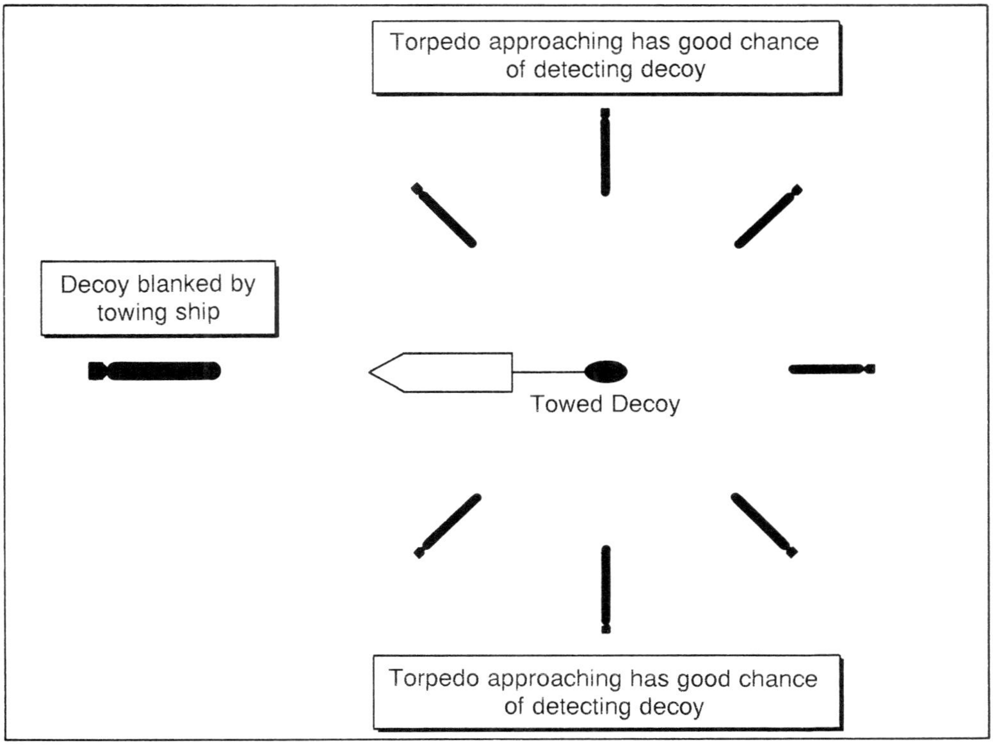

FIG. 8.5 Torpedo decoys and knowledge of approach angle

Secondly, if the decoy does its job properly, it will be lost to the torpedo and it will be necessary to stream a replacement before a torpedo re-attack happens. It is possible that such a decoy may have paid the ultimate price and done its job properly in 1982, saving a British frigate from an Argentine torpedo.

This approach is unlikely to work for an ASW submarine, which may already may be deploying several towed devices, such as passive sonar arrays and radio aerials. The concept of being able to deploy, far less replace, a substantial towed body is problematical. Instead, a system of ejected disposable decoys is used. Historically, these derive from the German *Pillenwerfer*, which was merely a chemical bubble generator. Although static, this was often effective in producing an alternative sonar target. The sophistication of modern homing weapons demands a much more complex solution such as is to be found in the American ADC Mks 3 and 4, British *Bandfish* and Israeli *Scutter* systems. Some of these will actually take account of the transmissions made by an active homing weapon and provide it with what it expects to hear. There may also be a form of propulsor attached to the decoy to feed the weapon 'target movement', usually away from the firing submarine. The exact characteristics and effectiveness of such systems are closely guarded.

These decoys are unlikely to be effective against such techniques as wake-homing torpedoes. Here, a more radical look is being taken at the whole field of torpedo defence in the Surface Ship Torpedo Defence (SSTD) programme being examined in both the USA and UK. Such work, as far as is known, has not yet resulted in the operational deployment of any equipment. It is thought

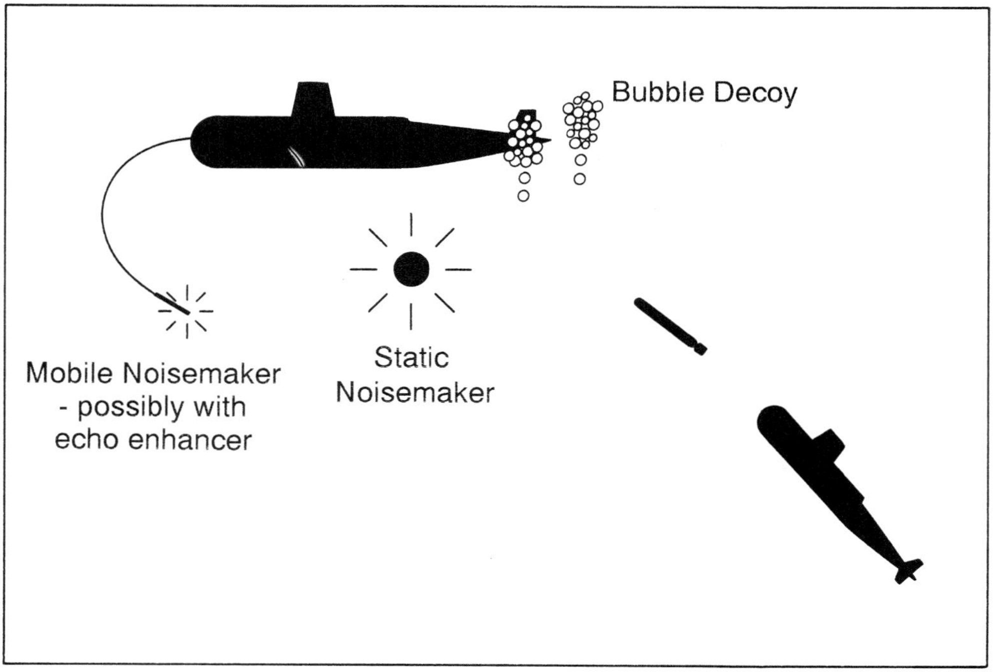

FIG. 8.6 Submarine torpedo decoys

that both hard- and soft-kill methods are being considered. Developments of existing decoys can be looked on as soft-kill, whilst anti-torpedo torpedoes or mortar-fired charges might be used for hard-kill options. One useful analogy might be that of an underwater SDI. The demise of the USSR and the subsequent perception of the Soviet underwater threat fading away may play a crucial part in the fate of such programmes as SSTD.

TRAINING

A nation engaged in ASW may field the best aircraft and ships in the world, and they could be equipped with the finest sonar and weapons that money can buy; but unless this is used with sound tactical doctrines and underlaid with thorough training, the investment will be wasted. Tactical aspects will be considered in the next chapter. Basic principles of operating equipment can be achieved at early stages of personnel training. However, the effectiveness of any ASW unit is unlikely to depend entirely on individual skills, but rather on the efforts of teams within the unit itself, and ultimately of the unit as a whole. Beyond that, the ASW unit itself is likely to form part of a group and that formation itself has an effect proportional to its competence. There should thus be a pyramidical aspect to training, as it is not rational to go ahead with the higher level of training without having at least basic competence at the lower level.

Technology has a part to play at all these levels, providing ready simulation of many situations and problems which would be difficult, costly and sometimes even impossible to replicate at sea. Perhaps more importantly, the passing of all new operators through a common system with uniform standards of teaching and supervision ensures a consistent product, whose standards are known and recognised in the units which the training organisation serves. Many such training equipments operate in the western navies and air forces, although the systems operated in the former Soviet Union (FSU) are less well known. There is also a requirement in operational units for the continuation training of crews and again it is now possible to provide a high degree of on-board simulation. Usually, this makes use of operational equipment.

Operators of sensors and weapon systems form only one part of the unit. It is also necessary to train the command team and this too can be carried out both ashore under supervision and independently on board. The blending together of groups can also happen both at sea and ashore, but perhaps is subjected to its most strenuous test at sea, both in exercise and operations. Without the test of hot war, it is difficult to say how good any equipment, tactical doctrine or training actually is. It can be suggested, however, that the nation which invests nothing or little in training is unlikely to do well when subjected to any worthwhile trial.

OPERATIONAL ANALYSIS

Operational Analysis (OA) is one of the hidden supporters of ASW, and indeed of most aspects of modern warfare. The origins of the modern discipline lie in the Second World War, where Britain and America had the foresight to introduce and exploit such methods to maximise the effectiveness of the sensors and weapons they had, as well as producing pointers to the future. Perhaps the best illustrative example comes from those days: the question of the best depth setting for air-launched depth charges. Here many attacks had been made, and only a very few had been successful before scientists were turned loose on the problem without any preconceptions. What they discovered was that only those attacks made on a surfaced, or only recently submerged, submarine stood any chance of placing charges near the target. But the existing depth setting was based on a point mid-way between the surface and the known maximum operating depth of German submarines. This was, of course, much deeper than the submarines in the 'successful attack' category just defined would be. The settings were modified to a shallower depth to take account of this and greater success ensued, almost immediately.

Today, the techniques of OA are applied in a number of ways including:

- Studies to select the most effective and economical system.
- Aiding the precise definition of selected systems.
- Extracting important points from exercises.
- The post-event determination of operations.

It is difficult to point to any hardware that is used exclusively for OA, but several decades of computer use have led to much software which has been applied in the form of either small- or large-scale modelling. The extremes might be suggested by considering torpedo terminal homing at one end of the scale and complete campaign run-throughs at the other. Contemporary models allow the analytical luxury of replicating many runs, varying many details in order to extract useful conclusions.

There is, of course, the potential snag of ensuring that the model is an adequate representation of reality and that seemingly minor (but often important) details receive sufficient prominence. Here, as in all forms of OA, there is a need to combine the rigorous analysis of the scientist with the experience, military judgement and gut feeling of the practitioner.

With the two applications above, exercises and operations, there is probably more scope for the latter naval skill than strict science, although there is clearly a place for both. Here the aim is to discover what happened as opposed to what people thought happened at the time so that useful objective lessons can be drawn. This one of the more obscure, although arguably most worthwhile, supporting activities in ASW.

UNDERWATER COMMUNICATIONS

If ASW involves the efforts of ASW submarines, then there is likely to be a requirement to communicate with them for tactical purposes. It has been suggested that the submarine is the best of all single platforms for ASW. Its combination of good sensors, heavyweight weapons and covertness is excellent, but there is the disadvantage of communications. Here it is not intended to deal

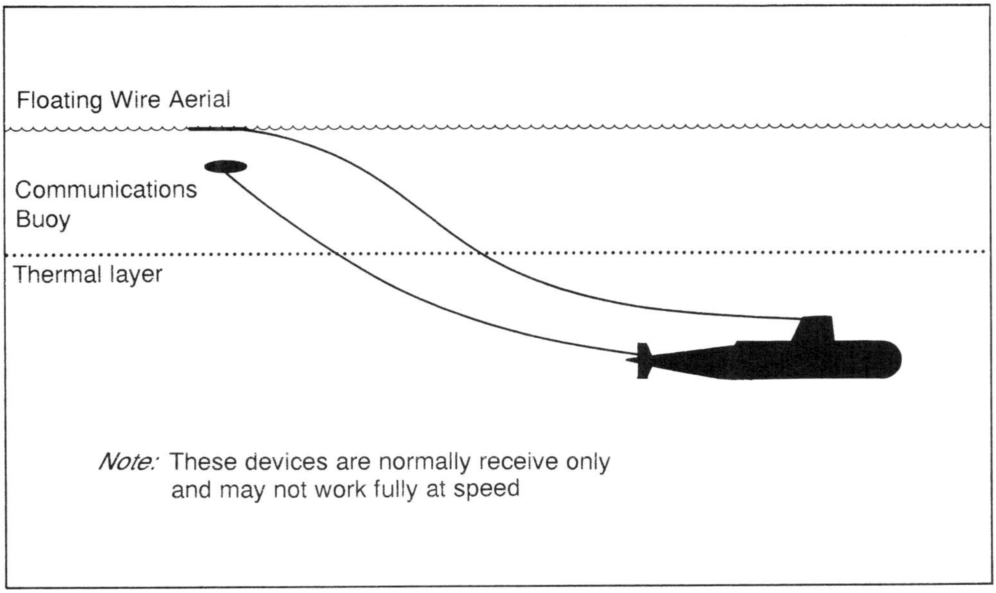

FIG. 8.7 Submarine communication buoys and wires

with long-haul communications, submarine-to-shore and shore-to-submarine. It should be noted, however, that such means may provide the only practicable bearers for 'tactical communication'.

For preference, there should be other means available. These divide broadly into those using the radio spectrum, and the use of underwater acoustic frequencies. Dealing with radio first, the problem is that a submerged submarine has only a limited ability to receive RF without putting up an aerial of some sort. Certainly towed wires and buoys improve both reception and tactical freedom, but such devices operate best at frequencies which are difficult to radiate practically from surface ships and most aircraft.

The only alternative would appear to be piercing the surface with a mast-mounted antenna. This is probably most suitable for use with aircraft, because of the limited RF horizon of a relatively low mast. Here again, the cost is that of tactical freedom, with the submarine constrained in both depth and speed.

One option is that of using buoys. Different types can operate in either direction. For example, the Sippican BRC-6 expendable transceiver allows two-way UHF voice communication for the life of a 45 minute battery, or until the submarine moves beyond the limit of the 3,000 m wire connecting it to the buoy. Alternatively a one-way device such as Sparton's AN/SSQ-86(XN-1) allows an aircraft (or surface ship) to be linked by RF to a buoy, which then translates the signal into acoustic form for transmission to a submarine.

A device like this introduces the acoustic method, which has been in use for some time in underwater telephone systems. These systems can either use voice or radio-type signals and may be either omni-directional or narrow beam. Their range is not very great, perhaps in the low tens of thousands of yards, and the data rate is slow compared to radio, but this may sometimes be a useful form of tactical ASW communication. Examples of equipment are the British Graseby G732 Mk III and the American Model 5400 made by the EDO corporation.

SHALLOW WATER ASW

The ways in which the elements of ASW are brought together to form a system are considered in the next chapter. There is, however, one very specialised form of ASW described here. Shallow water ASW poses particular challenges not encountered elsewhere. This is not the realm of high-speed nuclear submarines, towed array frigates and open-ocean systems. Rather it is the field of slow and small submarines and, possibly, submersibles; difficult water conditions; and actions which may be geographically constrained, as well as sometimes lasting for days. In short, it is a different form of ASW, spawning different solutions and tending to be of greatest interest only to certain nations. Thus, a country such as the USA had virtually no serious interest in shallow-water ASW for the duration of the Cold War, whereas it has always been of prime importance to Sweden.

Firstly, it is necessary to define shallow-water with a little more precision. One useful definition might be the 200 m or 100 fathom line, which takes in such areas as the Baltic Sea as well as a large area of water surrounding the United Kingdom and Ireland. As well as shallowness itself, several areas such as the

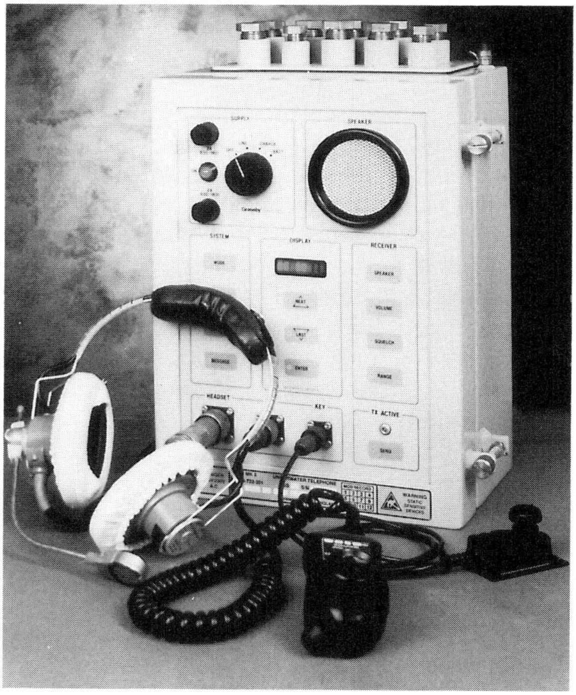

PLATE 8.5 Underwater telephone terminal *(Photo: Graseby)*

Norwegian fjords (some of which are actually quite deep) and the Stockholm Archipelago are also characterised by many ragged islands and islets.

To be fair, this is probably more to the submarine's disadvantage than it is to ASW. However, these areas often abound in rocky bottoms, with added wrecks. Although a hazard to submarine navigation, the greatest importance of these features is in providing a wealth of shelter to submarines and false targets for ASW sonars. It is probable that submarines found in such waters are smaller and slower than those used for ocean warfare. But this is often an advantage as the type of submarines built for coastal use are of several hundred tons displacement only, and by size alone are difficult sonar targets. Further, operating inshore, they are unlikely to use their diesel engines and are thus very quiet.

All these points make shallow water ASW a rather different animal from its deep water cousin, and consequently different solutions to different problems are in evidence. That said, as in all ASW, there has been little hot warfare in recent decades, with the prominent exception of the incursions into Swedish waters, particularly the Soviet *Whiskey* class submarine which grounded in Swedish waters in 1981.

What then are the particular problems and solutions of shallow water ASW? What follows is a very brief run through the material presented earlier making the necessary changes for the shallow water case. Detection can be very difficult for the reasons mentioned above. In addition to fragmented bottoms creating multiple false targets, water types may be very complex, possibly with mixes of salt and fresh water. Conditions can thus be very difficult for sonar. Variable depth sonar may provide some of the solutions to these difficulties, and the general lack of pace in shallow water ASW also suggests the option of deploying dipping sonar (of the helicopter type) from surface ships. Here, too, the limitations of the helicopter (often shore-based) are less salient than in open-ocean ASW. Indeed, its ability to move slowly and stay still may be positive advantageous in comparison with the high speed of the fixed-wing ASW aircraft.

Another of sonar's problems in shallow water is the level of reverberation from not only the water column – which is always present – but also from the bottom. Certain receiver techniques may palliate this situation, but can never totally get rid of the problem. For the same reason, high transmitted power is not usually useful in this situation. Modification, or even fundamental design, of sonar to optimise for such water can be done, but usually at the expense of other characteristics. If the sonar is to operate purely in this environment, then these compromises are acceptable, but the levels of performances, such as ranges, are unlikely to be of the same order as in the open ocean. In the past, some specialist sonars for bottom classification such as the British 162M have been used, but it is probable that their functions are now either no longer considered to justify a separate sonar or that sonars designed specifically for shallow water use have supplanted them.

The relatively poor performance of shallow water sonar also tends to suggest the use of as many vehicles as possible, to compensate for the relatively poor sensor performance. In any case, the physical confines of the area suggest small ships and aircraft. It is not known whether the principal exponents of shallow water ASW employ submarines for the task. Although having many advantages for ASW in general, as pointed out previously, they suffer the same constraints of manoeuvre as their opponents. The lack of headroom or depth under the keel is a particular disadvantage, leading to a very much increased risk of underwater collision, especially in operations short of war.

Nor are all problems of shallow water ASW limited to sensors. The general trend to homing torpedoes has not always translated well to the particular requirements of this environment. A technique commonly used in active homing weapons is that of the 'Doppler gate'. Here, in order to reject all targets which are stopped, including objects on the bottom and the bottom itself, valid returns have to register a speed of at least a small number of knots. This is a very useful device for the open ocean, but is a disadvantage in shallow water. Although true bottom target rejection is useful, the slow progress of a submarine in shallow water may be insufficient to allow the true target to be classified as such by the Doppler gate. The problem is made worse by the effects of tidal stream, often very strong in coastal waters. Here the tidal rip over bottom objects can generate apparent target speed and present what seems to be a perfectly valid submarine to the weapon's guidance system. Thus, shallow water ASW, if not quite the last refuge of the thrown or rocket propelled weapon with an explosive warhead, is certainly a place where apparently primitive weapons have a useful role to play. Further, in peacetime these weapons have the advantage that, if used with either a reduced charge or deliberately fired to explode some distance from the submarine, then they may play a part in attempting to persuade the target to move or even surface.

Shallow water ASW can thus be seen as a distinct category of warfare with challenges and solutions which are not of use in the blue water prosecution of submarines. Obviously, its basic techniques are broadly similar to general ASW; but the variations and scale changes and the probable exclusion of both the ASW submarine and fixed-wing aircraft all suggest a different category of warfare. Whether it will continue to exist is largely a function of potential threat – watch this lack of space.

9

Bringing It All Together: Platforms and Large-Scale Systems

INTRODUCTION

So far, the elements of ASW practice have been discussed under such headings as detection and prosecution. Although there has usually been some larger unit associated with each part of the description, what has not been considered as a whole has been the individual units, or platforms as they are often currently called. By this is meant the ships, aircraft and submarines employed in ASW and their particular characteristics. This chapter will discuss types of ASW unit as well as the combination of their properties and efforts, and illustrate by example different approaches taken to this warfare skill in terms of these platforms. Obviously these will reflect the sensor and weapon system chosen by the owning nation, but other significant factors are also likely to emerge, such as the relative stress laid on ASW by different countries, and the extent to which national style – if there is such a thing – intrudes into choice and design of platform.

It is also important to see how ASW works at levels above that of individual systems and even platforms: ASW is fundamentally a group or team activity. There are examples where the key player is a single unit, perhaps a submarine operating by itself in a patrol area, but even in this apparently simple case it is likely to be supported by other activities and facilities. It is often the case that the operators of such teams do not always consider or name their organisation as an ASW system, but nevertheless that is what it is. Its effectiveness often hinges not just on the quality of individual components, but also on the way in which they fit together. It is possible that several high quality components can be let down by poor linkages in the system. A good historical example of this was in the Battle of the Atlantic, when in the earlier part of the conflict there was little Allied ability to locate, far less do anything about, a German submarine between its leaving base and reaching torpedo range of a convoy. This was rectified largely by means of radar, shipborne high frequency direction finding (HF DF) and cryptography, producing a good ASW system.

PLATFORM CHARACTERISTICS - PLANES AND BOATS AND SHIPS

In this section aircraft, submarines and ships used for ASW are examined and examples described. This gives an idea of the way in which such platform types influence and set limits to the types of ASW which any country or alliance can pursue. There are certain common factors running through such an analysis. The first is size which tends to be related to range or reach. In comparative terms, larger aircraft have greater range than small ones, and the same applies to ships. There is also a connection to seaworthiness, which can be considered too in terms of the ability to operate fully in more extreme conditions. Further, size can permit more and better sensors and weapons, as well as greater stocks of the latter. If C3 is an important consideration, then a smaller platform is likely to be a more awkward choice. For aircraft carriers, size is probably the most important determinant in permitting or denying fixed-wing operations. This in turn allows or forbids the use of more capable ASW aircraft at sea.

The next important factors are speed and endurance: for surface warships, with the possible exception of the very smallest, there is very little significant speed difference; for submarines, there is a significant variation in speed largely dependent on propulsion type, multiplied further by the current ability of the nuclear submarine to sustain its higher speed over days, rather than hours. This tends to affect speed of deployment most of all. With aircraft, there tends to be a step change between the relatively slow, short endurance helicopter and the faster, longer-legged fixed-wing aircraft. In the latter case, however, this may be offset by shore basing placing the aircraft's home hundreds of miles from the action.

Aircraft The first classification to note here is that suggested above of helicopters and fixed-wing aircraft. The latter tend to be more aerodynamically efficient, thus faster and with longer endurance; but against this must be balanced two important points. Firstly, the ability of the helicopter to hover motionless with respect to the sea surface allows it to deploy larger and more powerful sonars than can the fixed-wing aircraft which can have no physical link with its sonar. This is an advantage for the helicopter and a limitation of the MPA which has implications not so much for data transfer (easily accomplished using modern techniques) as physical size and, in the case of active sonar systems, power transmission.

The other important facet of the helicopter is that it can be operated from ships of only a few thousand tons, such as frigates. There are many of these ships worldwide. Few are now designed without the ability at least to land helicopters: a great number also have support facilities, of which the most necessary and basic is a hangar to provide weather protection, and thus allow sustained operations. This significant innovation has allowed the relatively ready expansion of ASW into the midfield, from the few thousand yards around an ASW vessel to perhaps the 20-30 mile range, or even beyond.

PLATE 9.1 *Sea King* helicopter *(Photo: L & L van Ginderen)*

Some nations have taken this yet further by the use of sensor systems deployed from the helicopter, which can cover significant areas. These can be used either independently of the parent ship or perhaps in reaction to a cue such as a towed array sonar contact. On the other hand, a small helicopter may only have the lifting capacity and endurance to allow it to carry and drop a torpedo in a place directed by its parent or another ship holding submarine contact. Some indication of the equipment, capabilities and types of helicopters is given in the Table below.

There are other less obvious aspects of capability. The first concerns operating constraints – to what extent is the helicopter capable of operation from its home platform in all weathers, day and night. The Canadians were to some extent the leaders in this field, having demonstrated the ability to operate one of the largest maritime helicopters, the *Sea King*, from frigates of only a few thousand tons for several decades.

There, special flight deck equipment was designed to permit such operations in high sea states. But there is more to this than the admittedly difficult task of landing and take off in hazardous conditions. There is little point in having a dipping active sonar if the helicopter is incapable of hovering safely, both by day and at night. And neither of these theoretically attainable activities – flight operations around the clock and 'dipping' in all weathers – are of much practical use unless they are regularly practised by aircrews.

The fixed-wing aircraft is often more tolerant of such conditions. It is likely to be operated either from larger seagoing platforms – aircraft carriers – or from shore. Currently, the seagoing fixed-wing aircraft is one of two classes, ancient and modern. Ancient is the propeller-driven S-2 *Tracker*, now only found in

HELICOPTER TYPES

Characteristic/Type	*Basic*	*More Advanced*	*Medium Helicopters*
Role(s)	Radar/Visual search Torpedo carriers	ASW local/coastal search Localisation Weapon carriers	Long range search Autonomous/ semi-auto search Localisation Weapon carriers
Equipment	General duties radar Torpedoes Depth bombs	Dipping sonar or sonobuoys Specialised radar ESM MAD FLIR Torpedoes Depth Bombs	Dipping sonar and sonobuoys Specialised radar ESM MAD FLIR Torpedoes Depth Bombs Mines
Examples	Aerospatiale *Alouette* III Aerospatiale *Dauphin* A365F MBB Bo 105	Kaman SH-2 *Seasprite* (LAMPS I) Kamov KA-27/29 *Helix* Sikorsky SH-60 *Seahawk* (LAMPS III) Westland *Lynx*	Westland/Sikorsky *Sea King* Boeing/Kawasaki 107 Westland/Augusta EH101
Owners	Argentina Belgium Chile Colombia – and others	Netherlands Russia UK USA – and others	Italy Japan Russia Sweden UK USA – and others

South American navies which operate obsolete aircraft-carriers. These ships' demise is likely to mean the end of the seagoing *Tracker*. The French operate the even smaller *Alizè*, which will probably suffer a similar fate

The service life expectancy for the American jet-engined S-3A/B *Viking* is somewhat greater. This is a very capable ASW aircraft deployed in all USN carrier air groups. It can carry a sensor and weapon load little short of the much larger land-based P-3 *Orion*. But the *Viking* is likely soon to be the only example of its type. Although aircraft carriers are becoming more widespread, the VSTOL type is preferred by such nations as India, Spain and Thailand, where aircraft such as the *Harrier* are complemented by helicopters for ASW, amongst other uses. Thus there appears to be no more place for the fixed-wing ASW aircraft at sea. Even the tortuously realised Russian carrier capability has taken this route: despite operating conventional fixed-wing combat aircraft, it will only deploy helicopters for ASW. For the sake of completeness it should also be noted that a few countries – mainly Russia – still operate flying boats for ASW. Fixed-wing aircraft types are indicated in the table below.

ASW Ships ASW ships come in a vast variety of sizes and types. It is rare now, however, to find a ship whose sole purpose is ASW, just as it is almost as rare to find a mainstream warship which has no ASW capability at all. The basic ASW equipment fit can be regarded as self-protection: a sonar

FIXED WING AIRCRAFT

Characteristic/Type	*Carrier*	*Shore-based*
Role(s)	Towed array ship support Radar/Visual/Sonar search Torpedo carriers	ASW area search Localisation Weapon carriers (roles other than ASW ones)
Equipment	Radar FLIR MAD ESM Torpedoes Depth bombs	Radar ESM MAD FLIR Torpedoes Depth Bombs
Examples	Grumman S-2 *Tracker* Breguet Br 1050 *Alizè* Lockheed S-3 *Viking*	Shin Meiwa US-1A (flying boat) Tupolev Tu-95 *Bear* F Lockheed CP-140 *Aurora* Hawker Siddeley *Nimrod* Lockheed P-3
Owners	Argentina Brazil France USA	Canada Japan Russia UK USA – and others

PLATE 9.2 US *Spruance* class destroyer *(Photo: L & L van Ginderen)*

set, a weapon (usually a lightweight torpedo system or ahead-thrown weapons) and possibly a torpedo decoy. Even vessels as small as around 100 tons, such as the Swedish *Hugin* class, which are nominally Missile Fast Attack Craft have sonar and light mortars; some even have VDS as well. At the other end of the scale are the several classes of cruisers and destroyers of around 10,000 tons deployed by the USA, propelled by either gas turbines or nuclear power.

Above even these stand the three or four so-called battle cruisers of Russia's *Kirov* class at over 24,000 tons. As size increases ASW reach is added to with a selection of sensors and weapons from multiple sonars with greater capabilities, especially in the open ocean such as towed arrays; rocket-launched weapons such as ASROC and SS-N-15; and, perhaps most importantly, the ability to deploy several, often up to medium-sized, helicopters.

It would be wrong to consider such ships as the *Kirovs* and the American *Aegis* cruisers purely in terms of ASW; their principal attributes lie in other fields of naval warfare. It would also be misleading, however, to ignore such capabilities totally. At the very least such ships have the ability to protect themselves in depth with systems which can be effective out to several tens of kilometres. On the other hand, their other roles, such as anti-ship cruise missile firers (*Kirov*) or area air defence (*Aegis*) suggest that they are the wrong ships to be used in a positive and aggressive fashion for ASW.

Indeed it could be argued that the surface ship is not the platform of choice for engaging in close combat or even medium-range fighting against submarines: it is fairly vulnerable. Nevertheless, it will often be necessary to risk surface ships to some extent against submarines, and for this a degree of specialisation, or at least emphasis of type, becomes apparent. It has become increasingly

ASW SHIPS

National/ Type/ Year	*Tons*	*Speed (kts)*	*Sonars*	*Weapons*	*Helos*
Canada – *Halifax* 92	5235	28	HM, TA	LT	1M
France – *Leygues* 79	4490	30	HM, V, TA	MT	2L
Germany *Bremen* 82	3600	30	HM	LT	2L
Germany – *Brandenburg* 94	4490	29	HM, TA	LT	2L
India – *Delhi* 95	6200	28	HM, V or TA	LT, DC	2M
India – *Godavari* 83	4000	27	HM, V	LT	2M or 1M/1L
Japan – *Asagiri* 88	4200	30+	HL, TA	LT	1M
Netherlands *Karel Doorman* 91	3320	30	HM, TA	LT	1L
Russia – *Udaloy* 80	8700	30	HL, V	HT, RM	2M
Russia – *Neustrashimy* 93	4100	32	HL, V or TA	HT, RM	1M
Russia – *Krivak III* 84	3600	32	HM, V	HT, RM	1M
Spain – *Santa Maria* 86	4017	29	HM, TA	LT	2M
UK – *Duke* 90	4200	28	HM, TA, AL	LT	1M
UK – *Type 22 Batch 3* 88	4900	30	HM, TA	LT	1M
USA – *Spruance* 75	8040	33	HM, TA	LT, ASR	1L
USA – *Oliver Hazard Perry* 77	4100	29	HM, TA	LT	2L

Key:
HM – Hull mounted, V – Variable depth sonar, AL – Active low frequency, TA – Towed array, LT, MT, HT – Light, Medium, Heavy Weight torpedoes, DC – Depth Charges, RM – Rocket Mountings, ASR – ASROC, M, L – Medium, Light helicopters

difficult to produce a universal classification of ships by name as definitions have shifted over the last few decades by both function, size and (to some extent) national fashion. To avoid such difficulties it might be helpful to define what might be termed a generic ocean-going ASW ship, drawing on the characteristics of the examples produced by several different nations.

PLATE 9.3 British Type 22 frigate *(Photo: L & L van Ginderen)*

PLATE 9.4 Canadian *Halifax* class frigate *(Photo: St John Shipbuilding)*

What becomes clear from looking at such an aggregation is that there is much common ground. The majority of ships are within 1,000 tons of 4,500 tons full load displacement: all but two are in the 28–32 knot maximum speed bracket. Hull-mounted active sonar is invariably present, either of medium or low frequency. The transducer itself is likely to be found either underneath the forward hull or in a bow dome. Of the 16 examples, VDS is found in 6 and towed arrays – the most significant recent development for surface ships – in 12, although in some cases these may be alternatives. The main weapon built into the ship itself is the lightweight torpedo fired from deck mountings or sometimes from within the ship's above-water structure.

There are some additions and exceptions to this rule: Russian ships favour heavyweight torpedoes and also deployed rocket-propelled charges to several kilometres; larger US ships deploy ASROC as well as torpedoes. Perhaps the most unusual, if not anachronistic, ASW weapons feature is that of the Indian *Delhi* class which is reported by a normally sober and reliable annual source to be fitted with depth charge rails.

It is noticeable that the helicopter has become a commonplace of ASW ships. What are also marked are two expansionary trends. Firstly, this is manifested in the ability of about half the ships listed to carry two (usually light) helicopters. Secondly, there is an even more significant trend towards the deployment of larger helicopters at sea. In helicopter terms, these are usually referred to as medium, but no bigger helicopters are normally used in direct combat roles. The larger variety are certainly used for troop transport and cargo delivery, but rarely at sea and not for ASW. It is thus noteworthy that the standard ASW unit can now deploy one of the most capable organic ASW air units as a matter of course.

PLATE 9.5 Westland *Lynx* helicopter – in many ASW ships
(Photo: L & L van Ginderen)

At the other end of the scale the very light helicopter such as the Westland *Wasp*, capable of doing little more than taking a weapon to an ordered drop point, has tended to disappear from the orders of battle of the first line ASW navies.

ASW Submarines Any submarine is in theory an ASW unit. In practice its capability is formed from sensors, weapons, doctrine and practice. Many of the first two items are often dual-, or even multi-purpose, capable of being used against either surface vessels, submarines or other targets. This diversity in role may actually militate against capability in any single field, limiting for example the number of each type of weapon carried. Doctrine is sometimes declared or can be inferred from known characteristics of sensor and weapon systems. Practice is less easy to determine. It is, of course, possible to exercise a nation's submarines purely against its own sisters or those of co-operating allies and this provides some insight into submarine ASW. But similarly it would be difficult to imply a significant ASW role to the three *Daphne* class submarines of South Africa with neither friend nor enemy equipped with submarines within thousands of miles.

Moving up the scale of possibility a previous lack of ASW interest, now rectified, may be deduced from the French wish to upgrade the earlier *Rubis* class SSNs to the same ASW standard as the later boats. Indeed the relatively late arrival of the French in the SSN business tells an ASW story in itself.

The French Navy is broadly comparable in size with the British, but with different priorities. The latter put its first SSN to sea in the early 1960s; it was

PLATE 9.6 French SSN *Rubis* *(Photo: L & L van Ginderen)*

to take the French more than two decades to follow. Merely having SSNs is in itself a commitment to ASW, notwithstanding the multirole nature of such ships. But the equipment fitted to British SSNs clearly implies the primacy of the ASW role. The equipment fitted to Russian SSNs also suggests ASW as a principal role; and this is confirmed by a reasonable amount of published tactical doctrine. In the American case, ASW is publicly stated as a main task, and this has been underscored recently by emphasis on under-ice warfare, whose only practical application is ASW.

What then are the characteristics of the submarine as ASW unit? Firstly, it must not itself be over-susceptible to enemy ASW; this is usually a function of stealthy aspects of its design and operation. It must not be vulnerable to detection and attack by a potential opponent; much of this can be achieved by attention to the detail of emission control, most especially noise. Secondly, it should be capable of detecting an enemy submarine first and this usually implies acoustic sensors of increasing size and complexity such as, especially, the towed passive sonar array.

But detection is only the start of prosecution and the ASW submarine has to be capable of refining its initial detection and then producing a fire control solution adequate for whatever weapon is to be employed against its target. Perhaps most importantly, with the possible exception of an initial steer or cue from some external system, such as IUSS (see page 137), all these other stages will most likely have to be achieved without assistance from, or communication with, any external body. Here lies the submarine's greatest source of strength as an ASW vehicle – and its greatest weakness. As a single platform, it can deploy almost (not quite) the best in sensors; and it has almost certainly the best terminal weapon in the heavyweight torpedo with its much greater explosive payload. But it possesses neither the aircraft's speed nor lack of vulnerability to the submarine. Further, it cannot match the surface ship's symbiosis of best individual sensor (the towed array), constant access to external information and ability to co-ordinate the efforts of other units, especially ASW aircraft.

There are two domains, however, in which this surface benefit is either eroded or does not obtain at all. The first is in open water when surface operations are either impossible or needlessly costly because of enemy surface or, more probably, air domination. The second is brought about by a physical barrier in the shape of ice. Operations under ice are not only the sole domain of the submarine, but it is only some submarine-operating nations which have chosen to exploit the difficult world of the North Polar ice cap. As far as is known the only countries which use this remote part of the world are Russia, the UK and the USA.

Canada expressed an interest in its territorial areas under the northern ice, but its plans to exercise its sovereignty by means of a transformed navy dominated by nuclear submarines proved unrealisable.

ASW TACTICS

Modern ASW tactics tend to be equipment-driven, especially at the small scale level. Nevertheless, the usual considerations of own mission, enemies' capabilities and intentions have to be assessed first. Is the aim to seek out contact with enemy submarines as was the case in part of the US's Maritime Strategy, or is it rather the safe and timely arrival of a body of shipping, be it naval or mercantile? In the latter case encounters with enemy submarines are to be avoided rather than sought out. Nevertheless, attacks by submarines may not be avoidable in which case defence and counter-attack must be considered.

At the lowest level a single unit, such as a ship or aircraft, must use its own sensors and weapons to detect, track, classify and attack the submarine. As the latter will probably be aware of at least the last of these processes, two consequences tend to flow from this alerting of the submarine. Firstly, it will know that it is necessary to counter this attack in one way or another; secondly it may in this process be distracted from its present purpose. Thus any forceful ASW attack may, without being successful in terms of sinking or damage, still succeed in ASW terms by depriving an enemy of the effective use of his submarines.

What principles inform the attacking of submarines? Firstly, unless the attack is to be a reaction to the submarine's own attack, it is necessary to find the submarine – preferably before it finds the attacking unit or the ships which it may be protecting. For many years, this was difficult to the point of near impossibility, because of the relative merits of surface ship and submarine sensors. ASW tactics were largely reactive to submarine events, such as spending too long on the surface or, worse still, the submarine attacking a friendly unit – the

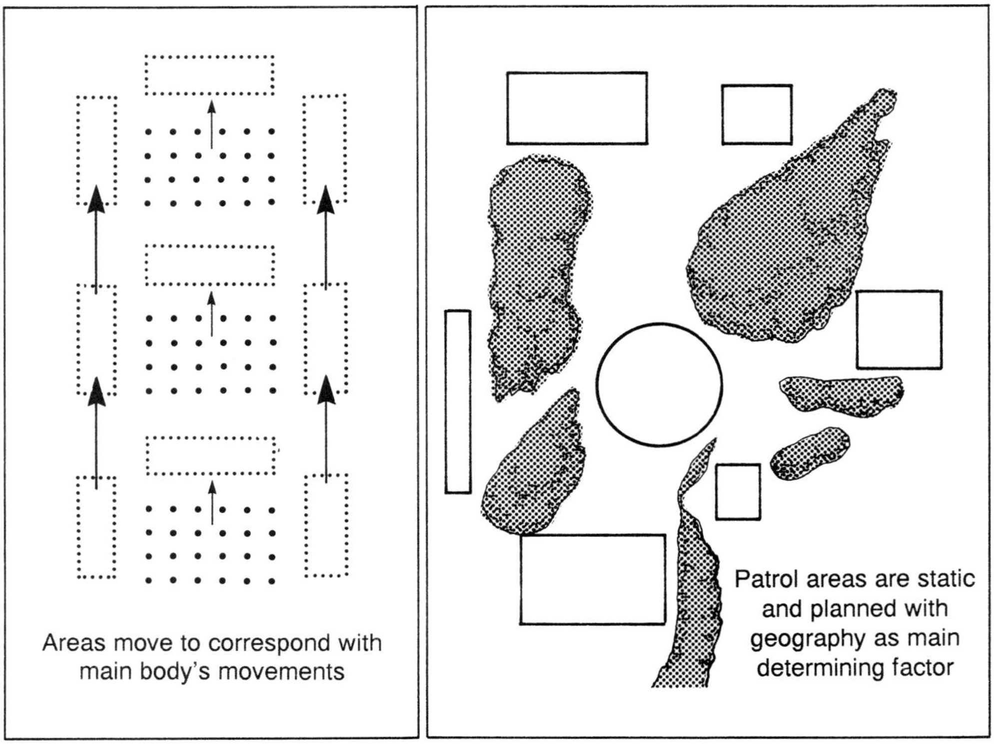

FIG. 9.1 Dynamic and static operations

so-called 'flaming datum' search. The combination of surface ship towed arrays and readily available ASW aircraft has recently and perhaps radically redressed this balance.

The first principle must therefore be to detect the submarine before it detects ASW forces. This is in itself a complex study, but at the tactical level this usually refers to the detection of one or a small number of submarines by mobile ASW assets. How should these be positioned to obtain such early contact? What factors are significant? In broad terms ASW search is usually carried out either with respect to a formation that is being protected, or else geographically.

The former tends to have a dynamic associated with the entity being protected. If this is a convoy or warship formation moving east at 10 knots, then the protective assets are likely to move generally at the same speed in the same direction. This does not mean that they will always be at this speed, but that successive search areas will average this motion. This may well have to be modified to take account of conditions for detection. Thus good conditions will allow further and wider spacing of the search unit, whilst poorer will dictate narrower and closer placement. Some account also needs to be taken here of the vehicle characteristics: surface ships fitted with towed arrays may have vast potential ranges, but

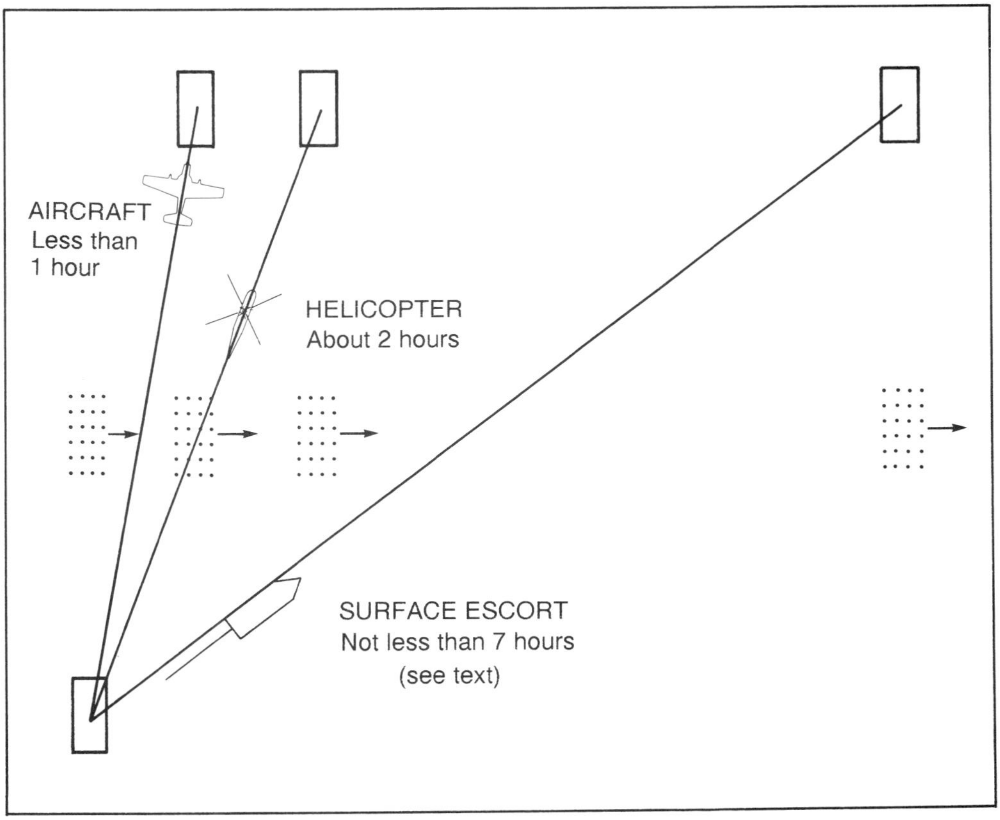

FIG. 9.2 Changing station

they are relatively slow at changing search areas. To look at a worst case example, a towed array frigate stationed 100 nm on the starboard beam of a 10 kt formation could be reallocated the corresponding station on the port beam.

There is a cross-track distance of 200 nm to be made good, but also the forward speed of the formation to be allowed for. At a frigate speed of 30 kts, this change would take seven hours. But such a transit speed might not be allowable for reasons of quiet operation or fuel economy. Further, if the main body's speed was greater, then the differential would be reduced and the process take much longer. Most medium helicopters could carry out the manoeuvre much more quickly, and fixed-wing aircraft could do this in much less than an hour. It is probable that neither helicopter nor aircraft could provide as good area coverage as the ship but here the ASW commander must balance coverage versus speed. It might be thought that a nuclear submarine would be in just the same situation as a surface ship but here the added dimension of communicating with the submarine and the problem of providing assurance that the submarine in transit is not attacked by friendly forces complicates and lengthens the procedure further. Such characteristics tend to define the roles of the various platforms: ASW ships with long-range sensors in advanced or at least remote stations with some long-term potential; aircraft in the shorter-term positions, or those of a reactive nature; and submarines in the longest term positions, or those in which it may be difficult, or even impossible, to deploy either ships or aircraft. Examples of such would be positions well in advance of a CVBG, outside the air defence coverage of such a group; and under Arctic ice.

Similarly, less capable units are likely to have their role defined by their limitations. The diesel-electric submarine, because of its relative lack of mobility,

PLATE 9.7 Tanker refuelling frigate – surface warship vulnerability
(Photo: L & L van Ginderen)

is suitable for allocation to a search area defined geographically, but not to the direct support of a moving group of ships. Surface ships without long-range sensors – in practice, this means a towed array – are likely to be found close to the main body. The optimum stationing of all units for ASW is likely to be compromised by the demands of other threats and duties, as well as the realities of logistics. For instance, the possession of an area-defence SAM system or powerful air warning radar is more likely to dictate the stationing of a surface unit in the face of a significant air threat than the fitting of a medium-range sonar and a set of torpedo tubes. The presence of an unlocated enemy heavy surface force may be a higher command priority for a fixed-wing aircraft, and land attack cruise missiles such as *Tomahawk* – often found now in American SSNs – can be of more importance to the submarine's placing in some circumstances. The impact of logistics is likely to be most felt in the case of towed array frigates operating some distance away from main bodies.

If the main body's speed is relatively high, then a search policy of sprint and drift will impose high fuel consumption on the frigate. In turn, this implies either a periodic return to the main body to make use of its tanking assets, leading either to significant gaps in coverage or to the use of more ships to relieve and

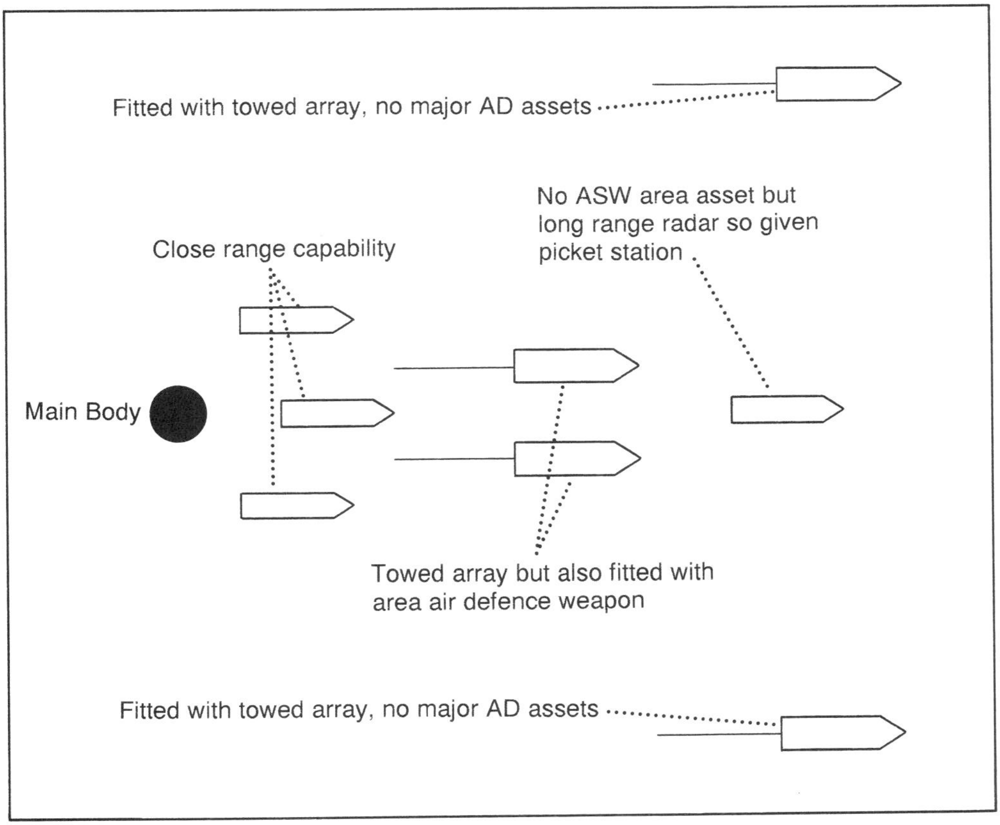

FIG. 9.3 Formation figure – showing compromises

ensure gapless cover. Alternatively the fuel can go to the frigate in the form of a tanker moving from frigate station to frigate station. This, too, is expensive in asset usage: in heavy threat conditions, the tanker itself may require a close escort to ensure its survival. Lastly, with a high speed of advance (SOA), and noting the relatively low speeds of tankers, such a method, sometimes called Delivery Boy, may simply not be feasible.

Such considerations result in a formation design which is inevitably a multi-dimensional compromise for any given set of circumstances. An example of such a process is shown in Fig 9.3.

A further implied dimension to all this is time. With time, the perceived threat will change; the geographical and environmental conditions will alter; even the numbers, capabilities and serviceability of the ASW force will change. Above all, the strategic and operational task can vary drastically. A vivid example of this was during the Falklands War of 1982. After the long passage from the UK (increasing submarine threat against moving formations) a period of relatively static operations followed with the main battle forces deliberately stationed outside the range of most air threats (relatively static ASW operations). On moving the amphibious force inshore to conduct landings there was a significant ASW problem, but once inshore, the air threat predominated. As the force moved towards the shore, the obvious priority for helicopter usage was in support of the landings, not ASW. Few examples are as stark as this, but an invariable problem a commander has to face is the trade-off, or more probably multiple trade-offs, between constant tuning of formations to ensure optimum performance and the time taken to effect such changes.

When operations are geographically defined, rather than being related to a moving body, some of these problems are eliminated, but only to be replaced by others. A body moving at 15 kts simply leaves enemy diesel-electric submarines behind: at most they only get one shot at their targets. In a static situation this will not apply: the submarine cannot be evaded. It has either to be driven off or sunk. Here there can be less emphasis on mobility, but there often has to be even more on defence in depth and the impermeability of search cover. There is more scope for what might be termed the mathematical approach to search tactics. This can be seen in many of the Russian tactical methods laid down, where geometry appears to be of the greatest significance.

Once search has led to detection, the processes of classification, tracking and prosecution can take place. This may lead to the involvement of other units, depending on circumstance. Examples of this not occurring are if an ASW submarine is able to attack its own target whilst remaining within its own allocated water and rules of engagement, or a surface ship detecting a submarine very close to it when immediate independent action is necessary. But more normally, if time and assets permit, the detecting unit might be joined by at least one other in order to prosecute the contact. This does not usually apply in the case of ASW submarines as the difficulties of co-ordination are considerable. A further reason is that a surface ship consort might actually interfere with the process, especially in acoustic terms; co-ordination with an aircraft would also be difficult. A surface unit will benefit from another similar ship in order to provide mutual support and complicate the submarine's problems. If the contact

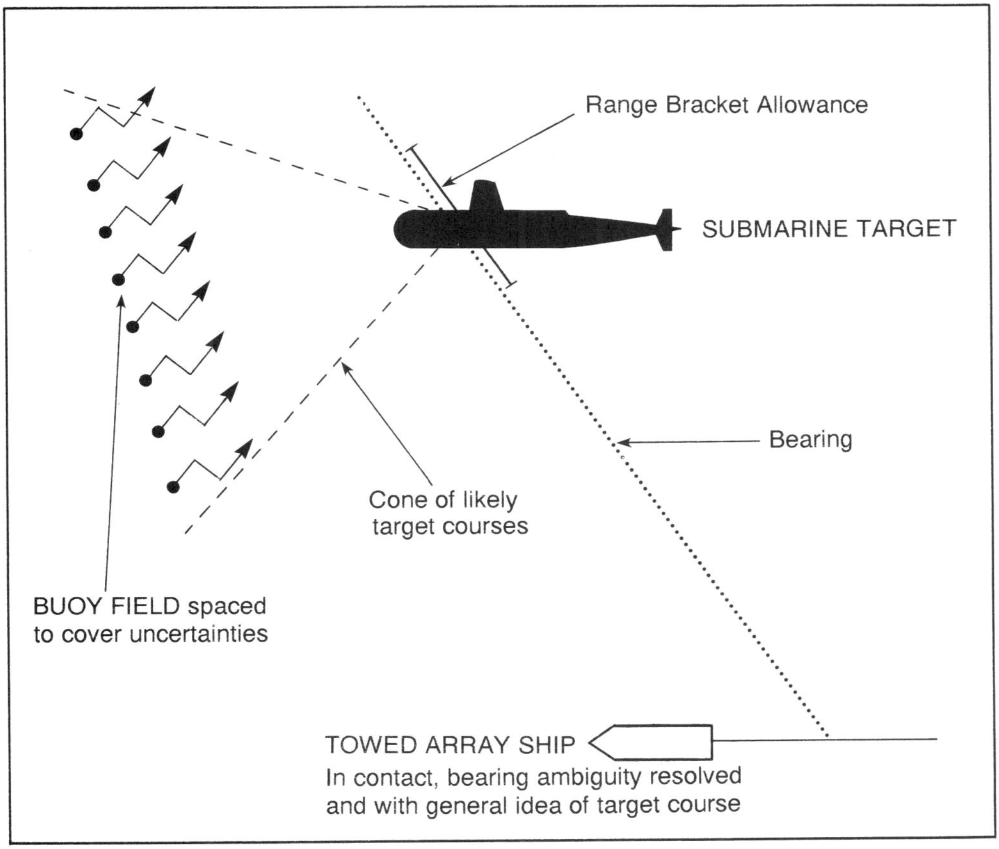

FIG. 9.4 Sonobuoy field to exploit towed array bearing

is at long range, quite probably the case if the contact has been gained on a towed array, then an aircraft is the only practicable supporting unit. Only a helicopter or fixed-wing aircraft has the speed to lay a sonobuoy field in the hope of localising the target in a reasonable timeframe.

As mentioned in an earlier chapter, a towed array's great strength is its ability to make long-range contact, its weakness a lack of knowledge of range. In placing the sonobuoy field, considerable judgement has to be exercised in determining its distance down the bearing.

Under most realistic conditions it is unlikely that an aircraft-placed field can cover the entire range of possibilities. The submarine contact might be at any range from ten to over 100 miles, but it is unlikely that a sonobuoy field can cover much more than several tens of miles. Here external intelligence and the experience of the detecting unit may be able to refine the placement somewhat. Some offset ahead of the bearing may also need to be made to allow for target movement during the time that the field is capable of operation, often a period of several hours. Buoys should also be placed sufficiently apart to take advantage of the predicted conditions against a particular likely target, but sufficiently close to allow some

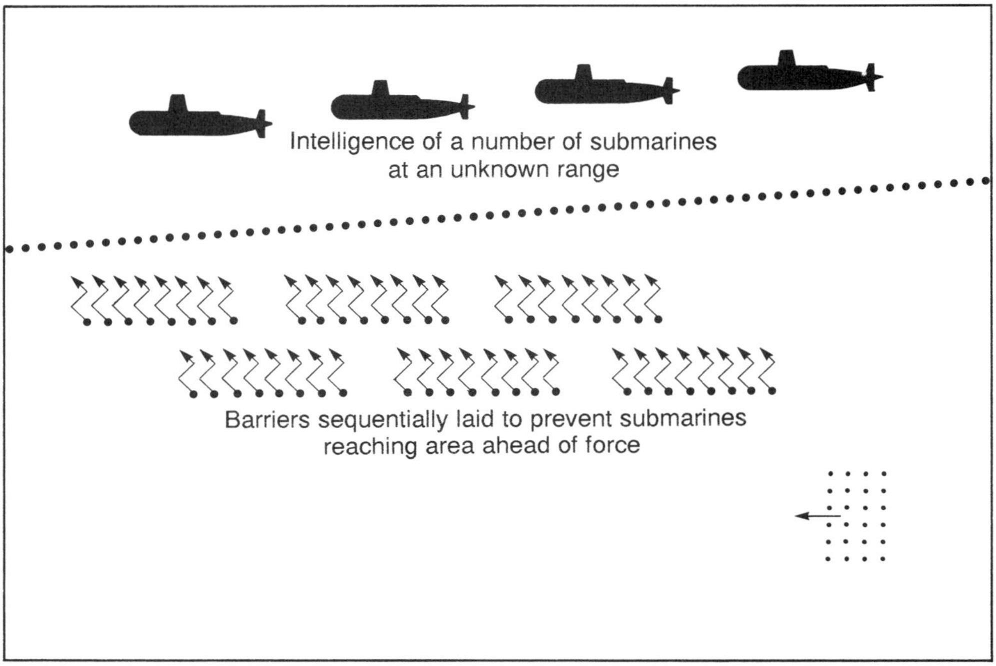

FIG. 9.5 Sonobouy barrier/field placement

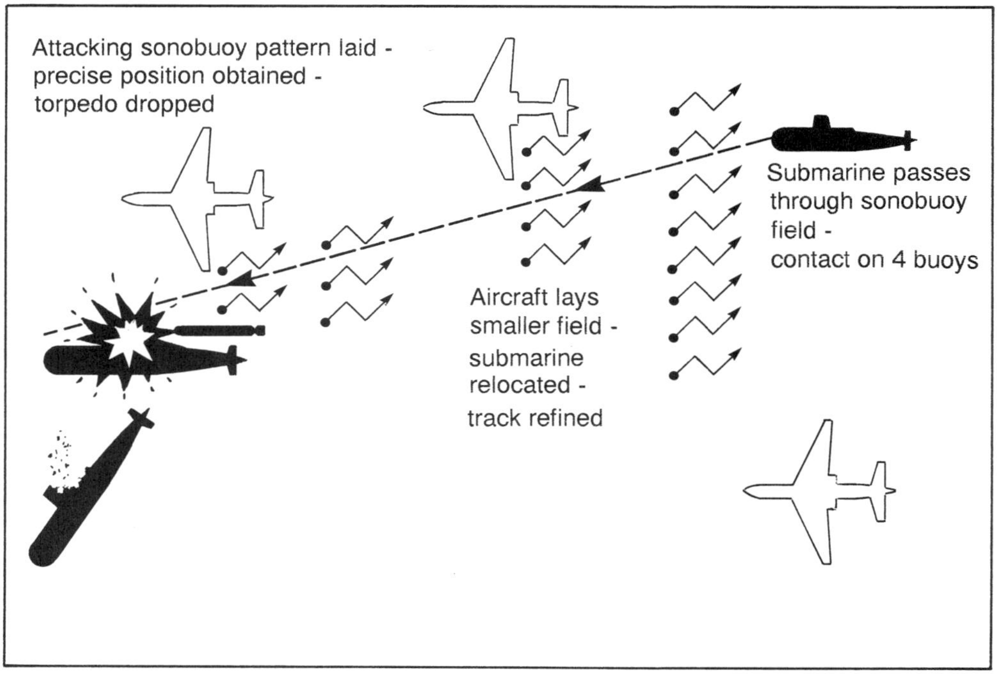

FIG. 9.6 Sequential buoy location

overlap for assurance of gaining contact. Although the surface detecting unit cannot determine range by itself, it could possibly have enough time to conduct a ranging manoeuvre which at least rules out the possibility that the submarine is very close, say within 20 miles. The placement of the buoy field may also have to take account of the most dangerous possible (rather than the most likely) position of the submarine. For example, if a body of transitting ships is being protected and the air-laid field can cover a 40 mile front, it may be more prudent to position the field at 20-60 miles down the bearing even if the detecting unit feels that it is more likely that the submarine is at 100 miles.

Once initial sonobuoy contact is gained, it is normal practice to use further buoys to refine the position and determine target course and speed. The latter parameters can often be supplied by the original detecting ship but their refinement is best left to sonobuoys. Localisation is usually achieved by managing to put more than a single buoy into contact. If these are directional, then a simple bearing crosscut provides position. As the bearings change with time, tracking is also achieved. Doppler shifts, either obtained from a single sensor or again correlated with a second buoy are another method of estimating target course and speed. When a solution of sufficient confidence has been generated, with the position fixed to within a mile or less, with submarine course and speed reasonably refined, it is time to attack. Then a torpedo may be dropped, usually some distance ahead of the target submarine to compensate for target motion and to allow for the torpedo enabling its search sensor and reaching its best depth for search. In some circumstances, the solution may be refined even further by use of a second sensor. This could be either an active sonar (sonobuoy or dipping sonar if a helicopter is used) or MAD. The former has the disadvantage that the submarine is likely to be alerted prior to weapon release, allowing it to make evasive manoeuvres and release decoys. The latter calls for precise low-level flying (in itself increasing the possibility that the submarine might hear the aircraft) and may well be ineffective against a deep submarine, because of the limited range of this sensor.

Whatever sensor or method is employed for the first attack, the unit making it is unlikely to assume that it will immediately be successful. The torpedo may not function properly, the submarine may successfully evade the weapon or it may hit but do minimal damage. During the run of the weapon, the submarine will still need to be tracked and this may well become more difficult than before, as the submarine will now be alerted to the attack and may be using drastic evasive manoeuvres. It is not normal to release more than one torpedo at a time, as each may interfere with the other's chance of success, creating both an alternative underwater target as well as another source of noise.

The problem of having to attack several times may pose a logistical difficulty, especially if a helicopter is the prosecuting unit. Even the heavier of these, such as the *Sea King,* are unlikely to have many torpedoes to use. In deploying the helicopter, trade-offs will have to been made between sensor and weapon load, and fuel. Numbers of weapons may have had to be sacrificed in the interests of endurance; in any case the number of weapon carrying stations will be limited. Whatever the circumstances, it will normally be wise for the ASW commander to ensure the availability of further weapons. This is best provided for by a further aircraft, although the bigger MPAs usually carry quite large stocks. There may be a role still for the lighter helicopter, which may be unable to locate submarines themselves, although its endurance may be tested somewhat at longer ranges. With such lower capability units, there is also more likely to be a problem of timing. Should such a unit not be launched early enough then there will be a gap in the pressure on the submarine; if it is deployed too early, then it may become low on fuel and have to return before its weapon is required.

One commentator suggests that Russian ASW doctrine may be different in two respects from western practice. Firstly, it is thought that MPA may operate normally in pairs, rather than singly. Here, one is principally for search and detection and one for attack. The other difference, less strongly indicated, is that the co-ordination of helicopters and surface ships is achieved by helicopters being the main search units. Once detection has occurred, the prosecution is handed over to the surface ships who would then carry out attacks with ASW torpedoes and multiple-barrelled rocket launchers. Despite the ranges of such systems being at least as great as western lightweight torpedo systems, such a method would appear to be not only relatively slow but seems to put the surface ships to unnecessary risk.

Returning to more general considerations, in areas immediately surrounding formations the first priority must always be the urgent attack of the submarine. Here method is most likely to be determined by the availability of detecting and attacking units in time: an ASW unit of the highest capability which is some 20 minutes distant will be much less useful than a medium or low capacity unit within two minutes of coming into action. Finesse and deliberation have to be sacrificed to urgency. The range or location at which the changeover from urgency to deliberation takes place will be determined by a complex amalgam of enemy capability and the capacity of own forces, all measured against a background of environmental factors and the objectives of the ASW force. In the nearfield, urgency dominates all other considerations; further afield, the conduct of an ASW incident or battle has more to do with the organisation of assets.

FORMATIONS AND SCREENS

Reference has been made several times before to main bodies of ships, and the disposition of these and their protecting forces is a small science in itself. It is not intended to address this fully, but rather to sketch the elements of this before looking at the ASW aspects of formations and screens. The fundamental principle involved is that of balancing requirements, assets, threats and circumstances. It is normal to consider the division of warships into main body units and escorts, but there are complications. An American aircraft carrier has an enormous capacity for projecting military force over hundreds, even thousands of miles: by means of its S-3 *Vikings*, it can project considerable ASW capability out to several hundred miles. But it is at least as vulnerable to a torpedo-firing submarine at close range as any other ship. Indeed a combination of its size and its necessity to take up a great deal of searoom to operate aircraft may actually render it more liable to attack. Other units, too, are likely to need protecting, although few pose quite such difficult challenges as the fixed-wing aircraft carrier.

Others which need protecting may include underway replenishment ships, other logistic units, troop transports and, sometimes, ships which carry force or even strategic assets, such as land attack cruise missiles. Examples of the latter category might include *Aegis* cruisers or *Tomahawk* carrying ships.

In general, the principle that informs the protection of these forces is defence in depth, by means of layering ASW forces, so that multiple opportunities of detection and attack are afforded. But the main body itself merits some consideration in ASW terms. Self-evidently, the smaller the area (fixed or moving) that has to be protected the better. However, there is a limit to how closely packed ships can be. This is partly a function of size, but also of their operating characteristics. Tankers and other replenishment vessels, if carrying out their principal functions from within the main body, need more space to operate prudently than if they were by themselves. If force air defence assets are scarce, they too may be concentrated in or close to the main body. But the largest enemy of compactness is undoubtedly the fixed-wing aircraft carrier. This will often have to steam directly into wind to operate aircraft, both for takeoff and landing. It is rare that such a course will correspond exactly with the direction needed to be made good by the body as a whole. During intensive carrier operations, this requirement will recur every few hours in accordance with the carrier operating cycle. Protection of the carrier demands the suitable placement of assets to cover these movements. Thus, the effective size of the main body may be greatly increased. A further complication is introduced by the addition of further carriers. Here, the commander has to make a decision whether to keep them together or put them in separate groups, each with its own escorting forces. If the latter are in adequate supply, and if the commander has confidence that enough anti-air and anti-missile forces are available to cover all groups, then a separated scheme is feasible; if not, then the carriers may have to be concentrated. In either case, ASW defence may have to be provided to a main body which can operate over several hundreds, or even thousands, of square miles of sea.

PLATE 9.8 *Nimitz* class carrier – protector that needs ASW defence
(Photo: L & L Van Ginderen)

Normally, the units whose capabilities are relatively limited are confined to the areas in the vicinity of main body units. Some of these may be there in any case, mainly because of other weapons with which they are fitted such as SAMs with more than a self-protective capability. Traditionally a defence against the torpedo-firing submarine, some doubt must now be cast on the efficacy of such placement, at least when faced with a highly capable submarine force, such as that of Russia. This comes about because of two developments: the long-range super-heavyweight wake-homing torpedo and the submarine-launched anti-ship missile. In the former instance, a close escort (say out to about 10 miles) can have little effect against a weapon with a range in excess of 20 miles. However, the wake-homing weapon is thought to be somewhat indiscriminate and a submarine may have to close well within theoretical range in order to attempt at least rudimentary target identification and selection. Nevertheless it would be imprudent to assume that this will be the case and the close escort's effectiveness in this situation must be considered questionable at best. If this is so for these torpedoes, it is even more so for the submarine-launched missile.

Does this mean that the ASW close escort is a dead concept? It should be noted that only Russian nuclear submarines can currently use the super-heavyweight torpedoes and that the tube-fired anti-ship missile has spread little beyond the major naval powers.

For most submarine operators, there is no alternative but to move fairly close to the target in a diesel-electric submarine of limited mobility and use relatively short range torpedoes; the close escort fitted with medium range sonar (MRS) and lightweight torpedoes thus retains some utility beyond that of self-protection. A further point in favour of this apparently outdated method is that it complicates the task of the firing submarine in finding and selecting the most important target.

The area next out from such short range escorts is probably dominated by the helicopter fitted with active sonar. Here a combination of aircraft speed – typically up to four times the absolute maximum of the surface escort and something like eight times greater than optimum search speed – and the random nature of the dipping position make the helicopter a feared opponent of diesel-electric submarines and respected by nuclear ones. Such is the versatility of this ASW unit that it can just as easily fill a gap in a surface ship screen, be part of an advanced screen (conferring defence in depth) or be used to attack other units' contacts. Its sensor, although limited in size and power in comparison with a hull mounted sonar, has the advantages of variable depth operation, whilst operating in a low self-noise regime.

When integrated in the design of the screen for a main body, the helicopter has to take account of the main body's positions and movements. This can either be achieved by means of a radar fitted in the helicopter, or by positive or advisory control by a radar operating in a main body or screening unit. Although flexible, an ability to operate helicopters on a round-the-clock basis demands a relatively high number of aircraft and crews. It also assumes a reasonable degree of servicing facilities and the ability to deal with at least the most likely range of defects within the force, if not on board the owning unit itself. A further prerequisite is helicopter equipment suitable for day and night operations in the majority of weather conditions likely to be met. The critical tests tend to be takeoff and landing, together with the ability to maintain a hover at night suitable for dipping sonar deployment. Such equipment and skills are by no means present in the helicopters operated by all navies. Even if helicopters are operated from shore, largely obviating the former constraint, night dipping in heavy weather is still a decisive matter.

Further out, three types of ASW unit may be used. The heavier longer-ranged helicopter still has a place here, although there is an obvious trade-off between range and time on task. A good rule of thumb might be that, providing the helicopter with an operational load has an endurance of around four hours, then one hour may be spent on transit to and the same back to its base, allowing two hours for operational tasks. This tends to suggest a practical limit of about 100 miles from its base, but this may be extended either by using a forward based deck – some frigates are suitable – or by taking fuel from a similarly based unit, known as HIFR (Helicopter In Flight Refuelling). This limited endurance and the relatively constrained weapon and sensor fit (when compared to a fixed-wing ASW aircraft) tend to mean that the helicopter is unsuitable for large-area search without any previous form of tactical cueing. The helicopter at these ranges is thus more suited to supporting a unit such as a towed array frigate already in contact.

The fixed-wing ASW aircraft is less likely to be constrained by a relatively light fit of equipment and short times on task. It is, of course, perfectly capable of supporting the prosecution of contacts gained by either frigates or submarines: indeed, this is arguably one of the most potent ASW combinations of all. But the fixed-wing aircraft is also capable of independent area search as well as responding to cues from area search systems. The aircraft also has little difficulty in communicating with other ASW units, other than and unlike the submarine.

The submarine, be it SSN or SSK, is also most likely to be deployed well away from the main body. This is caused by a combination of factors, some driven by unsuitability, some to take advantage of the submarine's own characteristics. The SSK cannot match the speed of a main body's likely advance; it is thus likely to be employed in areas well ahead of the force. These space allocations are likely to be overtaken by events and the option then presented is to jump the SSK ahead to a further area by means of a surface passage. This is only likely to be feasible if the main body's SOA is low and the SSK's surface transit is unlikely to be opposed, especially by aircraft. The use of SSKs is, therefore, most suited to static operations. The SSN is less likely to be constrained by speed and is capable of carrying out fast transits submerged. Here the limiting factor tends to be the problems of communicating reliably with a submerged submarine; these have been mentioned earlier.

Thus it can be seen that when ASW resources are available the submarine attempting an attack faces a challenging series of layers in order to attain its aim.

The strength of the ASW forces depends not so much on the capabilities of any one unit or type of unit but rather on the combination or synergy of their abilities. The skill lies in the ordering of these forces; taking account of threat and environment; building on strengths and taking account of weaknesses; and always being able to bear in mind the fourth dimension – time. Once a plan has been made, it is

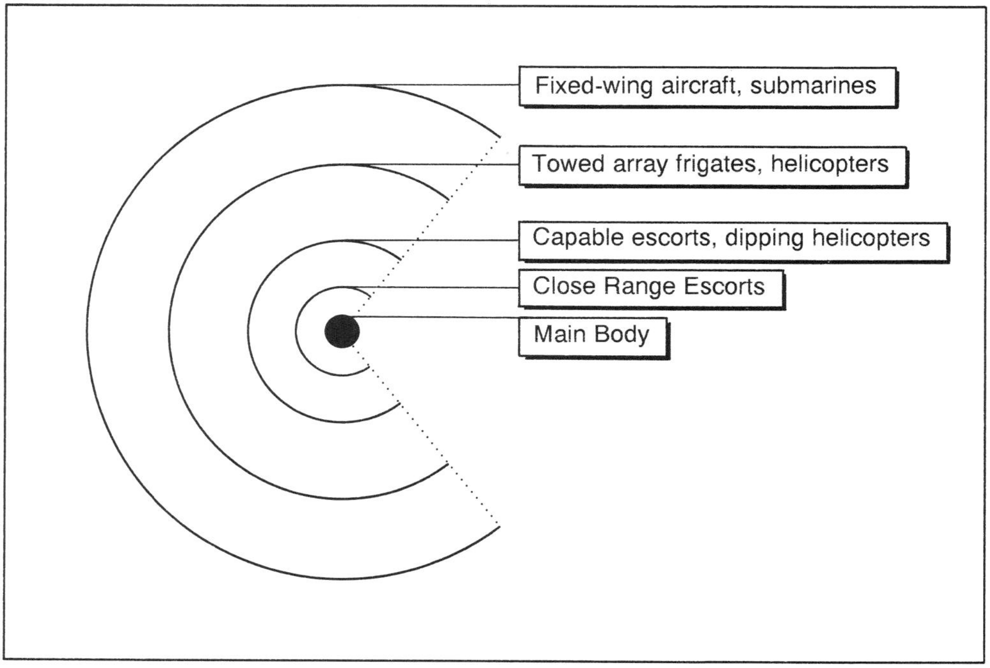

FIG. 9.7 ASW layers

then essential to deal with the incidents of enemy action, detection of submarines and their prosecution which arise. It was once normal to distinguish attacks as urgent or deliberate but a better classification would probably be very urgent or urgent. In the former case fast reaction demands extremely prompt action without too much regard to the exact fitting of the most suitable weapon and platform to the target: time is all. In the latter instance, some heed can be given to suitability and the task of the ASW commander has more to do with resource management. This is likely to involve the despatch of supporting units to the scene of action and possibly having to re-order the disposition to take account of this.

Before leaving the subject of dispositions and formations it is important to address the topic of protecting non-naval shipping. Ensuring the continuance of trade and the shipping in support of military operations has been a requirement for centuries, stretching back to the 16th century Spanish bullion *Flotas* and beyond. Evidence in to the mid-20th century was strongly in favour of the convoy as a method of protection, most especially against the new threat of submarines. Latterly it has been argued that convoy has lost its importance, because of:

- The increased mobility and destructive capability of the nuclear submarine.
- Space and other forms of surveillance making convoys easier to find.
- The increased speed of contemporary merchant vessels making it difficult for escorts to operate effectively against submarines.

Among other means of dealing with this problem, the defended lane tactic was devised. This envisaged areas of water either side of a shipping route being searched by ASW submarines, aircraft or towed array frigates, while shipping passed safely through the middle. Although exercised, this tactic has never been proved operationally. Further, although theoretically valid against noisy earlier generation nuclear submarines, its efficacy against more modern nuclear and all diesel-electric boats must be considered unproven.

A further doubt might be introduced by the knowledge that radar surveillance from space – the most likely means of identifying formations of ships including convoys – is only available to a very few nations. It is one of the more expensive, if not more exotic, forms of space technology which is liable to limit its general spread in the world. It is also important to note that not only would such systems be required to exploit the potential of space surveillance, but so too would fast (probably near real-time) methods of transmitting data to submerged submarines. Such solutions are complex, technically advanced and expensive.

In summary, therefore, the realities of available technology still leave many questions unanswered about the practical application of advanced principles to contemporary submarine warfare: the lack of recent operational experience leaves the matter further open. Convoy may not be quite so dead as its recent critics have suggested.

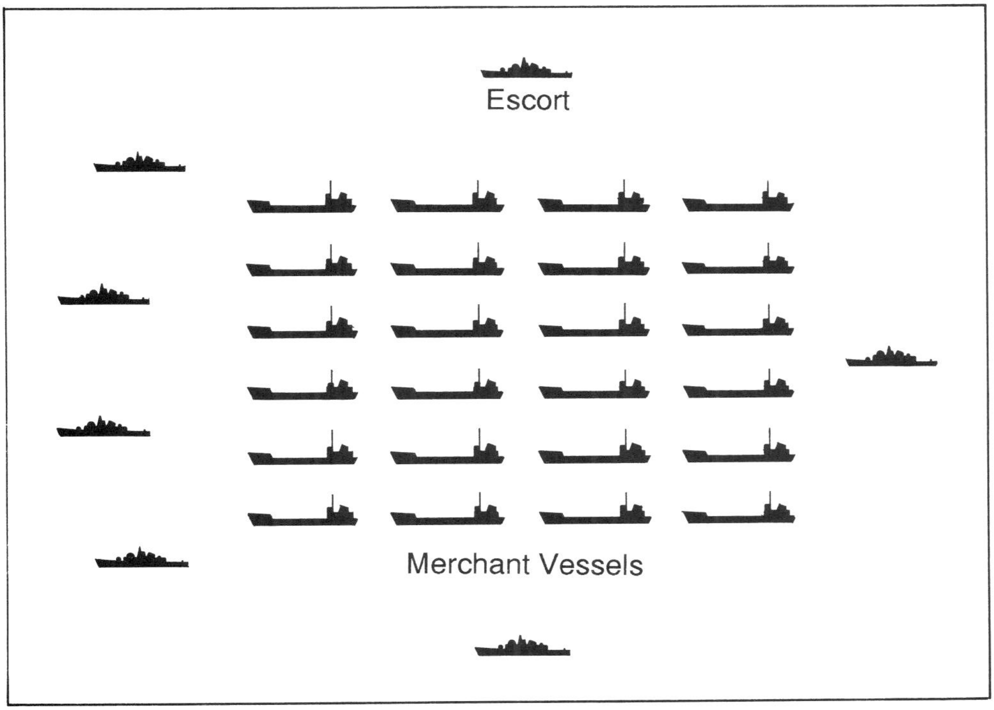

FIG 9.8 Convoy – still a useful protection

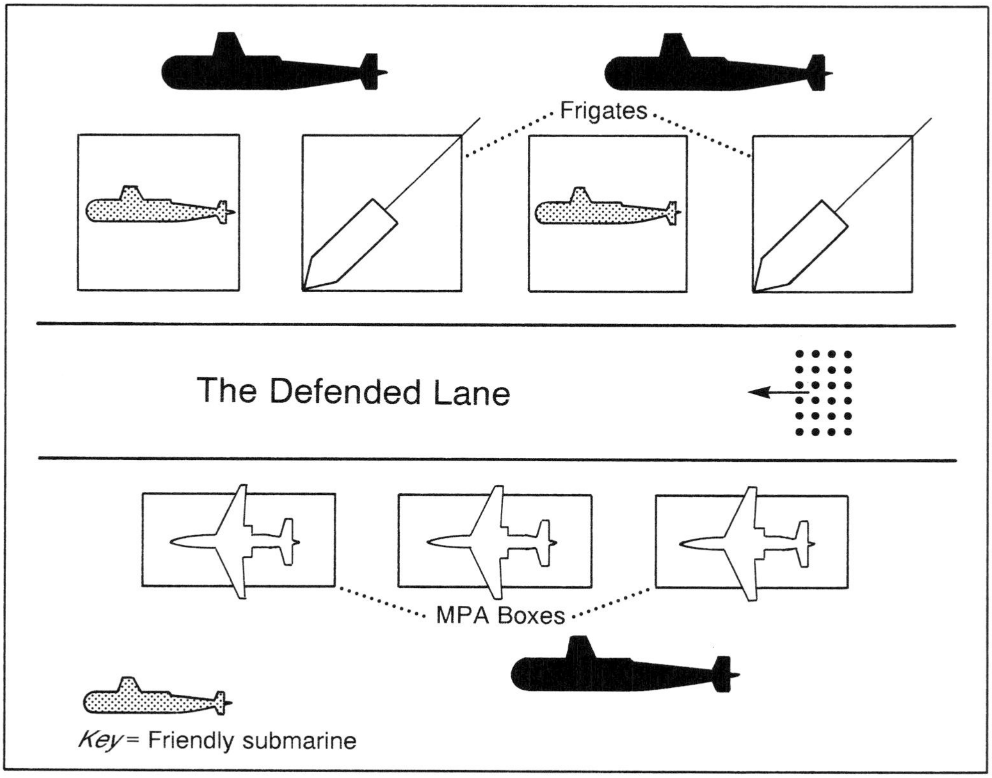

FIG. 9.9 Defended lane

THE SHORE ELEMENT

By the time of the Second World War, ASW was becoming a matter beyond the interest and sole control of the commander at sea. Convoy battles against submarines were directed at the higher level from shore headquarters. The redisposition of ASW forces at the operational level was ordained from there, major diversions of convoys initiated from shore, and the fullest intelligence picture was only maintained in such places. Nevertheless, the detailed conduct of the ASW battle always remained the prerogative of the commander at sea. When working properly, the sea-shore relationship formed an effective ASW partnership. The same remains true now and into the foreseeable future. What can a command organisation on shore contribute to an ASW battle at sea and how does it achieve this?

Firstly, it is important to note that certain assets belong to, or at least are best controlled from, shore rather than sea, almost at all times. Examples of this are shore-based ASW aircraft, submarines not in the immediate vicinity of the ships at sea, certain strategic assets such as IUSS (see page 137) and some surveillance systems – those using space-based sensors and intelligence collection mechanisms. There tend to be two reasons for shore control of assets, one or

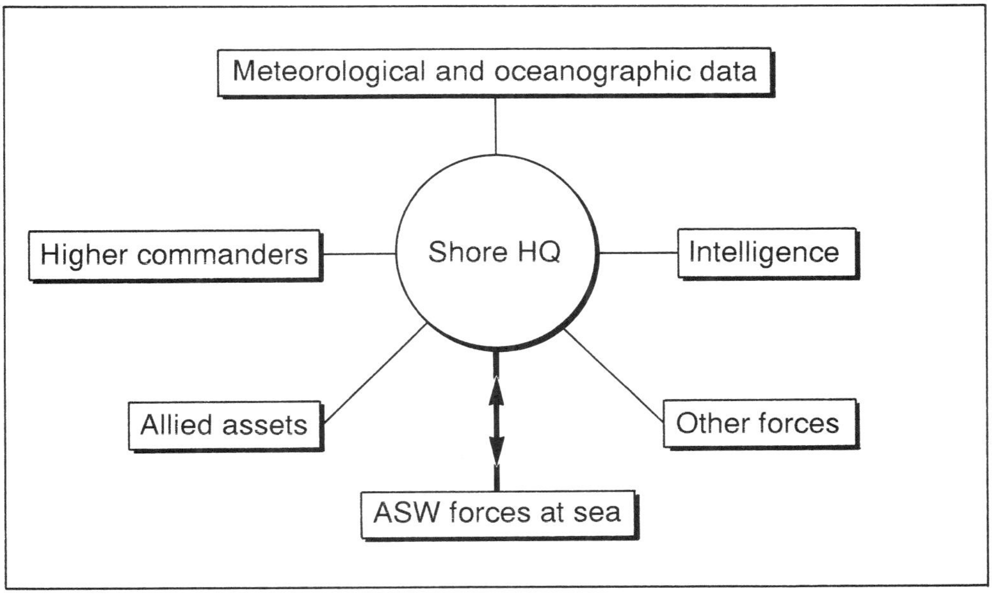

FIG. 9.10 Shore headquarters – access to other entities

both of which may apply in given circumstances: these are system constraints and the control of strategic assets. The practicalities of communicating with submerged submarines virtually dictate the use of long-haul shore communications, be they VLF radio or satellite communications (SATCOM). Further, the waterspace allocated to submarines, even if they are operating in support of a specific force at sea, is unlikely to be of interest merely to the commander of that force. Waterspace, just as much as any weapons system or surveillance asset, is a strategic commodity which has to be managed at that level.

Similarly, although it started life as an entirely static shore-based system SOSUS (Sound Surveillance System) has now been supplemented by T-AGOS (Towed Array Ocean Surveillance System) ships to become IUSS.

The T-AGOS ships are capable of deployment either in the gaps of the fixed system, or else in areas directly related to the protection of friendly forces. Clearly, here is a strategic asset allocated or even controlled from shore. In intelligence matters, too, the same general principle is likely to apply.

The detail here is unlikely to be the subject of open debate, but it seems unlikely that intelligence assets can cover all threats comprehensively all of the time in all places at a speed desired by the fleet commander. There is also the consequent point that if the assets are adequate and available, they will almost certainly be supplying not just the right amount of information, but probably too much: a competent shore authority can do much by way of editing or tailoring such a product to support the force at sea in the optimum manner. It is probable that some of these strategic assets, such as SIGINT, are also competed for by commanders not engaged in ASW or even maritime warfare.

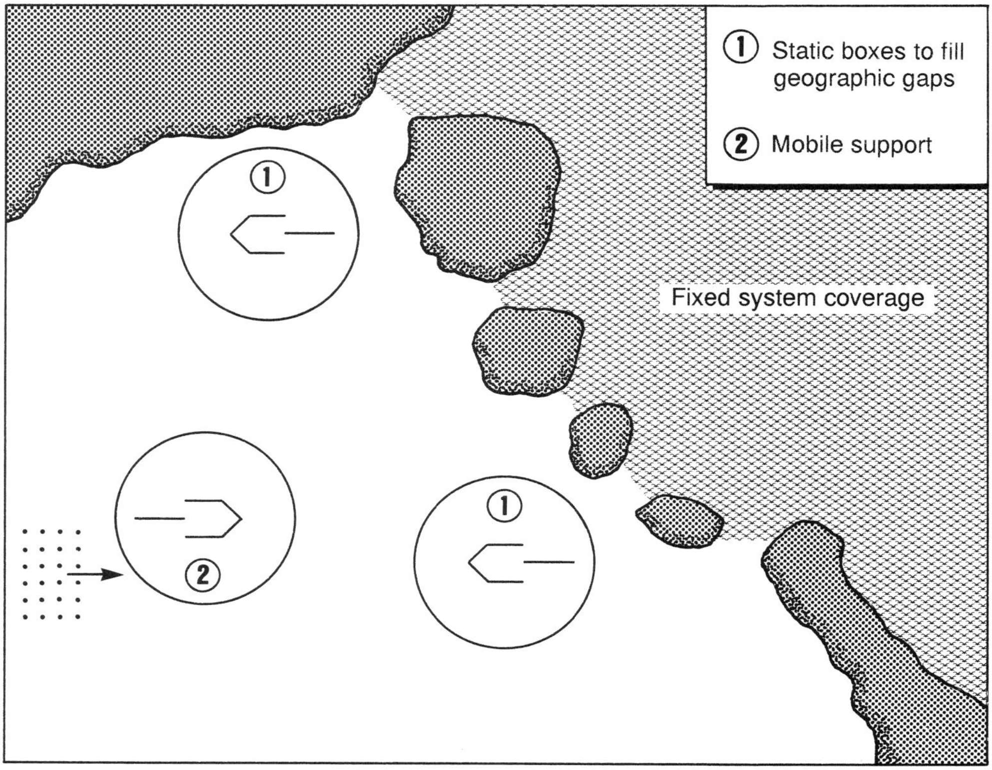

FIG. 9.11 T-AGOS ship deployment

This combination of strategic priority determination and practical constraint tends to highlight the necessity for the role of a shore headquarters. However, there is a third factor which may apply during some operations. If covertness of operations is essential to a commander at sea, then it is likely that radio, radar and even active sonar emissions may be restricted, or even banned totally. Control of such a force, especially when it is spread out well beyond line of sight or UHF radio range, may be beyond direct control of the commander at sea. A shore organisation, usually with secure long-haul communications under its control, can thus play an important role in the command and control of the force until the time when such restrictions are lifted. In the process, it may be in a position to understand what is happening in the whole force better than the commander at sea.

There is, of course, a danger that the volume and quality of information, together with the ability to communicate quickly and reliably with a force at sea, may lead to micro-control from shore. A balance has to be struck between the ability to do such a thing and the temptation to over-indulge in it. It is probable that this is a fundamental and ancient tension in warfare, and in hierarchic structures: modern communications have simply highlighted this problem.

Integrated Underwater Surveillance System (IUSS) There are many advantages to deploying bottom-laid passive sonar arrays. Unlike mobile systems, they are inherently quiet, enjoy virtually no restriction in size and can be laid in depths which practicable mobile systems cannot reach. It is possible that they may be able to exploit the deep Reliable Acoustic Path (RAP). There are limits to their capability: able to detect sound sources out to possibly hundreds of kilometres, the system will also be aware of any source, not just those of interest, that is submarines. Further, it is probable that the diesel-electric submarine – at least when using battery-electric drive – is virtually immune from detection. There are also areas where environmental factors render detection unlikely if not impossible. Lastly, although extremely sensitive detectors, these systems are less effective as locators: in this they might be considered as towed arrays writ large. In optimum circumstances, however, such as when two or more arrays are in contact, it may be possible to localise the target to circles with radii of 8-45 nm.

The best known system is the American SOSUS system, which together with Surface Towed Array Sonar System (SURTASS) and T-AGOS and other inputs forms the larger scale IUSS. SOSUS itself was conceived as long ago as the 1950s. Since then it has been deployed in both the Atlantic and Pacific Oceans, using shore terminals in allied littoral countries such as Canada, Iceland, Japan and the UK. It is probable that the system has grown incrementally, expanding both in capability and geographic scope over the ensuing decades. Its exact capabilities and limitations are not in the public domain, but the continuance of the system over such a long period suggests that it is fundamentally effective and that it has kept up with the reduction in noise signature of the Russian submarine fleet.

It is probably capable of directing economically the activities of either ASW submarines or maritime patrol aircraft with sufficient accuracy to let the mobile unit's sensors relocate and subsequently track submarines with a greater degree of precision. Conjecturally, this may be good enough to permit subsequent weapon firing by these ASW units in wartime. Alternatively in high periods of tension, it is probably important to know the exact location of opposing submarines, most especially those threatening allied forces or even in the case of SSBNs the territory of the USA itself. This was especially important when a significant part of the Russian SLBM force had to patrol well west of the GRIUK gap.

It is thought that Russia probably deploys systems similar in concept, but much more limited in scope, both technically and geographically. The 'Cluster Lance' planar array has been noted in the Pacific. One view is that Russian systems are likely to be deployed in gaps and chokepoints where their limited performance allows them to be perfectly adequate tripwires, rather than true area surveillance tools. It is possible the Russians may perceive acoustic sensors as being of limited utility in any case and that they are turning their attention in other directions for area surveillance (see Chapter 10).

10

The ASW Future

INTRODUCTION

Predicting the future is never easy: it is simply too complex a problem. There are many factors which will determine the future of ASW. Most of these will be known now, but some currently thought important will dwindle to triviality whilst others, apparently minor or even barely visible at present, will assume greater importance when viewed from the perspective of the year 2020.

This is an important caveat to any look into the future, but does it mean that it useless to look even up to 20 years hence? As in the past century, there have been revolutionary changes to consider as well as evolutionary ones. For submarines, nuclear propulsion and SLBMs were revolutionary; torpedo development tended to be evolutionary. In ASW, long-range passive systems and the helicopter operating from relatively small ships were revolutionary; sonar evolutionary.

This mixture of fast- and slow-moving developments together with the factors external to strictly-defined ASW itself has typified the last century. These other causes are concerned with a number of areas, principally political and military rationales, which for this purpose can be swept together into one term: strategy. Then, economics, which tends to be a limiter rather than an enabler and, most importantly, technology. These subjects form a useful starting point to a consideration for the future of ASW. The reactive nature of ASW (emphasised in Chapter 3) means that a consideration of the future submarine should form an important part of this analysis. Lastly, these elements can be brought together to form a view of ASW in the period from the present until about the year 2020.

THE BEST OF ENEMIES – STRATEGY AND ECONOMY

A national strategy might be defined as what a state wants to do; economy is what it can afford to do. Sometimes the first will override the second, usually in wars of national survival or even periods of prolonged tension. The Cold War was probably an example of the latter, and this feature was an important contributory factor to the demise of a military superpower, the USSR. More normally in periods of lower tension or peace, economy will limit strategy. Arguably, the post-Cold War change of attitude on ASW expenditure may already be discerned in American economies in the operation of the IUSS system as well as a drastic slowing down of the SSN 21 *Seawolf* SSN programme.

It is worth noting that retrenchment in production and running costs is also likely to be reflected in research and development funding cuts. Thus not only will there be fewer new equipments, but the pace of specialist technological progress, at least in certain fields, will possibly also slow. The latter effect will, however, take some time to become apparent. The process as a whole has now been active for some years and it is thus difficult to suggest a reversal in general progress until beyond the turn of the century.

Looking around the world, defence drawdown is a general trend in western nations. In eastern Europe (never very important in the ASW league tables) this is very evident. However, in the former Soviet Union a different effect may also be at work. Although some selected programmes seem to be being maintained, it is nevertheless clear that widespread economic decline cannot continue to support a defence sector on the previous scale. Here, however, there are factors which suggest that undersea warfare remains a most important priority. This is manifest in strategic nuclear forces where START II, assuming ratification and implementation, will shift the emphasis in basing over the next decade or so from land to sea, and to submarines specifically.

Elsewhere, the same trends are not necessarily in evidence. In Asia, a small and probably sustainable boom in defence force procurement is under way. To

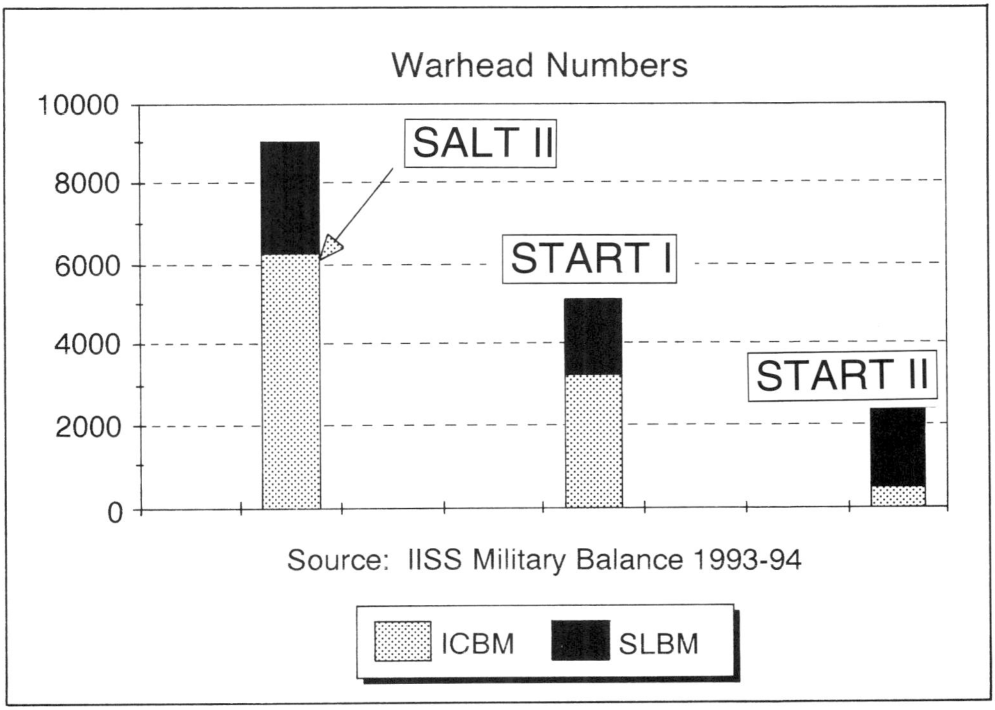

FIG. 10.1 Post SALT II, START I and START II basing proportions

what extent this is a general expansion or whether this is a response to the growing strengths of two potential regional superpowers, India and China, is difficult to say. Countries such as South Korea, Japan, Indonesia, Malaysia and Thailand have expanding economies, growing defence budgets and increasing interest in naval forces. Submarine and thus ASW awareness has grown in these nations, and this may well soon be translated into the procurement of more equipment. It may be a little early to suggest that the maritime nations of southern and eastern Asia in 2020 will be rather as South America is today, with a marked degree of both submarines and ASW capability, but this conclusion would be both possible and plausible. The main difference would be the added presence and probable proportional rise in the capabilities of both China and India. In these circumstances, it would also be reasonable to suggest that Japan – currently deploying over 50 destroyers and frigates, around 15 large and modern diesel-electric submarines fitted with towed arrays, and MPA – is unlikely to reduce its ASW forces significantly. Indeed, this is an area of potential expansion with ASW aircraft-carriers a distinct possibility. Nuclear-propelled submarine procurement might be an even more speculative surmise for this nation.

Before turning to other continents, it is also worth noting the recent acquisition by Iran of up to four *Kilo* class SSKs from Russia. ASW awareness (possibly even submarine panic) in the Gulf region has therefore increased considerably, and the fundamental instabilities in this region suggest that the Iranian acquisition should be interpreted as a ratchet step rather than a blip. The Gulf may

PLATE 10.1 *Kilo* class submarine – worldwide spread
(Photo: L & L van Ginderen)

thus become a substantial growth area for ASW; later in this chapter, acquisition of leading-edge sonar equipment by at least one nation is described – this could well be the start of a larger-scale trend.

Most of the South American littoral states – with the minor exceptions of Uruguay and the three Guianas – have maintained ASW and submarine forces for some years. Moves to modernise these suggest that this may be a longer-term phenomenon in some of those navies than, say, the use of old aircraft-carriers. Lastly, Africa. Other than the North African littoral and South Africa, this has not been even medium level ASW territory. The numerous other problems of that continent, and the fact that it has many land-locked and land-oriented states all suggest that this position is unlikely to change significantly in at least the medium term.

Looking globally, therefore, the position appears to be one of near stasis. The end of the Cold War may lead to a short-term decline in ASW forces, but this may not be sustained for a longer period. At the same time, there are other areas of the world, especially in southern, central and eastern Asia in which the beginnings of increased ASW interest are evident. Whilst the short-term impact of recent conflicts, against Iraq and in the former Yugoslavia, tend to suggest the dominance of land warfare, all that is needed to change this perception is a limited use of submarines by one nation, especially in sensitive areas.

Perhaps the leading potential example of this might be the use of Iranian *Kilo* class submarines in the waters around the Straits of Hormuz. Through these pass the tankers carrying much of the Gulf's oil being exported to the world. Although untested in the supertanker era, it is probable that the torpedo would be a more decisive weapon against such ships than the missiles used against them during the Iran–Iraq war of the 1980s. The underwater weapon would be at least as difficult to counter as these missiles. Further, in these difficult detection waters, the *Kilo* could prove a significant threat to warships which might be deployed to this potentially volatile region. An added difficulty is that the submarine would be an ideal vehicle with which to conduct sporadic warfare over a long period of time. Countering a submarine threat would be expensive in resources, especially if no declared, or at least established, state of war existed. It might for instance be difficult initially to establish with certainty that submarines (and if so, whose) rather than mines were responsible for losses.

THE TECHNOLOGICAL LIMITS

A look back over the last 25 years suggests that the next 25 may bring about equal change. In ASW, the emergence of long-range passive systems, the progress in weapons systems, the advent of the helicopter in even relatively small ships and the use of space sensors have all been important developments. What will be the comparable advances in the next quarter century? ASW cannot exist without the submarine problem, so this is the point where any assessment has to start.

Submarines If the emphasis on littoral warfare continues, which seems evident from such documents as the US Navy's *From the Sea*, then the age of the giant submarine such as the current Russian *Oscar* class may well be at an end. Another trend working against the large specialised submarine is the opportunity provided by improved weaponry for multi-role submarines. The leading current example of this is the American *Los Angeles* or 688 class which can be used against surface forces (at ranges of hundreds of miles with anti-ship *Tomahawk* and shorter-range torpedoes), submarines and even land targets. The proliferation of nuclear propulsion around the world may now slow down still further. This is not so much a matter of technological incompetence as a growing realisation of the full costs of such systems, including the disposal of spent plant. At the same time, the diesel-electric submarine may be entering into a new and very significant stage of its development with air independent propulsion (AIP). This holds out the promise not of equalling the nuclear submarine's underwater speed and endurance, but of greatly decreasing the diesel-electric boat's already limited reliance on the surface. For details of how such systems might be used, see Admiral Hervey's book in this series which makes it plain that a series of technological advances promises a much more capable conventional submarine. One very short cautionary point is that such developments have been promised before. In the 1970s, there was much talk – not apparently realised in practice – of how similar performance improvements might be realised by better batteries. However, with several classes of submarine about to put to sea fitted with AIP it would now seem safe to predict that this technology will be widely available and deployed by the year 2020.

At the same time, the growing trend in the past 20 years to put ever cleverer weapons into smaller packages will probably continue to the advantage of submarines, although to some extent this may be limited on economic grounds. Would it be too fanciful to see a small diesel-electric submarine, belonging to an Asian or even Middle Eastern country deploying anti-ship or even land-attack cruise missiles? This may be going a little far as the latter depend not only for full effectiveness on the missiles themselves, but also on a sophisticated degree of support from space and other systems. However, the possibility remains open.

The torpedo is likely to remain important as a sinker of ships. Operating in the medium where it can have the greatest possible effect, it is difficult to conceive any radical replacement for this weapon system. However, it may evolve further in becoming more of a 'fire and forget' weapon. The current combination of good automotive performance allowing long-range firing and various homing systems, especially the Russian wake-homing one, already permit this to some extent. However, the range cannot always be fully exploited because the weapon will probably attack the first valid target, not necessarily the most valuable. It might not be too imaginative to suggest that a weapon be evolved which could actually evaluate a potential valid target, rank its desirability for attack, and then move on to look at several others, before deciding which of these to return to and attack. If, however, the first target found met certain predetermined criteria, it would move straight in to the attack. No such weapon exists, nor is any known to be in development, but such an advance would do little more than to take advantage of several known and emerging technologies and put them together in one package. Current and near-term techniques which could contribute to this include intelligence systems (to determine the composition and disposition of the target force and transmit this to the firing submarine); submarine passive sonars to refine both qualitative and positional data for the weapon prior to firing; large-scale data storage on the weapon so that it can compare its own observations with database information; and lastly artificial intelligence and 'fuzzy logic' systems, so that the necessary target selection choices can be made. An intermediate step on the way to such a super-smart weapon might be to utilise an optic-fibre link to allow some of the post-launch decisions to be made in the firing unit.

Submarine sensors may progress, but recent trends seem to indicate that the high point in acoustic performance may have been reached some time ago. This indicates one of two possible ways ahead: improvements in above-water sensors or better access to external sources of information. In the first case, with the exception of the well established trend to multi-sensor periscopes and such devices as low light and image intensification sensors, it is difficult to see how much more can be done with such a limited aperture into the above-water world. The latter would appear to offer much more scope for progress, but it tends in practice to mean access – directly or indirectly – to space-based systems. These tend to be the prerogative of the prosperous and technologically-advanced, so even if one of these better-off nations chooses to share them with a poorer ally, the option of switching off by the donor always remains open. During the Cold War, the concept of similar support for surrogates – as opposed to long-term allies – was fairly common: although such relationships and ideas are now in recession, they could return.

THE ASW RESPONSE

The previous sections have painted a picture of the future submarine problem as it might turn out over the next few decades: what is to be done? Practicable ASW must not only adhere to the important principles spelt out in Chapter 3 of taking full account of the nature of the submarine, its roles and activities: it must also take account of technological advances in submarine warfare, whilst exploiting the same and other advances in the cause of ASW. How will it be possible to deal with the submarine problem in 2020? One answer must be in much the same way as today; this is certainly likely to hold true for the case of the more rudimentary submarine operating nations, who will probably have technologies and orders of battle of the sort likely to be found at the more modern end of *Conway's All the World's Fighting Ships 1947-1995*. Emphatically this will not be the case against the more advanced submarines and underwater systems.

The earlier chapters of this book have indicated that ASW may be conducted in a number of broad circumstances or operational contexts. It may be helpful to look at ASW first in these terms before turning to look at the specific technologies which may help or hinder ASW.

Types of ASW – Strategy Starting with the highest levels, it is difficult to suggest that the strategic nuclear dimension will disappear from global strategy. In some senses, it may well be limited; in the gross size of superpower arsenals, for

PLATE 10.2 SLBM being loaded – still the greatest ASW challenge
(Photo: Conway Maritime Press)

example. This assumes the full ratification and implementation of the START II Treaty. More importantly for the ASW future, however, than the overall reduction in arsenals is the growing trend to the sea-basing of these forces, clearly evident among the main current owners of these systems. This, alone, is liable to maintain at least some of the impetus ASW has enjoyed over the last 50 years. It would be rash to suggest that it will either stay at the same pace, far less increase, but neither will progress dwindle to insignificance. So huge is the investment – both economically and strategically – in submarine-based forces that no national player of that game would risk being surprised by advances in ASW.

Similarly, it is difficult to suggest that there will be any radical change in the way in which the world's bulk commodities will be transported. There may be certain long-term trends indicating that the total of such transport may decrease, such as growing energy awareness and efficiency in the developed world leading to lower consumption, or the accelerated development of areas closer to the energy sources (thus obviating or greatly reducing the need for sea transport), but the continuance of the belief in ever-rising economic growth as a necessary of national progress indicates the necessity for international trade. The trend away from manufacturing industry towards information technology may well continue, but the former will continue to be important: man cannot live by travelling on data highways alone. This and air transport will not supplant carriage by sea of bulk commodities and anything other than very small mass and very high value manufactured goods. The defence of shipping will therefore continue to generate an ASW need.

In terms of these strategic roles, perhaps conventional ASW suggests the greatest possibilities for change. Certainly, non-ASW technology especially, in such fields as access to instantaneous and secure communications, intelligence and global navigation information (such as GPS), tends to suggest a potential flexibility in dispositions away from the large scale but relatively concentrated American and Allied groupings of the late Cold War years: we should no more expect formations such as SACLANT's strike carrier groups – sometimes referred to as a 'flying circus' – in the Norwegian Sea. This alone is good ASW as the targeting problems it is liable to induce for opposing submarines go some considerable way to countering the potential of submarine-based weapons.

But, as has been suggested earlier, a type of warfare previously considered to be a special case may take on greater prominence than in the past half century – littoral warfare. Arguably the first examples of this have already occurred off Kuwait and – at much lower intensity – on the sea borders of the former Yugoslavia. This, it has been suggested, is the pattern of the future. It is fairly

PLATE 10.3 Large cargo ships – still vulnerable to submarines
(Photo: L & L van Ginderen)

easy to accept this as a short- to middle-term prediction, but less easy to be certain of it in the longer run. What would be its implications for ASW? On the limited sample so far, the message would seem to be that there is virtually no future in ASW: warfare is conducted by other means. Why build expensive submarines when ground attack aircraft can be used against shipping: so the argument might appear to run. The consequent stress is laid on land operations, with the sea only seen as a method of mounting these, then maintaining them, both with combat support and logistics. The judgement that ASW is dead is probably premature, as the number of submarine-owning nations is large and growing, albeit slowly. Assuming the continuing recurrence of such low- to medium-intensity conflicts, it is only a matter of time before a modern western or Russian navy has to deal with submarines. Arguably, this has already occurred during the Falklands War in 1982. Here, after the loss of the cruiser *General Belgrano,* the Argentine Navy only carried out operations with aircraft and submarines. The unwillingness to work on the surface reflected the disparity, both real and perceived, between a modern SSN force and relatively poor ASW capability. On the British side the potential of a single enemy diesel-electric submarine, which was both modern and serviceable, caused much ASW effort to be expended. It is therefore reasonable to suggest that the trend from ASW will continue until the first submarine-equipped enemy is encountered.

The nature of littoral ASW warfare will vary greatly with circumstances of geography and enemy submarine capabilities, but certain general characteristics can be identified. Initially, it can be described in terms of what it is not. The speed and other large-scale facets of blue-water oceanic ASW will not be present: no high speed SSNs; no long-range detections; little role for the vast and complex systems of the Cold War. These will be replaced by short range, possibly short duration, actions against small targets which will be very difficult to locate and detect. The mine is likely to play a much greater role, both as a submarine-laid offensive and defensive weapon, and as an ASW tool. To distinguish between ocean warfare and inshore operations, some commentators have dubbed this 'green water warfare' with 'brown water' being reserved for operations in the very close inshore area, such as has already been seen sporadically in the Stockholm Archipelago.

FUTURE ASW TECHNOLOGY

The general nature of future ASW has been sketched in terms of strategy, economics and type of warfare, but how might it actually be carried out in terms of technology? What follows depends crucially not only on the rate of technological progress itself, but also on a willingness to apply research to ASW. The approach taken here is to consider the main ASW activities and to look at how these might be supported by future equipment. Three areas to be considered are detection, attack and supporting activities.

Detection In submarines, the trends towards non-nuclear propulsion and diesel-electric enhancements such as AIP suggest that passive sonar is not going to be as important as it once was. However, the operational performance of AIP is yet to be established and its acoustic performance in its engine driven mode (as opposed to battery-electric drive) has yet to be established: this may still be fairly noisy. Further, no matter how power has been produced it still has to be transmitted to the water through a propulsive system, which may remain a significant producer of noise. The eclipse of passive sonar has often been forecast over past decades, but it has never quite done as badly as predicted. Nevertheless, it is difficult to suggest that it will be quite so important as it has been in the last two decades. Evolutionary improvements will continue to be made; improving materials, increasing processing power and better operator aids are some obvious areas which will be improvements in current systems. But physical limits, significant in ships and submarines and even more important in airborne vehicles already set a bound to performance and it is somewhat difficult to see how this can be overcome.

All this suggests a return to active sonar technology, but in a different way to the traditional hull-mounted set. The higher frequencies – of the order of a few kiloHertz – used for search and attack purposes in ships, submarines and aircraft systems have been limited both in range and against modern submarines designed to minimise sonar reflections, often by means of anechoic tiles applied to the hull. A way out of this is to use much lower frequencies – typically around 1 kHz and below. Recently systems such as Active Towed Array System (ATAS) have started to come into service. This is produced by Thompon Sintra Activitès/BAeSEMA and uses a 250 kg body with a stack of 10 flextensional transducers working at around 3 kHz and operating down to 235 m. In addition

PLATE 10.4 ATAS modern low frequency active sonar *(Photo: BAe SEMA)*

to this a number of modules may be added giving different lengths of line array and permitting:

- ► LF reception or,
- ► VLF reception or LF active sonar or,
- ► VLF reception *and* LF active operation simultaneously.

all depending on the version selected by the purchaser. It would appear that Taiwan, Oman and Pakistan are in the process of purchasing ATAS.

Such systems pose considerable technical challenges, however. Firstly, there is the problem of generating and transmitting such frequencies. As frequency is lowered, more power is needed for the same acoustic level and the larger the size of the transmitting device to put this into the water. This may have the effect of excluding sonobuoy-based systems in practice. Nor is life very much easier for other platforms. LF active systems may be more difficult for a submarine to combat, but they introduce their own problems such as reduced bearing discrimination and relatively low data rates. But it may be possible to use such a system multi-statically, that is with one or a few transmitting units and many receiving ships: a likely component of any such system would be the necessity to know fairly precisely the position of the transmitting unit(s). On the other hand, the more modern torpedo with its tendency towards smart weapon

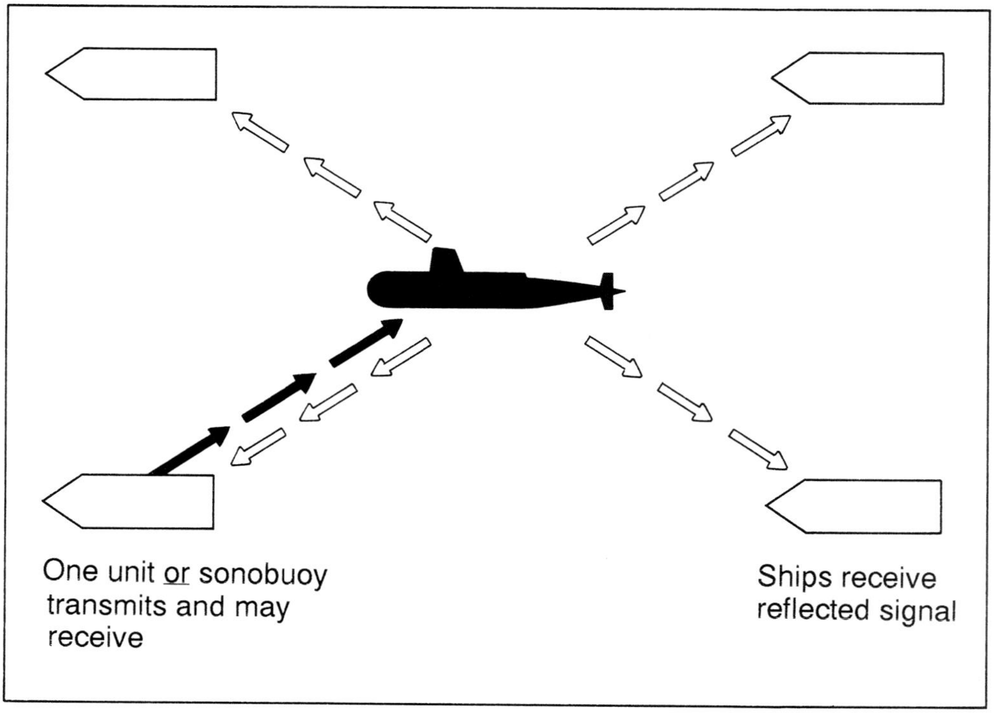

FIG. 10.2 Multistatic sonar detection

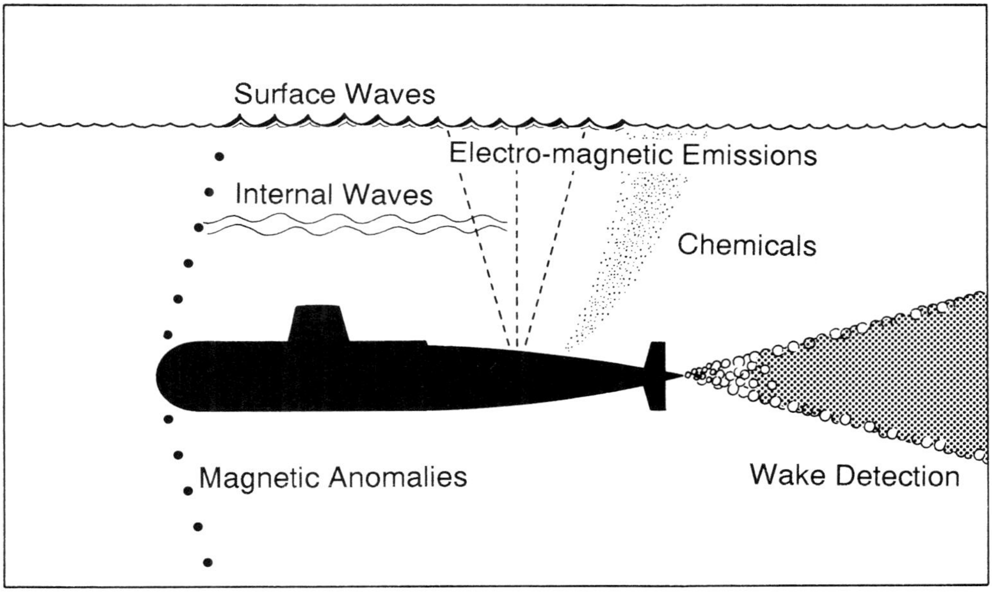

FIG. 10.3 Submerged submarine – potential for non-acoustic detection

techniques may well be able to cope with the resultant uncertainties and ambiguities.

Space Systems Perhaps the greatest change in the next decades may come about through the greater deployment of space-based systems. It is difficult, however, to be certain about both the potential of these systems and the likely range of their capabilities in practice. Further, this technology seems unlikely to be cheap and the combination of the demise of the Cold War and the consequent refocusing of spending priorities may well limit their deployment. It may nevertheless be useful to outline some possibilities for such systems.

Some of the systems which are already in service have some ASW capability, although this is likely to be severely limited in any tactically practical sense. Thus, existing radar ocean reconnaissance satellites (RORSATs) and their electronic detection counterparts (EORSATs) can detect surfaced and radar transmitting submarines respectively. But these are postures and activities which the prudent submariner seeks to avoid. The important questions are: can space systems be used to detect submerged submarines and, if so, how well, both in terms of area covered and accuracy of location? Several mechanisms have been suggested for detection. These include:

- Electromagnetic effects such as magnetic anomaly.
- Surface waves.
- Internal waves.
- Biological effects, such as bioluminescence.

- Temperature anomalies caused by the submarine.
- Wake detection.
- Detection of chemical (and in the case of nuclear submarines, radio-active) emissions from the submarine.

Detection methods do not need to be space-based to hold out the promise of detecting a submerged submarine. Although the sea generally allows few emissions to penetrate it significantly, with the general exception of sound and the case of VLF/ELF radio transmissions, there may be other limited 'windows of transmission'. One may be the blue-green laser, a particular frequency band of this by now familiar technology. This may have been investigated by the USA, Australia and Sweden, the latter being interested in the detection of small submarines in shallow water, where limitations in depth on the sensor's performance are not important. In the open-ocean case such a system may have already been deployed aboard Russian *Bear*-F ASW aircraft. Known as *Amethyst*, this requires precision low flying at a height of 100 m. Apparently the sensor only covers 100 m wide swaths and target depths down to a maximum of 50 metres. This latter dimension is probably the system's greatest limitation, analogous to the early MAD systems, but even more restrictive. A further difficulty apparently arises from the inability of many operators to recognise targets on the display.

Attack The fundamental problem in attacking a submarine is likely to remain the same in the next few years. Since the submarine remains a difficult target, this is unlikely to become an easier task. Certainly, electronics may make existing weapons more reliable both in an engineering sense and in their ability to sink or at least cause significant damage to a submarine. It would be a fairly risk-free speculation to suggest that any radical breakthrough in warhead technology (such as became possible in the 1950s with small nuclear devices) seems unlikely. This would require a considerable change in world sentiment as a whole, as well as in the minds of high technology nations. What might seem more likely, especially in the light of the moves, noted earlier in this chapter, towards fast-reaction, short-range engagements would be:

- Fast delivery systems for terminal weapons.
- Faster terminal weapons
- Smarter weapons with greater ability to discriminate between decoys and submarines – these could use technology of a level similar to that described for submarine weapons earlier in this chapter.
- More lethal warheads (but not approaching the level hitherto used in nuclear-tipped weapons).

In short, the answer would look remarkably like a torpedo. If the trend towards littoral warfare is sustained, then there could also be more of a role for the ASW mine.

Other Activities The latter part of this chapter has largely dealt with equipment for either detection or attack. It is also probable that the supporting technologies which have acted as force multipliers for the more sophisticated ASW nations will continue to develop. Again it can be suggested that the rate of growth will also slow; two effects may also be in evidence although they may appear to have one result. The first is that of diminishing returns in which an ever-larger outlay of resources will be necessary to make smaller incremental improvements. The second is that the present technologies may become more accessible to a greater number of nations. One example relating to detection equipment might be ATAS described above which seems to be reaching not just export customers, but also those with no previous interest or experience in ASW such as Oman. It may then be that experience and training become even more crucial factors than they now are; conversely the supportive software for future equipments may reduce the importance of these factors, although this would seem unlikely. A further area of potential development concerns measures against the old underwater enemy, the torpedo. This, however, is a complicated and difficult technical challenge, and programmes such the joint US/UK SSTD will have to steer a path between ineffectiveness and becoming a short-range underwater version of the late SDI in space.

Platforms for ASW may also change markedly. For now, the vast investments of the Cold War years will take time to work their way out of the inventories. Even then, there will be stabilities and instabilities. Looking back over the last half century the Maritime Patrol Aircraft *as a platform* has been very stable. The ones operated by advanced ASW nations have all had four engines, and flown at roughly the same speed for the same order of time. There may have been some increase in speed and some reduction in endurance, but none of great significance. What has changed has been the equipment fitted to the aircraft. Similarly with surface warships, although there has been a rather more than marginal increase in size, the fundamental type has remained unchanged. What therefore might be the impact of the growing emphasis on littoral warfare of ASW? Assuming that ASW is of relevance at all, it might be assumed that there would be a growing role for mines, relatively light short-range aircraft (including helicopters) and shore-controlled systems, such as sensor fields. However, this tends to assume control or at least use of the proximate shore belonging to the side conducting ASW. This might not necessarily be the case, in which instance, then perhaps the more 'traditional' platforms such as surface ships, large MPAs, helicopters and, possibly, nuclear submarines would have a part to play. The sheer flexibility of such units may render them very necessary to changed circumstances.

CONCLUSION

It seems unlikely that the impetus given to ASW by the Cold War will continue into the future. Nor will it dwindle to insignificance; this is ensured almost entirely by the continued reliance by the USA and Russia on submarines as a major component of their nuclear weapons systems. A further factor for sustaining ASW may be the slow but perceptible spread of submarines in the world. As in all forms of warfare, economic features will also set limits to growth. Technology, especially in the form of information processing and remote sensing from space has much potential for driving future ASW, but this may well be limited by the other factors.

11
Conclusion

ASW is a warfare skill that will be needed for as long as there are submarines. The principles that inform it are relatively simple to understand, but often rather more difficult to put into practice. This is partly because there is no universal submarine problem, so there can be no universal solution. The technological aspects of ASW, largely concerned with the equipments needed to detect and destroy submarines, represent some of the most advanced materials deployed in the defence sphere, but such a material approach by itself can never solve the problem of combating submarines entirely.

It is also crucially important to have the best possible understanding of two other fields: the submarine and the sea in which it operates. The latter only comes from a combination of appreciating the various mechanisms of the sea as a medium, the application of these principles to the particular environment in which ASW is to be conducted and measuring key parameters at the time of operating. The submarine, too, has to pay heed to such considerations and if the ASW practitioner can make better use of this factor then at least he has a chance of winning the battle. If, however, the submariner is the more knowing user of the maritime environment, then ASW success is unlikely. This point applies with equal force to the deep ocean or coastal waters.

Similarly, successful ASW must be underpinned by as full a knowledge of the submarine as possible. This implies an acquaintance with its operating principles, the particular characteristics of a specific enemy and the submarine's own objectives. The practicalities of intelligence mean that such information in practice is likely to be incomplete and possibly misleading. However, the main tenets of submarine operations are fixed by characteristics of the environment and submarine construction, and there should be no excuse for an ASW operator not to know and comprehend these facts thoroughly.

Over the next few decades, there will be advances in both science and technology as they affect ASW (and indeed submarine warfare). It is difficult, however, to suggest that any radical change in principles is on the horizon. If any medium- to large-scale underwater conflict should occur, then it is liable to have many of the characteristics of previous ones. This is not to say that it will closely resemble the 1940s Battle of the Atlantic or any other historic campaign. On one hand it might imply global conflict involving nuclear submarines and ocean assets on, over and under the sea; alternatively very small submarines operating within 50 miles of a coastline could be the more likely enemy. But the long-lasting themes of success going to the side with superior technology, larger forces and, above all, both the proper doctrine and the will to take on a difficult and resourceful enemy will persist.

ASW is, after all, just one subdivision of maritime war, in itself a division of war in general. However, it cannot be denied that it is one of the most fascinating and challenging aspects of armed struggle and although good ASW has never won a single war, it has prevented a great many, both hot and cold, from being lost.

Further Reading

Donald C. Daniel, *ASW and Superpower Strategic Stability,* London, 1985

Dr. P. J. Gates and N. M. Lynn, *Ships, Submarines and the Sea,* London, 1990

Willem Hackmann, *Seek and Strike: Sonar, Antisubmarine Warfare and the Royal Navy, 1914-1945,* London 1984

Rear Admiral John Hervey, *Submarines*, London, 1994

Rear Admiral J. R. Hill, *Anti-Submarine Warfare*, London, 1984

Group Captain B. C. Laite RAF, *Maritime Air Operations*, London, 1991

Hung P. Nguyen, *Submarine Detection from Space: A Study of Russian Capabilities*; Annapolis, Maryland, 1993

Tom Stefanick, *Strategic ASW and Naval Strategy;* Lexington, Mass., 1983

Robert J. Urick, *Principles of Underwater Sound*, 3rd edition, London, 1983

Annual Publication, *Jane's Underwater Warfare Systems*, London

Index